VOLUME 10

tribute plays

SERIES EDITOR **VIJAY PADAKI**

COMMENTS ON THE PUBLICATIONS

Glocal is the word that comes immediately to mind when I think of BLT's long history and ambitions. One can be local in one's view, without being insular, and one can be global, pulling voices from elsewhere into the context one inhabits, without becoming deracinated. BLT's house is strong because it has been built in the here and now; it is doubly strong because its windows have been open to the oxygen from elsewhere and from other times.

Ecosystem is another word I would use to pinpoint BLT's aspirations. It has understood that its strength is derived from the strength of the field in which it works. Whatever BLT knows, it has shared, and this sharing has taken many forms — from the training it has imparted to budding actors and directors to the support it has provided to fledgling theatre groups. The same commitment has propelled BLT's initiative to publish multiple volumes of plays that have been spawned by its admirable play development programme. There is a hunger for strong dramatic texts in India, where theatre production has grown far more rapidly than playwriting. In that context, these volumes will be seen as yet another precious gift that BLT has given to the theatre community.

Anmol Vellani
Theatre Director and past Director of India Foundation for the Arts

I am delighted that you are presenting all these plays that are at one and the same time enjoyable, revealing and memorable!

Roddam Narasimha
Science Historian and Professor,
Jawaharlal Nehru Centre for Advanced Scientific Research

This initiative would allow theatre practitioners from other parts of the world to access this work and look at the possibilities of staging these plays in multiple languages and in multiple cultural contexts.

Vidyanidhi Vanarase
Founder-Dirtector, International Association
for Performing Arts and Research

This volume addresses the critical need for more actable and accessible versions of classic Indian plays in English. Good plays around important historical ideas are unfortunately scarce. The second admirable volume helps correct that deficiency.

Ira Hauptman
Professor of Drama, Queens College, CUNY, New York

We have eagerly awaited the publication of these volumes. They have finally arrived. They will reach performers and audiences right across national borders and far beyond.

Sai Paranjpye
Theatre personality and award winning film director

An international leader in our field, especially its serious investment in new play development, including the publication series that can benefit all of us theater makers across the world.

Bill Rauch
Artistic Director, Perelman Performing Arts Center
at the World Trade Center, New York City

The new publication series produced by the Bangalore Little Theatre are an important and most welcome addition to world theater knowledge. Bravo!

Arthur Giron
Founding Member of Ensemble Studio Theatre, New York, formerly Head, Graduate Playwriting Program, Carnegie Mellon University

Bangalore Little Theatre has reached veteran status in Indian theatre with their powerful theatrical interventions in the community, spanning 60 years...these volumes enrich our understanding of the capacity of theatre to create spaces for potent ideas, that demand our engagement.

Yvette Hardie
President: ASSITEJ (International Association for Theatre for Children and Young People)

This work is not only important for India, it also makes plays from Indian writing known across the world. It is a very important and necessary project.

Ursula Werdenberg
Dramaturg-Playwright,
Secretary General of The International Playwrights' Forum

My warmest congratulations. This is a significant milestone and a wonderful achievement that gives readers an opportunity to think about our pasts and our presents through a history of ideas.

Anuradha Kapur
Past Director, National School of Drama

These are a valued resource.... they celebrate authors past and present and their translators as well, making the local, global.

Richard Crane
Playwright-Director,
Co-founder of Brighton Theatre

Your contribution to the goals of the International Playwrights' Forum, to the artistic treasures of your country, as well as for universal culture in general is indescribable indeed.

Gad Kaynar (Kissinger)
Professor, International Theatre Institute
The Yolanda and David Katz Faculty of the Arts, Tel Aviv University

ये नाम केश्चिदिह नः प्रथयन्त्यवज्ञां
जानन्ति ते किमपि तान्प्रति नैष यत्नः ।
उत्पत्स्यते तु मम कोऽपि समानधर्मा
कालो ह्ययं निरवधिर्विपुला च पृथ्वी ॥

Those who deride or ignore my work —
let them know: my efforts are not for them.
There will come along someone who shares my spirit:
the world is vast, and time endless.

– Bhavabhuti

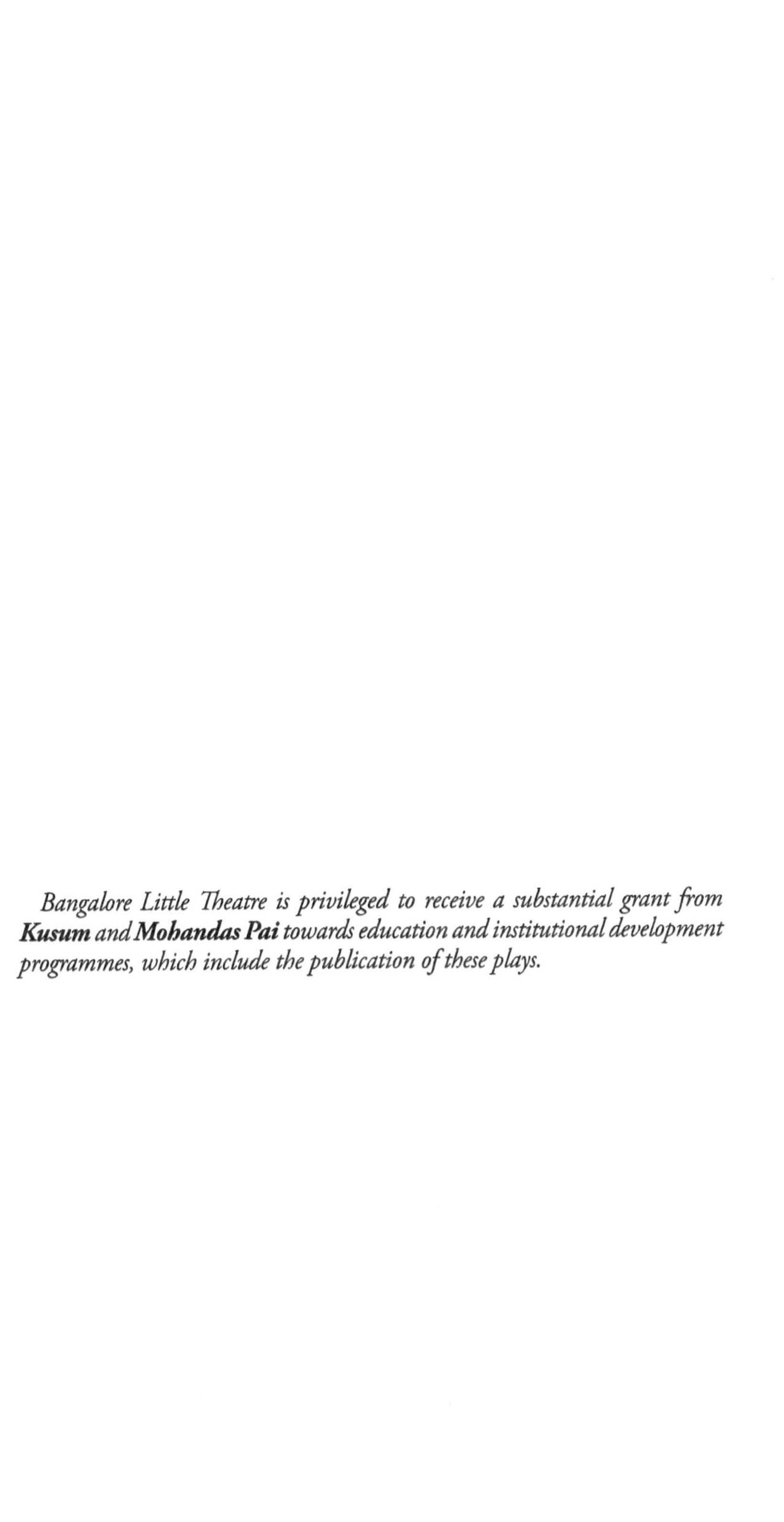

Bangalore Little Theatre is privileged to receive a substantial grant from **Kusum** *and* **Mohandas Pai** *towards education and institutional development programmes, which include the publication of these plays.*

ISBN 979-8-89556-006-8

CONTENTS

FOREWORD

Bangalore Little Theatre is an enormous exercise in imagination. It remains an aspiration for theatre performers and a source of inspiration for practitioners. The passion, perseverance, toil and grace is the hallmark of this intimate Institution, which has embarked on many pathbreaking initiatives, programmes and productions. If the History of Ideas programme was unique, the translation and adaptation of Indian classics in English is a huge service. In the programme Vijay Padaki has presented a pertinent model, wherein the play scripts transcend the cultural specificity and period in time to speak in a universal language that addresses our contemporary concerns. Although we read the text in English, we experience the content in the original. A truly remarkable feat.

BLT has had a strong play development programme for a long time. It is most appropriate that the plays are being published now. Several volumes of plays can be expected in print very soon. This is a huge contribution to the institution of theatre in India. We can be sure they will be received with enthusiasm world-wide.

Feroz Abbas Khan
Theatre director and award winning film maker

A SPECIAL MESSAGE

For nearly 60 years, Bangalore Little Theatre has been instrumental in promoting theatre arts in Bengaluru and across the country. The ambitious project of publishing their most successful plays in a multi-volume anthology marks a great point in their story – another marker of the tremendous success they have attained.

In translating to English and adapting the plays for the modern stage, Mr. Vijay Padaki (BLT) is conserving the best of Indian theatre. Each play is especially relevant to contemporary situations, from environmental concerns to resurgent regional identities, to introspecting the carnage of wars and finally the complexities of court politics.

I am certain that such a project provides us the perfect opportunity to understand, perhaps for the first time in recent years, the sheer wealth of Indian theatre spanning different cultural and linguistic traditions in the subcontinent. In producing such plays, and putting them together in this volume, BLT has undertaken a public service, one which every Indian living in the 21st century can profit from, for a long time to come.

With this, I wish BLT the very best for this and their many future endeavours.

Shashi Tharoor
Member of Parliament for Thiruvananthapuram

SALUTATIONS

It is well known that the huge collection of play scripts in BLT had remained unpublished for years. We are thankful to the Managing Committee of BLT to take on the publication task with determination in 2019 – and for pushing us into its execution. There has been an even more powerful hand behind the publications project, invisible but relentless in drive over several years. Rupande Padaki, known to all of us as Rupa, was in many ways responsible for the publications to be taken up. She succeeded at last.

We also extend our appreciation to Suraj Menon for illustrating the titles of all plays in this volume.

Deepak Mote • Vijay Padaki

PREFACE TO THE VOLUME

BLT and Outreach

Bangalore Little Theatre had recognized the importance of outreach activity in its earliest years. At that time it was a gut feel, without a proper articulation. Anything other than ticketed public performances might be viewed as outreach, done with the general objective of creating a larger 'constituency' for the theatre arts. It did not matter that BLT had neither a 'policy' nor a 'programme' of outreach at that time. What did matter was that members were committed to giving time to things other than stage performances. Play readings and appearances in schools and colleges were not uncommon events through the year.

When BLT restructured into a Public Charitable Trust in 2008 it was done with the purpose of reinforcing the strength the organization had gained in outreach activity. The Mission document referred to *rededicating the commitment to social development goals beyond performance*. The restructuring led to the creation of an *Academy of Theatre Arts (ATA)*. One of the programme thrusts adopted at ATA was *Theatre Appreciation*. It encompassed both earlier activities and new ones:

- The Summer Project on Theatre (SPOT)
- A niche programme of documentary theatre called *The History of Ideas*
- Short Theatre Appreciation workshops for the general public
- Community play readings

The Preface to Volume 3 in the publication series *(Children's Theatre)* has a lengthy description of the long term programme for children and schools at BLT. This, too, came out of the conviction for sustained outreach.

Theatre Appreciation

The annual Summer Project on Theatre, popularly known as SPOT, has been a major vehicle for Theatre Appreciation. While participants enrolling in SPOT think of it as 'actor training' on applying, BLT has always maintained that it is, in fact, a Theatre Appreciation course. Two 'prototype' workshops were held in 1979 and 1980. It came to be called SPOT in 1988, and has been conducted every summer since then, sometimes with two batches of participants in parallel. The current model of SPOT runs over 12-14 weeks, with all-day training sessions on Sundays and work on a chosen production through the week. A large number of artists now pursuing the theatre arts in Bangalore have had their start in SPOT.

In the early years of SPOT, the group chose a genre of some historical significance to work on in some detail. This included an author strongly representing the genre. The performance by the group at the end of the SPOT course was around the chosen writer.

The typical format in these plays was:
(a) Ensemble acting, the artists playing multiple parts on stage and off stage
(b) Originally scripted narration by on stage actors about the author and genre, thus extending the Theatre Appreciation objective to the audience
(c) The narration interspersed with representative scenes from the author's works

The performance was, in effect, a tribute to the author, built into the Theatre Appreciation objective. The excerpts chosen for inclusion were what appealed to the workshop group. A performing group using these Tribute Plays may well choose other excerpts. The format was adopted for the plays on Ionesco. Lorca and Moliere. The tributes to Strindberg and Tagore are through completely original play scripts.

It is useful to regard the theatre audience as a *constituency*. One strategic task for a theatre organization may thus be viewed as *constituency development*. It can be said that the theatre constituency in many societies is large and also well evolved. The task before us in India, at least in the English language theatre of Bangalore, appeared to be well defined by the constituency framework – to work towards an expansion in number and a better informed audience.

The Plays

This Volume has scripts developed in workshop mode for such genre-author explorations. It includes the plays developed around the life and work of Federico Garcia Lorca, Eugene Ionesco, August Strindberg, Jean-Baptiste Poquelin, known better by his stage name Molière, and Rabindranath Tagore.

The last needs a further explanation. In 2011, there were world-wide celebrations taking place to commemorate the 150th birth anniversary of the internationally renowned multi-faceted artist. A prolific creator of works in poetry, drama, novels, short stories, music, painting and dance, Rabindranath Tagore, often referred to as Gurudev, was indeed the complete artist. In addition, he was a social reformer, a pioneer in education, a champion of the poor and oppressed, and a passionate supporter of the freedom movement. Quite justifiably, there were innumerable performances planned all over the country, including Karnataka State, around Tagore's best known and most loved works of dance, drama and poetry. BLT decided to pay a tribute to Gurudev Tagore highlighting his work for and with children. It was done through the play script *Robi's Garden.* It was an original adaptation of Tagore's work for and with children, not much known outside Bengal.

The material for the theatrical production is drawn from a great fund of Tagore's writing, a lot of it for children, but enjoyed by grown-up audiences widely. These include verse, prose, short stories, plays, sketches (his "riddle plays"), fantasies, autobiographical writing, (esp. his childhood memories), and the letters to his grand-daughter and other children. In the play a small group of children is on an excursion to Jorasanko where Tagore's ancestral home is located in Kolkata. They enter the courtyard theatre in Thakur-badi and sense a magical air surrounding them. The caretaker of the estate shares an important mantra of Robi-da with the children: that the first step in getting what you want in life is...*imagination.* It is the surest way to have Robi-da's stories come alive on the courtyard stage. And they do – in Robi's Garden!

The play went on to become a highly acclaimed BLT production. It had a London production in 2013. More recently BLT developed *Robi's Garden* as an abridged Storytelling Theatre format of the play for performances in a wide variety of spaces – drawing rooms, libraries, seminar halls, art galleries, banquet halls, and so on. The presentation is by two actors only, with audience participation.

Other authors explored in SPOT have been:
- David Campton and the British resurgence of the 'sixties
- Sophocles and Greek tragedy
- Samuel Beckett and the distinct stamp he gave to his imagery
- Bertolt Brecht and his Epic Theatre, also called Dialectical Theatre
- Badal Sircar and the Third Theatre
- Mahasweta Devi and the rights movement
- Vaclac Havel and the unique Czech movement

These SPOT workshops focused on performing the chosen plays, while also exploring the socio-political context. The plays included in this volume emphasize the life and work of the authors. It can be said that the early SPOT explorations were precursors to the current highly successful long term programme of docu-theatre called *The History of Ideas.* Paying a tribute to a writer through a play script is such a neat vehicle for Theatre Appreciation!

The play scripts published in this volume are built upon narratives developed at Bangalore Little Theatre as part of the workshop productions. The works of Garcia Lorca, Moliere and Tagore are in the public domain. However, scripting for the workshops benefited from several excellent available renditions. In *A Little Bit of Lorca* the helpful suggestions of AS Kline at *Poetry in Translation* are acknowledged with gratitude. For *Ionescapes* we had the ready support of Marie-France Ionesco. The adaptation of Tagore's work for *Robi's Garden* was done in-house by a small team. It involved some original translation as well.

Vijay Padaki

STAGE DIRECTIONS
with the actor facing the audience

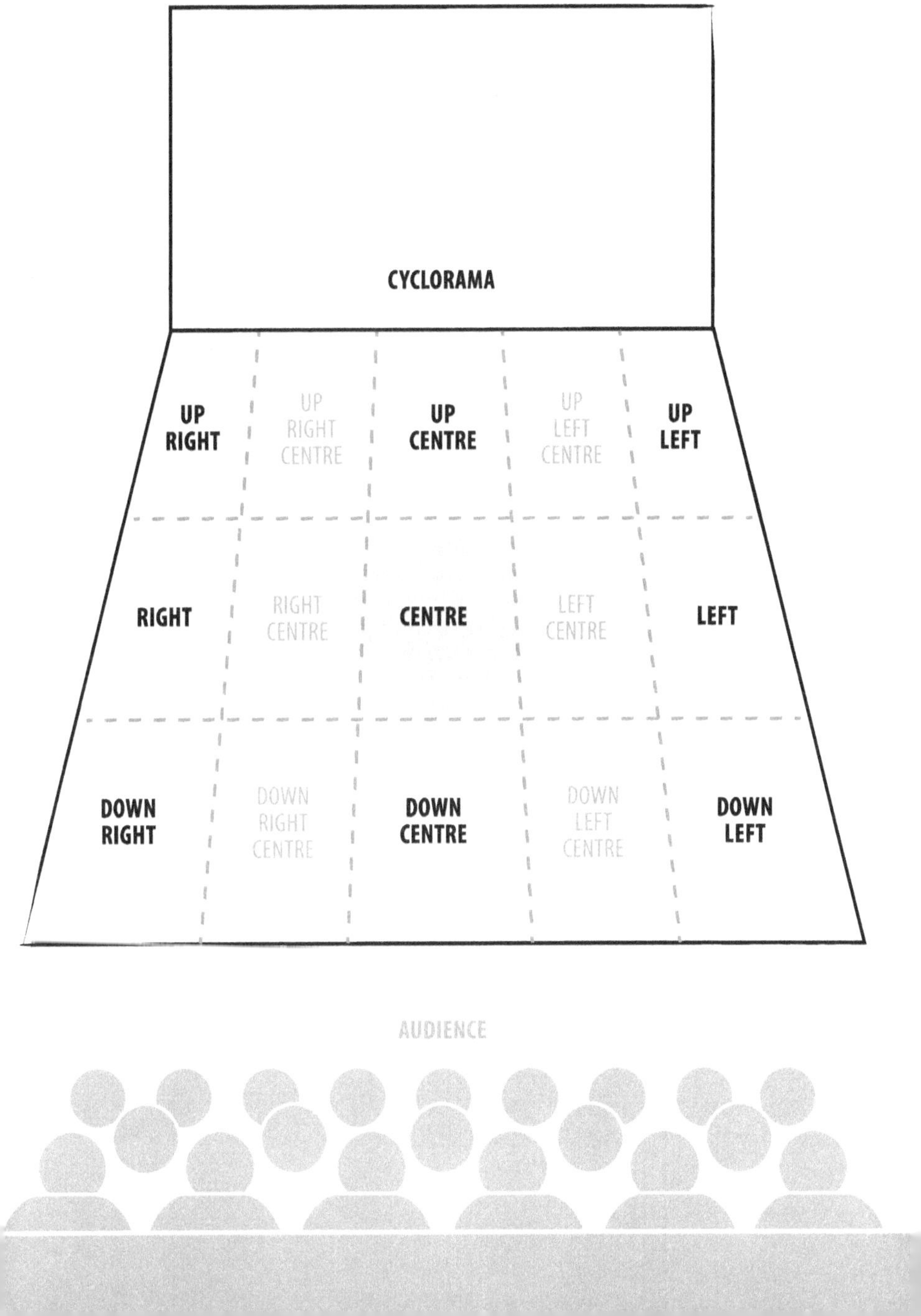

Robi's Garden

*Rediscovering Rabindranath Tagore's work
for and with children*

Vijay Padaki

FOR
PRIYALAKSHMI RAO

CHARACTERS IN THE PLAY

Chorus ensemble
The chowkidar at Thakurbadi
A group of children on an excursion

THE ARYAN
On religious bigotry and our gullibility with godmen
  • A PUBLISHER • THE ARYAN • VISITING AUTHORS

THE GENTLEMAN JACKAL
About aspiring to be somebody other than ourselves
  • MAN •WOMAN • HOO-WAH • SURGEONS
  • CHATTER-DI • JACKALS

LAST RITES
The importance of having the right guest list at a funeral
  • SONS • FATHER • DOCTOR

IN THE PINK OF DEATH
About dying by being persuaded into it
  • TRAVELLER 1 • TRAVELLER 2

TIGER TRAILS
A heady cocktail tapped from Tagore's tiger tales
  • CHIEF PUNDIT TIGER • TIGER LAL
  • YOUNG APPRENTICE TIGERS

THE BIRTH OF SHOES
An unlikely history lesson about the highly educated pitted against a humble son of the soil
  • KING HOBLOO • CHIEF MINISTER GOBLOO
  • MINISTERS • CONSULTANTS • COBBLER

NOTES

The Script

This adaptation is one in a long line in Bangalore Little Theatre's ongoing play development programme. BLT has promoted writing for the stage from the earliest years. In more recent times the group has acquired a reputation for its translations and adaptations. Play development is central to the programmes of the newly created Academy of Theatre Arts. Every one of the plays performed in the annual Children's Theatre project has been originally developed within BLT.

In 1961 the world-wide celebrations of the centenary of Rabindranath Tagore's birth included the Government of India's decision to create well equipped auditoria for the performing arts in every State capital of India. Among the first of these auditoria to come up was the Ravindra Kalakshetra in Bengaluru.

Fifty years later, there were world-wide celebrations taking place once again to commemorate the 150th birth anniversary of the internationally renowned multi-faceted artist. A prolific creator of works in poetry, drama, novels, short stories, music, painting and dance, Tagore was indeed the complete artist. In addition, he was a social reformer, a pioneer in education, a champion of the poor and oppressed, and a passionate supporter of the freedom movement. Quite justifiably, there were innumerable performances planned all over the country, including Karnataka State, around Tagore's best known and most loved works of dance, drama and poetry.

The questions arose: How should Bengaluru city pay a tribute to the great soul in whose memory we have one of the finest auditoria in the country? Secondly, how should Bangalore Little Theatre celebrate his 150th birth anniversary year? While most performing groups the world over preferred to pick up the "classics" and reinterpret them with renewed artistic fervour, BLT chose to reveal the lesser known side of the poet to the general public – the fun loving side. This is best seen in his work for and with children.

Once decided, it was a six-month project for a small team of dedicated researchers to locate the material, choose the right mix of prose, verse and narrative, seek expert advice on the context and meaning of the original work in Bangla, to get the right sound and rhythm in the English language adaptations and, above all, get the acceptance of the main audience – children. The principles of writing and performing for children set out in the preface to the first Volume of Children's Theatre plays (Volume 3) were, after all, inspired by Tagore's outlook as an educator. They were confirmed as most apt. The student audiences loved to have their imagination tested – teased – often surprising the grown-ups accompanying them. The team of writers, designers and performers was satisfied that the play had done justice to Robi-da in the year of his 150th birth anniversary.

For the purpose of this adaptation project the team examined several sources of available material. Some of these have been ready translations from the Bengali. Some others have been revealed to us by our Bengali friends. Not surprisingly, we have read more than one translation of the same piece in some cases. We are grateful to all of these sources of inspiration.

The team worked on a total of ten adaptations. The play script here has the six stories retained for performance. There are also short pieces providing links across the stories. Two of them were devised by the children in the cast as their own tribute to Robi-da.

The Approach

The task of creating a composite text for a theatrical performance, however, only begins with the translation done. We know it needs to go far beyond that. It is a responsibility we have undertaken with some trepidation, knowing fully the stature of the personality being represented. We hope it gives the viewer – and the reader – at least a small part of the satisfaction that we had in putting together the play. Any flaws that a discerning Tagore aficionado spots in the play script will be entirely on account of our own shortcomings.

The material for the theatrical production is drawn from a great fund of Tagore's writing, a lot of it for children, some for a general audience as well. These include: verse, short stories, plays, sketches (his "riddle plays"), fantasies, his autobiographical writing, especially his childhood memories, and letters to his grand-daughter and other children. Indeed, the main purpose of undertaking this play writing project was to celebrate Tagore's deep understanding of children and his unshakable faith in children. The treasure chest was loaded. It was very difficult to pick just the right handful of gems as a representative sample to display to the world.

All the stories included in this play are a reflection of Tagore's approach to the theatre as well: to create interesting images on stage, far from "realistic", highly improvisational in the use of materials, relying mainly on the imagination of the storytellers and then let the imagination of the audience take over!

Performing the Stories

In a brief prologue a group of children visiting Thakur-badi (Tagore's ancestral home in Jorasanko) is about to be treated to a few of Robi-da's stories. They are told that the first step in getting what you want in life is... *imagination*. (That is a line from the play!) This was the essential guiding principle in his educational philosophy as well. He believed that much of conventional classroom teaching destroys the child's god-given gift of imagination, and that the real objective of education was to enhance and strengthen that gift for life.

If there is one piece of advice to be given to the designer and director of the play, it would be to capture the atmosphere of fantasy and wonder that his writing so effortlessly evokes in the reader, and to recreate it on stage for the eyes and ears to delight in all over again. In thought, word and deed, Tagore's work for and with young persons combined a child-like innocence in making up stories with a profundity of content. Never one to talk down to children, his idea of storytelling accepted that the child was capable of a far greater level of imagination than the grown-ups around cared to recognize.

The format adopted for the play script is that of a moving collage. It attempts to interweave a few basic strands from Tagore's writing into a tapestry, to display a variety of patterns and colours as it sways gently with the breeze across the stage. The strands are selected from the colossal store of yarns (a fitting pun) and in a variety of forms of storytelling employed as already mentioned above.

Shifting seamlessly from one passage to another (and from one form to another) needed a "dramatic device" that would help the transition without being obtrusive. This requires, obviously, a combination of set design and action design and they, in turn, depend on the space available for the performance, the technical equipment available, the budget at the group's disposal, and so on. The suggestions in the play script should therefore be taken as one possible approach to the task of weaving the tapestry.

The Cast

The total number of characters from all the stories combined is naturally large. An ensemble of about twelve actors should be able to play all the parts, changing roles from story to story. Many of the characters can be played by either men or women. Some parts are, of course, gender specific.

It will be seen that the children in the cast have a rather special responsibility in presenting the play. While the script simply refers to them as a children's ensemble (with only two of them given names) it is useful to have a casting plan for the production.

The following casting plan is suggested for an ensemble of six children. CHILD 1: Girl (Pupli); CHILD 2: Boy; CHILD 3: Girl; CHILD 4: Boy; CHILD 5: Girl; CHILD 6: Boy (Debloo)

Stage Design

It is difficult to write a play script without a picture of the stage in the mind's eye. It is in submission to this weakness that the playwright has described below a set for the play. Naturally, the unfolding of scenes in the play has something to do with the suggested design. It can be the other way about too. The performing group is welcome to toss it out of the window and arrive at an original design for itself.

It would not be out of place to recall Tagore's own exhortation to dramatists of his time to shun the trappings of heavy and elaborate sets (which usually went with expensive mechanical devices as well), and to concentrate on the most important task of the dramatist on the stage... telling a story.

In the design chosen for the production of this play script, we have struck a compromise. There is a set, but it is simple and functional, meant primarily to serve two purposes. First, it is meant to evoke the atmosphere of Tagore's home environment in Jorasanko that seemed so central to much of the writing selected by us. Second, it is to aid the transitions across passages. An imaginative lighting design should help. That does not necessarily mean a very elaborate lighting set up.

Three levels of action are suggested for the set. The highest level would be the upstage area, to represent a balcony, including a balustrade. One part of the balcony can represent a small study next to a bay window, with an armchair next to the window. With no human presence in the balcony through the play, the construction can be light and simple to assemble.

The second level of action would be a rostrum, jutting out of the area under the balcony. This would perhaps be square shaped and occupy a good part of stage centre. Four pillars at the four corners of the stage might help.

The rest of the stage, at floor level, stretching from stage right, arching through down-right, down-centre and down-left to stage left would be the third level of action.

Dance and Music

Dance and song were integral to much of Tagore's drama. The play script suggests a group of children (much like a chorus) making brief appearances between stories with some narrative links. The performing group may decide whether it should be an exclusive chorus or an ensemble of actors with everybody being part of the link appearances some time or the other. Songs are not included in this script. We were not confident we could do justice to the task, especially in retaining a "Tagoresque" character in the total script. The idea of songs in Robi's Garden is not ruled out. Some time in the future, perhaps, a revised version of the script might be done as a musical.

The script suggests two versions for the prologue. The first version has an extended introduction to Thakurbadi, the ancestral home of Tagore in JoraSanko in Kolkata. This will work with high quality photographs or line drawings of the JoraSanko scenes for projection. The shorter version of the prologue is without these projections and is therefore shorter.

– VP

FIRST PERFORMED

By Bangalore Little Theatre
at Ravindra Kalakshetra, Bangalore, September 2011

Children's ensemble ....ANANYA, AYUSH, DHRITI,
GITANJALI, KRISHNA, MAHITI, MAYANK,
PRANAV, REHA, SAHIL, SUHAS, VAISHNAVI

Chowkidar .... NIRLEK DHULLA, RIJAS MUHAMMED

The Aryan
Publisher .... SHALINI NAIR, VIDYA BHARAT
The Aryan .... SUBRAMANIUM KRISHNAN,
AKSHAT ARORA
Authors .... LAWRENCE MANOAH,
KRISH BHARAT, RAVI SRINIVASAN
NIRLEK DHULLA, ANSHUL PATHAK, VIJAY KUMAR

The Gentleman Jackal
Man .... ANIRUDH ACHARYA
Woman .... RASHMI KRISHNAN, AMRITA SENGUPTA
Hoo-wah.....................SIDDHARTH JOSE, ANIRUDH ACHARYA
Surgeons....................PRUTHVI BANAWASI, KRISHMA SHETTY,
ROHINI GUPTA, VIBHA MISHRA
Chatter-di.............................DEEPTY SWAMY, ROHINI GUPTA
Jackals .... KRISHMA SHETTY, BHUVNESHWARI,
PADMAJA NAGARUR, DEEPTI SWAMY

Last Rites
Sons .... AKSHATH ARORA, NIRLEK DHULLA,
SUBRAMANIUM KRISHNAN, RAVI SRINIVSAN,
VIDYA BHARAT, SHALINI NAIR, KRISH BHARAT
LAWENCE MANOAH, VIJAY KUMAR,
ANIRUDH ACHARYA
Father .... RAVI SRINIVASAN, NIRLEK DULLA,
RIJAS MUHAMMED, NAVEEN TATER,
VIJAY PADAKI
Doctor .... RAVI SRINIVASAN,
VIJAY KUMAR, PRIYA RAO

In the Pink of Death

Traveller 1 .... PADMAJA NAGARUR,
SIDDHARTH SINGH, VIJAY KUMAR
Traveller 2 .... VIBHA MISHRA,
MUDASSAR KHATTAB, LAWRENCE MANOAH

PROFIT AND LOSS
*An interlude inspired by the Riddle Plays
presented by the children's cast as their tribute to Robi-da*

Tiger Trails

Chief Pundit Tiger .... ABHIJIT GANGULY,
LAWRENCE MANOAH
Tiger Lal .... LAWRENCE MANOAH, VIJAY KUMAR
Young Tigers .... SHALINI NAIR, VIDYA BHARAT,
KRISH BHARAT, NIRLEK DHULLA,
RAVI SRINIASAN, SUBRAMANIUM KRISHNAN,
AKSHATH ARORA, NAVEEN TATER

The Birth of Shoes

King Hobloo .... SIDDHARTH SINGH,
PRUTHVI BANASI
Minister Gobloo .... KRISHMA SHETTY,
SAMHITA SHASTRY, ROHINI GUPTA
Ministers .... BHUVANESHWARI, DEEPTI SWAMY,
PADMAJA NAGARUR, ROHINI GUPTA
Consultants .... SIDDHARTH JOSE, KRISHMA SHETTY,
SAMHITA SHASTRY, VIBHA MISHRA
Cobbler .... MUDASSAR KHATTAB,
SUSHANTH PATTANSHETTI

Lights .... SHASHANK PURUSHOTHAM
Sound .... ANSHUL PATHAK
Costumes .... SUNITHA RAJAGOPALAN,
ANUSHA MAJUMDAR
Stage Manager .... NAVEEN TATER
Publicity .... THE OTHER DESIGN STUDIO
Production Coordinator .... SHASHANK PURUSHOTHAM
Directed by .... PRIYA RAO
Assisted by .... VIJAY PADAKI

PROLOGUE

The version presented here is the short one. A longer version is available that uses projections.

The play opens to a dark stage. Sound of thunder, followed by rain. As the rain subsides, we hear the voice of a Guide taking a group through a conducted tour.

VOICE

This way! This way! Mind that puddle, stick to the right side, follow me... That is Kolkata for you! One ten-minute drizzle and the streets are flooded.

All right, you can step into the compound now. Good. Now... when you pass through that gate there you will be entering another world, another Kolkata. No kichad-wichad in there. Nice, clean surroundings, another world. Yes...

(The group has now stepped into a corner of the performing area, dimly lit. The guide is seen as a chowkidar in Pathan clothes. He continues.)

CHOWKIDAR

This is where all the drama and music and dance took place...artists invited from outside, the family's own shows, the jatra in season...Today people have big big theatres in the city where a thousand people can sit in fancy seats. They have carpets on the floor, there is air conditioning and all. People wear expensive clothes and jewellery, they eat popcorn paying fifty rupees a packet. Who eats moongfali from paper cones anymore? Four annas for a packet this big!

Who performs here today? Nobody. You can't perform here now. It is a heritage site. Yes, there has been an exception. Bangalore Little Theatre was invited to perform here some time ago. It was a play about letters exchanged between Mahatma Gandhi and Gurudev Rabindranath Tagore. Robi-da. Robi to his friends and family.

Wait! Look up there. What do you see?

(A tight spot on the study upstage with Tagore's armchair.)

That is where he often sat and worked...for long hours...in a world of his own, dreaming of kings and queens, heroic men and villains, clever animals, clever boys and girls, imaginary creatures, all of them crowding the pages of his notebook and urging him on: Write about me! Write about me! And you know what? He wrote about all of them! Every one of the characters in his stories were like dear childhood friends. He never abandoned them.

You know...it is said that in his childhood Robi would sit in the balcony and pretend that he was a schoolteacher.

(A voice is heard. It is Robi-da. This voice will appear in different parts of the play.)

VOICE

I made up games of my own. I was sometimes a teacher. The railings on the balcony were the pupils in my class. There were always a few pupils who didn't care about their lessons. I had to be stern with them. I warned them that if they didn't study hard they would end up as coolies. Ah, yes, they had to be punished too. A teacher had a cane in the classroom in those days.

(Cross fade down-right. A boy is sitting and talking to an imagined row of pupils, represented by plastic water bottles.)

BOY *(DEBLOO)*

You have not brought your home work? That is the second time this week. Go and stand in that corner. I will attend to you in a minute. And Potlu, why is your shirt not tucked into your pants? To the corner. Bantu, stop sniggering! First you have twenty spelling mistakes, then you snigger in class. To the corner!

(Boy picks up a cane and brandishes it menacingly.)

All right, put out your hands all of you. Remember, this is really for your own good. Going and squealing to your parents is not going to help!

(The light opens to reveal a group of schoolchildren on an excursion accompanied by a Chowkidar. Two of the children have names in the play – Debloo and Pupli. The children perform as an ensemble, sharing parts amongst themselves, providing the links to scenes.

Upstage is the set for the play, not clearly visible yet. The group is watching the boy down-right. We recognize the voice heard thus far as that of the Chowkidar.)

CHOWKIDAR

Debloo-baba, We have to stay together when I am showing you around. You must not go off on your own like that. You had us all so worried.

CHILDREN

>> Debloo!

>> Always wandering off!

>> Day dreaming!

>> And those are our water bottles!

>> We left them with our bags!

>> Give us the bottles back!

(The children pick up the water bottles, ending Debloo's game.)

DEBLOO

Oh, all right! Take your bottles back. I haven't taken a drop from any of them.

CHOWKIDAR

But you shouldn't have taken off on your own like that!

DEBLOO

They were making preparations for a play.

A CHILD

A play?

ANOTHER

A play? Here?

DEBLOO

It must be a jatra group.

ANOTHER

You must be imagining things!

ANOTHER

Just like you!

CHOWKIDAR

There hasn't been a jatra here for ages!

A CHILD (PUPLI)

I wish we could see a drama performed here today.

CHOWKIDAR

Ah, jatra, jatra! What fine performances they used to be!

ANOTHER

I wish Debloo is right! Not just another day dream.

(Crossfade. Spot upstage on armchair. The voice is heard.)

VOICE

Of course we also performed plays. The family loved to write plays for children and the children loved to perform them. All of us really looked forward to performing in the courtyard theatre. There was something or the other happening in our theatre all the time. It was also the place where visiting Jatra troupes performed their plays. Those were late night performances, going on through the night. We were never allowed to watch them, whisked off upstairs after supper by a servant. "Off to bed!" We knew that the jatra people were great storytellers and fine entertainers. But what they actually did in the courtyard remained a deep mystery. I could only wish I was there, and only imagine what they might be doing.

(Cross fade to the group.)

DEBLOO

I tell you I saw them. They were preparing for a play. They were laying out all the props and the costumes

A CHILD

Do you think...?

PUPLI

You know what? Robi-da believed strongly in the great power of imagination. If you really imagined something with all your heart it could appear just like that in front of your eyes.

ANOTHER *(To Chowkidar)*
What do you say? Is that true?

CHOWKIDAR
Well...

DEBLOO
Maybe it works for some, and doesn't work for others.

CHOWKIDAR
True, true! Sometimes two people see the same thing in two different ways.

PUPLI
Like yourself now. You could be a Chowkidar in Jorasanko. Or you could be the Kabuliwala in Robi-da's story.

DEBLOO
Or "Shey" in the stories.

A CHILD
"Shey"?

PUPLI
"Him". "He". That lovable rascal of a companion of Robi-da in cooking up stories.

CHOWKIDAR
Now that you mention it...

ANOTHER
You know, I wondered about that when he came to take us for a tour of Thakurbadi.

ANOTHER
Me too! I thought Oh my god, it is the Kabuliwala!

ANOTHER
Well, are you?

CHOWKIDAR
Ah...Well...You see...

DEBLOO
It's up to us! We can make him the Kabuliwala if we want to!

A CHILD
Do you think we can make him give us a play here if we want to?

ANOTHER
If we want to strongly enough?

DEBLOO
Tell you what! Let's sit down in a tight circle here and make our wish.
(They sit)
I think it works better if we hold hands.
(They do)

CHOWKIDAR
I think it works even better if you close your eyes.
(They do)
(The stage lights come on to reveal the main acting area. The rostrum is decorated. On one side, stage right, are two clothes horses with costumes. On the other, stage left, are benches with props laid out. It is a colorful sight. Appropriate music.
The Chowkidar has seated himself at the foot of the rostrum. He is now wearing a Pathani head dress and has a large bag with him.
The children open their eyes and see the stage.)

ALL
Kabuliwala! Kabuliwala!
(They rush to him)
What do you have for us, Kabuliwala? What's in your bag?

CHOWKIDAR
Aren't you frightened of the Kabuliwala?

A CHILD
Frightened? Why?

CHOWKIDAR
Am I not going to carry you away in my bag?

ANOTHER
But we know the story already. We know what you really carry in the bag.

ALL
>> Pishta
>> Badam
>> Apricots, walnuts
>> Nice things to eat!
>> Goodies!

CHOWKIDAR
Hmmm...I am afraid I have to disappoint you today.

A CHILD
No goodies?

CHOWKIDAR
The supply from Kabul has dried up, my dear friends. You have to get your badam from California now.

ANOTHER
Then what are you doing here in Kolkata?

CHOWKIDAR
Where else can I go? This is my home.

ANOTHER
And the bag? What do you have for us now?

CHOWKIDAR
What else? It is what you wished for a few moments ago!

PUPLI
Stories!

CHOWKIDAR
From my creator himself!

DEBLOO
Stories by Robi-da?

CHOWKIDAR
Right here! Right now!
Right! What stories do you want?

A CHILD
Animal stories!

ANOTHER
People stories!

ALL
>> Clever animals!
>> Stupid people!
>> Funny animals!
>> Funny people!
>> Tigers!
>> Jackals!
>> Kings!
>> Ministers!

CHOWKIDAR
Well, there are the animals, and there are the people. What would you like?

PUPLI
Give us both! Animal people. And people animals!

CHOWKIDAR
How much time do you have? Your bus leaves in one hour and thirty minutes from now. How much can you take in that time?

A CHILD
As much as we can take!

CHOWKIDAR
Clever! We must include clever children in the stories! Do you know how many stories Robi-da wrote?

A CHLD
Hundreds!

ANOTHER
Thousands!

CHOWKIDAR
Nobody really knows the exact number. But they were enough to fill a whole bag like this one. And his little plays for children? And his poems? His letters to the children he loved?
Oooh, add them all up, and we need many more bags!

A CHILD
I think you are going to begin with the Kabuliwala story. Right?

ANOTHER
Wrong! Everybody knows the Kabuliwala story. Let's have some other stories.

CHOWKIDAR
That is a point, you know. Let us look at some other stories. So many of them have remained hidden in this bag for so many many years.

A CHILD
Are you going to tell us all the stories yourself?

CHOWKIDAR
I don't have to. I have arranged a drama group to do that for you.

DEBLOO
I told you! And this is where they will perform, right?

CHOWKIDAR
Where else? This is where you imagined they would perform, right?!

PUPLI
Have you chosen the stories yet? Can we make up some stories too?

CHOWKIDAR
You imagined the drama performance. Why can't you imagine the stories?

ANOTHER
You mean...?

CHOWKIDAR
Of course! Go ahead!
(The group sits in a huddle again, eyes closed.
Change in lighting. Music. The cast and crew come onto the stage from all directions and stand in a semi-circle above the children's group. They look menacing! A few beats.)

AN ACTOR *(Bellowing, snapping the children out of their meditation)*
All right! What are we waiting for? Let's get on with it!

OTHER ACTORS
>> We don't have all night for this!
>> An hour and twenty five minutes now!
>> We have to get started!
>> Clear the stage!

CHOWKIDAR
Your time starts NOW!
(The children's group clears the stage hurriedly. The Chowkidar introduces the first story to the audience, as the actors set up for it.)

LINK – THE ARYAN

THE ARYAN

The scene is the office of a publisher. The principal characters are the publisher and a visitor. Other authors join in. They may be men or women. Only the visitor is given a name. The other characters may or may not be given names.

LINK

CHOWKIDAR
When people look at pictures of Rabindranath Tagore, they can only think of him as Gurudev. He is sooo serious looking in all those pictures, like a philosopher or a high priest or prophet Moses or something like that. They can't imagine another side to him. The fun loving side. Of course Robi-da was a philosopher as well, everybody knows that. But he was a philosopher with a twinkle in his eye. And you know what? He could be very philosophical while poking fun at things. What did he poke fun at? Oh, many things – the short-sighted caste system, the arrogance of the rich and famous, the chamchagiri of those went along with them, the Western orientation of the elite, self appointed godmen, their gullible chelas, doctors and their fees and their mysterious medicines – all of these seen as much today as in his time. He came from a wealthy family himself, but spent a lot of time with the poor, working on the family's lands. Maybe that is why he was able to laugh at people like his own. Maybe that is why he saw wisdom in the lives of humble people all the time. Robi-da was deeply spiritual in his personal life, but was constantly critical of blind faith and superstition. He had very little patience with religious bigotry.

For instance, in one of his short stories the publisher of a progressive magazine is visited by a man whose claim to fame is that he is born an Aryan.

(The Chowkidar withdraws. The Visitor enters.)

PUBLISHER
You are...?

VISITOR
I am an Aryan.

PUBLISHER
That means a Hindu.

VISITOR
No, I am an Aryan first, a Hindu by the way.

PUBLISHER
Your name?

VISITOR
Chintamani Kundan Chaturbhujdas.

PUBLISHER

And what can I do for you?

VISITOR

I wish to write an essay for your magazine.

PUBLISHER

Do you have a topic for the essay?

VISITOR

I shall write on the supremacy of the Aryan religion.

PUBLISHER

You will pardon my ignorance, but what is this Aryan business?

VISITOR *(Surprised)*

You don't know about Aryan heritage?! Look, sir, I am an Aryan. My father, Shri Nakul Kundan Chaturbhujdas, is an Aryan. His father, Shri Sahadev Kundan Chaturbhujdas was an Aryan.

PUBLISHER

A chatur-ful family, I can see. So, by religion you are...different from the rest of us?

VISITOR

I suppose so.

PUBLISHER

How do you tell the difference between Aryan religion and non-Aryan religion?

VISITOR

That which is not non-Aryan religion is Aryan religion.

PUBLISHER

And who would be the non-Aryans?

VISITOR

Those who are not non-Aryans are Aryans. For example, I am not a non-Aryan. My father, Shri Nakul Kundan Chaturbhujdas, is not a non-Aryan. His father, Shri Sahadev Kundan Chaturbhujdas was not a non-Aryan. His father –

PUBLISHER

I think I've got it. You are saying that since your father, Shri Nakul Kundan Chaturbhujdas, is not my father, and I have no relationship with his father, Shri Sahadev Kundan Chaturbhujdas, I am a non-Aryan.

VISITOR

Yes...No...I mean, I am not sure.

PUBLISHER (*Admonishing*)

What do you mean you are not sure? Are you not sure Shri Nakul Kundan Chaturbhujdas is not my father? Are you not sure whose son you are and who is not your father's son?

VISITOR

Sir, the issue is not about who is whose son? It is about their race. We must know what race we both belong to.

PUBLISHER

Your race or my race?

VISITOR

Do you not see that we are both Aryan by birth?

PUBLISHER

So you think Shri Nakul Kundan Chaturbhujdas and I have something in common after all?

VISITOR

Why not, sir?

PUBLISHER

Why, sir?

VISITOR

All right, have it your way. If you don't want to be an Aryan, that is your business. I am only sure that I and my father and grandfather are Aryans. All my ancestors on my father's side are Aryans.

PUBLISHER

How many generations of Aryan ancestors can you trace in your family line?

VISITOR

We are all descended from Sage Kashyap.

PUBLISHER

They say there was a sage Bharadwaj who started our line. But what about the fathers of sage Kashyap and sage Bharadwaj? I wonder which lines these sages came from.

VISITOR

I can see that no discussion is possible with you. This is all because of the miserable English medium education today.

PUBLISHER

What other kind of education can you get in Calcutta? Did you not also study in an English medium school?

VISITOR

That is a crime I cannot be accused of. I dropped out of school before I was twelve.

PUBLISHER
What did you do then?

VISITOR
I joined an Aryan Mission school.

PUBLISHER
Did the Aryans not come here from Europe?

VISITOR
Did the Aryans not go to Europe from here?
(Enter three other authors. The publisher greets them.)

PUBLISHER
Ah, welcome, welcome!
(A general exchange of pleasantries)
I hope you have brought a good supply of essays, as always.

AUTHOR 2
A pleasure writing for you, as always.

AUTHOR 3
You have another visitor, I see.

PUBLISHER
Yes, this is –

VISITOR
What do you people write about?

AUTHOR 4
Oh, various things – ants, bees, science, myths...

AUTHOR 2
Gods, goddesses...

AUTHOR 3
Puppy dog tails...

AUTHOR 1
Anything about Aryans?

AUTHOR 4
Well, scientific facts came to us from Europe, which is the land of Aryans.

VISITOR
BAH! European Aryans are an inferior race. The best science came from Indian Aryans. Don't you know that?

AUTHOR 2
You mean Hindu Aryans?

VISITOR
Aryan first, Hindu by the way.

PUBLISHER

This is Shri Chaturbhujdas III here. He believes —

VISITOR

Indian Aryan science was always far ahead of European science. Take your hair oil, for instance. You will have noticed in every Aryan household that even today they put three drops of oil on the floor before applying a palm-full of the oil to the head. Do you know why?

(An awkward pause. The publisher intervenes.)

PUBLISHER

Perhaps you will be good enough to educate us on the matter.

VISITOR

If you don't know something as elementary as this, how can you write articles on scientific matters? Do you know why Aryans snap their fingers while yawning?

ALL AUTHORS

>> No

>> Snap fingers

>> Yawning

>> There must be an explanation

PUBLISHER

We must find out.

VISITOR

And the Aryan ladies — have you seen what they do with a hand-held fan? *(Another pause. The authors look at each other)*

When she is fanning herself if the fan touches anybody by chance the lady taps the fan once on the ground. Why?

ALL AUTHORS

>> We never thought about it

>> We know nothing about it

>> We don't know anything

VISITOR

Look at yourselves! You proclaim that Europeans gave us science, and yet you know nothing about why Aryans yawn or sneeze or massage their head with oil!

(The publisher motions to the others, cautioning them that the first author may not be quite sound up there.)

PUBLISHER

Sir, about dropping oil on the floor before applying it to the head...A fascinating observation. What is the explanation?

VISITOR

It is called meghanashtamam. In English they have copied it to call it magnetism.

AUTHOR 2

That means you have studied the concept of magnetism in English texts?

VISITOR

Entirely unnecessary! You don't need to study English texts to know science. You don't need English to know anything.

ALL AUTHORS

>> True! True!

>> English confuses things

>> Especially the pro-noun-ci-ation

VISITOR

It is all Greek and Latin

PUBLISHER

Reductio ad absurdum
(He tries to caution the others again)

VISITOR

Don't you know what ancient Aryan science says?
(Another pause)
There are three kinds of energy. Within-Energy, Without-Energy and Out-Within-Energy. When the body is oiled, an out-within-energy is created in the soul within, leading to a magnetic field without. That is magnetism at work for you! To counter the magnetic field the Englishman invented the Turkish towel, to be rubbed vigorously on the head after a shower. Indian Aryans have had a thousand year old legacy of using a hand woven gamchha after an oil bath. A clearly superior alternative to the English practice. Think about it!
(Dramatic pause. The authors are dumbstruck.)
And all you can do is to keep parroting that Englishman Newton's utterances, which he picked up from Aryan science in the first place.
(The publisher takes the group of authors away for an aside. They break free and return to the Visitor.)

ALL AUTHORS

>> Wah! Origin of magnetism!

>> Purpose of magnetism!

>> Discovery of magnetism!

>> Invention of magnetism!

VISITOR

I could go on...

ALL AUTHORS
>> Oh, please do
>> Go on, please
>> Aryan physics, Aryan chemistry

PUBLISHER *(Snapping finger, yawning)*
And snapping fingers while yawning!

VISITOR
Reverse magnetism! The concavity of the palm converges charging power, setting off a parallel generating process in which receptive force, breaking free of impelling force, is reciprocally influenced by compelling force, transcending life, cause and retention. Then sattva, rajas and tamas are brought into an escape mechanism, in which gaseous heat is punctuated by the snapping of thumb with middle finger, thus causing neurological heat, that prevents solar heat from entering orifices of the human body and disturbing the essential heat equilibrium.
(A dramatic pause)
If this is not science, what is?

AUTHOR 2
Nothing else!

VISITOR
What is?

AUTHOR 3
Nothing more!

VISITOR
What is?

AUTHOR 4
Nothing ever!

PUBLISHER *(Aside)*
All he needs is a saffron robe.

VISITOR
Our sages knew everything about life long before Darwin.

PUBLISHER
Sir, about the ladies tapping the ground once with the fan...

VISITOR
Oscillating magnetism!

PUBLISHER
And defying gravity above the earth in an aeroplane...

VISITOR
Modulated magnetism!

PUBLISHER
How did you acquire all this knowledge?

VISITOR
It came to me.

PUBLISHER (*Incredulous*)
Perhaps you would be so kind as to wait outside while I attend to some business with these authors here. They are here for an engagement...

ALL AUTHORS (*Pushing the Publisher out*)
>> Perhaps you would put the kettle on
>> Perhaps some namkeen biscuits from the bakery
>> Perhaps a plate of paan
>> Not to forget the tobacco with the paan
>> Tea and namkeen biscuits please
>> Paan with tobacco please

(A short pause. The other authors stand facing Author 1 in a semi circle. He claps. They fetch a saffron robe and rudraksh beads and dress him. When they are done, he claps again. They kneel. He claps. They prostrate. He blesses them.)

LINK – THE GENTLEMAN JACKAL THE GENTLEMAN JACKAL

Pupli and Chowkidar down-left. She is reading a report. Chowkidar speaks

LINK

CHOWKIDAR
Time for an animal story! (*To audience*)
Ready for an animal story? Yes?
What animal would you like? A lion? A lion tailed macaque? A dinosaur?! Maybe a duck-billed platypus? A hare, a tortoise? Ah, we've heard that one a million times, no? Was it a turtle or a tortoise in that story? By the way, what is the difference between a turtle and a tortoise?

PUPLI
I asked my teacher and she didn't know. She didn't want to say she didn't know, so she made me work on it and write a report.

CHOWKIDAR
You want a story about a dog? Did you know that dogs came from jackals? No? It's true. Before dogs there were jackals. The same canine line. They were the first to make friends with humans.

PUPLI
How about a jackal story? Shall we try a jackal story of Robi-da?

CHOWKIDAR
The story of the Gentleman Jackal. The first NRJ – the Non-Resident Jackal.

PUPLI
In one of the stories by Shey – you know who that is by now, He, Him, that Fellow – he sends a report about an institution that has been set up to create gentlemen jackals. It is called the Association for Cultural Development of Canines – Jackal Chapter.

CHOWKIDAR
ACDCJC for short.

PUPLI
Shey is supposed to have sent this report about a success story.

CHOWKIDAR
Almost successful.

PUPLI
The almost successful making of a gentleman jackal.
(In the action area we see a woman in a chair reading a newspaper with her morning cuppa. A jackal steps in unnoticed, walks up to her and peers over her shoulder.)

WOMAN
It says here that there is a competition between onion growers and potato growers. It is about prices. Who can raise prices faster? Higher? They are racing to see who will be first to reach the price of gold.
(The jackal taps the woman on the shoulder.)
I've told you! Whoever gets to the newspaper first, reads it first. You have to wait. Pour yourself a cup of tea till I finish.
(A man enters, stops and takes in the scene. The jackal moves to pour a cup of tea.)

MAN *(To audience)*
It is working. We have got Hoo-Wah to take an interest in the newspaper. That's his name, Hoo-Wah. He can't read it, of course. That is going to take much more work.
(The jackal holds out the cup of tea for the man, who gestures to the jackal to take it.)
Getting a jackal to make conversation with us was not too difficult. Getting him to read a newspaper....

WOMAN
(Putting down the paper) An English newspaper!

MAN
Too much for Hoo-Wah at this stage. That's his name. Oh, there is so much more we can do with Hoo-Wah.

WOMAN
We are ready for the morning test now. Shall we?
(Hoo-Wah moves down to the Man enthusiastically. The Man uses hand signals to make the jackal sit – stand – drop – beg – etc. Finally he addresses the jackal.)

MAN
What is your name?

HOO-WAH
Hooooo- Waaah

MAN
Good! *(To audience)*
Now, we are ready for the day's work.

WOMAN
What shall we take up in class today?

HOO-WAH
Begging your pardon, ma'am, sir, you are very kind and generous and all that in taking me as your student. But you are only teaching me doggie tricks – sitting, dropping, begging, and so on. Any stupid Labrador can do these things. Surely a jackal deserves something more!

WOMAN
What would you like us to do with you?

HOO-WAH
Can't you make a man out of me?

MAN
You mean, like...?

HOO-WAH
A gentleman! So I can also sit in the verandah, have tea and biscoot, wear a suit with a tie, go to the cinema...

MAN
Why on earth would you want to do all that?

HOO-WAH
You know how all in the jackal tribe hold you humans in such great awe. You are like gods to them. If I can look like a human too, I will become a VIP jackal. Even a VVIP. Maybe a godman jackal.

WOMAN
Shri Hoo-Wahnandashankara...

HOO-WAH
Shri Shri Shri Hoo-Wahnandashankara!

WOMAN *(To Man)*
What do you say? Shall we take him on?

MAN

He seems ready for it. I say let's give it a go.
(Crossfade to Pupli and Chowkidar in their corner.)

PUPLI

It was a big project for them, wasn't it?

CHOWKIDAR

The first real challenge for ACDCJC. From little doggie tricks to the real thing.

PUPLI

Making a man out of a jackal!

CHOWKIDAR

Making a gentleman out of Ho-Wah.

PUPLI

Did Hoo-Wah's family know?

CHOWKIDAR

Of course not! He was going to surprise them!

PUPLI

How did they do it? What did they actually do?

CHOWKIDAR

The very first thing to do was to appoint a surgical Task Force. Four eminent members of ACDCJC were appointed as the team.
(We see Hoo-Waa being laid on a table. Four persons in surgeon's gowns stand around the table, their backs to the audience, hiding Hoo-Wah. The Man and Woman are joined by two others to form the team. On one side is a table with the surgical instruments laid out: a hand drill, a wood saw, a pair of garden scissors, butcher's knife, and so on.)

ONE

The very first thing to do is to get rid of his fur and make him hairless.
(We see a great big chopper brandished by a surgeon, descending on the table. A moment later a coat of fur is tossed aside.)

ALL

Aah! Look at his belly button!

TWO

Next! We must get him to stand erect on his hind legs.

THREE

This little surgical procedure should do the trick.
(We see a large hammer going into the circle, followed by a roll of bandage. There are heavy thuds from the operating table.)

FOUR

All right, let's get him to stand.

(All four help Hoo-Wah off the table and help him stand. He is looking bare. Both his legs have crepe/bandage above and below the knees. Hoo-Wah staggers for a while, with encouraging remarks from the others. Finally, he is erect. He is pleased.)

ALL

Aah!

(One guides him to a large mirror.)

ONE

There! How does it look? How does it feel?

HOO-WAH

Good...Good...

ONE

That doesn't sound too enthusiastic. Is something wrong?

HOO-WAH

No, no, this is good. You have done a good job.

TWO

But!

HOO-WAH

But it somehow does not feel complete. I still don't feel hundred percent human.

THREE

Ninety percent? Eighty percent?

HOO-WAH

A hundred and ten percent.

(The four close in on Hoo-Wah, examine him closely.)

ALL

AAHHH! The tail! The tail! Off with his tail!

HOO-WAH

Wait! Gentlemen, wait!

ALL

It has to go!

HOO-WAH

But it is the best jackal tail in the whole tribe! My fame far and wide is because of my superb furry tail! People recognize me from a mile away because of my tail!

ALL

Then it must go!

HOO-WAH

The English tailors in Calcutta are all after my tail for a lady's overcoat.

ALL

It must go!

(The four of them carry him back to the table. A large knife descends. A sharp "Owww"! A tail is flung aside. The bandage is taken off. They help him stand again.

He is led to the mirror.)

FOUR

Blessed is the beast that is rid of its beastliness!

ALL

Amen!

FOUR

Repeat after us ...Amen!

HOO-WAH

Amen...

ONE

Is that better?

HOO-WAH

I suppose it is.... If you think so...

ALL

We think so!

THREE

How should he be dressed?

FOUR

Very simple! It should be in keeping with his desires.

(Three others bring a strap-on shirt with bow tie, a tail coat and a bowler hat for Hoo-Waa.

A solar topi should also do.

He is dressed up now. One guides him to the mirror again.)

HOO-WAH

Hoo-Wah, Hoo-Wah, is that really you?

ONE

It won't do.

ALL

It simply won't do.

TWO

You cannot be called Hoo-Wah anymore.

HOO-WAH

Not Hoo-Wah? But that is my name! My aunt says it is the sweetest name ever.

ALL

Not any more.

THREE

As a human animal in human clothes and a human bearing, you must have a human name.

ONE

You will henceforth be known as...Jack!

TWO

Well! Our job is done! You are a man now!

THREE

A fine specimen of man, we must add.

FOUR

Just come back here after three days for a routine check up.

HOO-WAH

Any follow up treatment? Diet restrictions?

ONE

Just one. This is important. For the next thirty days and thirty nights you must not – repeat, simply must not – meet anybody from the jackal tribe.

TWO

You must not meet any of them. You must not speak to any of them.

THREE

You must never again speak your native jackal language. Put that behind you for ever.

ONE

Practice being yourself. Which is?

HOO-WAH

Hoo-Wah.

ALL

NO!!!

THREE

You are...?

HOO-WAH

Jack!

ALL

Good!

ONE

You must meditate for at least two hours every day. You must keep telling yourself that you- are-Jack.

HOO-WAH

How should I do that?

TWO

Try chanting "Jack be nimble, Jack be quick".

THREE

Keep repeating it to yourself.

(The four of them leave. Hoo-Wah sits in a corner, closes his eyes and meditates. Crossfade to Pupli an Chowkidar.)

CHOWKIDAR

Hoo-Wah's aunt, the one who gave him his name, was also the buk-buk of the tribe. She was in fact called Chatter-di. She dearly loved Hoo-Wah, who had left the village days ago and hadn't been seen by anybody since.

PUPLI

Anxious about his disappearance, she went to the Village Chief and demanded that he organize a search party to look for Hoo-Wah.

CHOWKIDAR

He was no ordinary jackal, after all. He had the finest furry tale in the whole tribe.

PUPLI

Meanwhile, Hoo-Wah, fully recovered and cheerful, was thinking about how he would astonish his family and tribe. And how they would make him their god.

(A search party of jackals, led by Chatter-di, is seen approaching the action area, crouched, catching the scent, advancing.)

CHATTER-DI

Stop! I think we may be near.

A JACKAL

We are at the edge of the human settlement.

ANOTHER

No scent of Hoo-Wah.

ANOTHER

Some other strange scent drifting this way.

CHATTER-DI

Smells like that spray the humans use under their armpits.

A JACKAL

Shall we try calling him.

CHATTER-DI

Good idea. Let me try first.
Hooooeeee Hoooo-Waaah !!

ALL

Hooooeeee Hoooo-Waaah !!

(A booming voice offstage)

Jack! Remember what you have been told. Ignore them!

ALL

Hooooeeee Hoooo-Waaah !! Hooooeeee Hoooo-Waaah !!

THE VOICE

Hold your ground, Jack! Don't move! They will go away.

ALL

Hooooeeeeoooooeeee Hoooo-Waaaa !!

(Hoo-Waa cannot take it anymore!)

HOO-WAA

Ayyeeaiyohyoowaaahh! I am here!!

(The search party steps into the clearing at the same time that Hoo-Waa does. There is shocked silence, broken by Hoo-Wah's excited proclamation in his newly acquired accent.)

Hellow, I'm Jack! How-do-you-do?

(The search party remains stunned)

Aunty! It's me!!

(The search party shrieks in horror and runs away in all directions.)

SEARCH PARTY

>> A ghost!

>> A mad ghost!

>> An English ghost!

>> A ghost freak!

(Hoo-Wah is left standing there, finely dressed, speechless. All he can do is moan.

Crossfade to Pupli and Chowkidar.)

PUPLI

Even his own aunt didn't recognize him?

CHOWKIDAR

Maybe she didn't. But again, maybe she did. Maybe that is why she ran away.

PUPLI

What did Hoo-Wah do after that?

CHOWKIDAR

What could he do? He was neither here nor there. Shooed away by the humans, and snarled at and snapped at by the jackals. He tried meditating to a different rhyme – to get his tail back. Any tail would do! A rabbit tail, a mongoose, one of Little Bo-peep's lambs. Nothing worked.

PUPLI

Poor Hoo-Wah!

CHOWKIDAR

Not really. He was last seen wandering over the hills giving lectures at ashrams and conferences. I hear the management institutes are also after him now.

LINK – LAST RITES

LAST RITES

A bench DC with an elderly gentleman lying on his back, arms crossed on his chest.

Around the bench are five chairs. A chair to the right of the gentleman has a doctor. Down-left or down-right is a huddle of women, heads covered, faces concealed. Three of the gentleman's four sons are seated in the other chairs at the start, but move about through the scene. All the sons return to the chairs at the end. The sons are all dressed alike, for mourning.

The sons may or may not be given names.

The feed-in link to this scene is a poem by the children, the lines suitably distributed.

LINK

POEM
There was a doctor of Chittagong
Whose list of patients was two miles long
On looking closer I read
That all of them were dead.
There was a doctor of Cooch Behar
With secret remedies in a jar
A spoonful here, a spoonful there
Corpses littered everywhere
There was a doctor of Bangalore
Rather proud of his hit and run score
Patients of every description
Despatched with a single prescription
The Right Honourable Krishna Kumar Rai Bahadur is going to die.
As you might have guessed from the name
He belongs to an important family.
A very important family.
The importance level
Of the important families of Calcutta
Is measured by the company one keeps
Who must all be important personalities themselves.

(The children exit. The scene opens.)

SON 1
Who all must be informed first?

SON 3
We must make up the list quickly.
(Weeping from the ladies huddle.)

SON 1

Can the ladies wait a bit, please? There is still time for your wailing. Just hold on.

SON 2

Yes, Welling saheb must be informed. And Holding saheb.

FATHER

What is the list you are preparing, boys?

SON 3

We must send a note to people informing them about your death, father.

FATHER

I am still breathing, am I not?

SON 2

We should be prepared, should we not? We must start writing now.

SON 1

We must collect the condolence letters from all important people as soon as possible.

SON 2

All the Englishmen's condolence letters.

SON 1

We must get the letters printed along with the news of the death. If they are delayed they will be stale.

SON 2

The obituary and the letters must be in print at the same time.

FATHER

Can you not wait till my hands and feet have turned cold?

SON 3

How can we wait, father? The work on the list must start straight away. At this time the Englishmen go off to Shimla and Darjeeling.

SON 2

Ah, remember to include Right Honourable Mr.Shimmerling.

SON 1

Let's see, we already have...the Governor General saheb, Macaulay saheb, Wilson saheb, Gilbert saheb, Sullivan saheb...

FATHER

Won't the sons chant at least one hundred and one names of Lord Vishnu for me?

Oh, Hari Hari...

SON 2

Of course, we must include Harrison saheb. I will add the name.

FATHER
At least chant Ram Ram, my sons.

SON 2
Yes, yes, Ramsey saheb...

FATHER
Narayan Narayan!

SON 1
Write down Norman saheb
(Son 4 enters)

SON 4
Good evening, doctor. Any progress?

DOCTOR
Well, it is looking like –

SON 4 *(To others)*
Why are we wasting time on non-essential matters? The most important matter is not being attended to.

FATHER
Thank you, my son.

SON 4
Taking part in the funeral needs enough notice, no? People must be informed, no? We have to get Police bandobast for the procession. It is very important.

FATHER
The most important thing for the funeral is for me to stop breathing. Then...

SON 1
Don't worry about that, father. *(To doctor)* Doctor?

DOCTOR
Yes, sir?

SON 1
What progress? How much more time?

SON 3
What time should we mention for people to gather?

DOCTOR
Well, I think...
(Weeping from the ladies huddle.)

SON 4 *(To the ladies)*
Shhh! There is important business being discussed here.

DOCTOR
Everything going well, probably about ten o'clock.
(Loud wail from the ladies huddle.)

SON 2

Ohho! What is the problem with you all? Weeping and wailing like this! Is that all you can do? We must get the tearful condolence letters from the Englishmen first. They must reach in time!

SON 4

What do you say, doctor?

DOCTOR

Everything should be over by about 2 am, at the latest.

SON 1

That means...Oh god! We must move fast! Hurry up with the list for condolence messages. Get the press release out, quickly!

DOCTOR

The medicine...We have to get that here first.

SON 4

Oh, the medical store on Park Street is open all night. If the telegraph office and the newspaper offices close, we will miss the bus!

DOCTOR

By that time the patient may...

SON 1

Exactly! That is why we must hurry. We cannot have him dying before the letters and announcements are sent out.

SON 3

Everybody, get to work!

SON 4

You can mention the time for the start of the funeral procession as 6 am.
(All the sons exit hurriedly.
The doctor remains by the father's side. The father hums a bhajan to himself softly.
The lights dim momentarily.
Fade in.
The scene is as at the start. All four sons are seated. The father is sitting up, looking cheerful. He has a packet of potato chips in his hands.)

SON 4

Doctor, it is almost five. You said 2 am.

DOCTOR

I know. What to do? The pulse rate is sound.

SON 1

What kind of doctor are you? You have landed us in deep trouble!

SON 3

It was the delay in bringing his medicines. Not taking them has made him recover.

FATHER

My sons, you are in danger of worrying yourself to death. Go and get some sleep. I am feeling better now.

SON 3

Tchha! Why could he not have gone at the appointed hour?

SON 2

We can't be punctual in anything we do. Look at the Englishmen!

SON 4

I am not feeling so well now. The cremation ground has been booked for seven o'clock. They have taken an advance payment.

OTHER SONS

>> I am not feeling well myself...

>> Me neither...

>> Oh, my head...

FATHER

Lucky, the doctor is here.

SON 1

All the trouble we have taken for you, father!

SON 4

All the expense.

(The father rises and exits. On the way he gets the women's huddle to move on too.)

DOCTOR

I have an idea.

(The four sons turn to the doctor. Pause.)

SON 1

Well?!

DOCTOR

If any of you would care to take his place and breathe your last, we can still go ahead on schedule.

LINK – IN THE PINK OF DEATH

IN THE PINK OF DEATH

The feed-in link to this scene is by the children, the lines suitably distributed.

Robi-da loved to joke about death.
Oh yes, he wrote about flowers and trees and birds in flight and sunrises
and sunsets.
But he could be really funny when he wrote about death.
Here is a poem we enjoyed working on for this play.

Knock knock! Who's there?
Your faithful servant, sir. If you would just care
To listen for a moment, it is not good news I bring
Just one ear please, the pillow you may still cling.

Go away! I rise when I hear the alarm ring
When I am on my feet, you may bring
News, good or bad, new or stale,
About floods, earthquakes or ministers in jail.

Sir, the house is on fire! No answer came
Did he not hear? Was he playing a game?
You must be up, sir, and out
No time to lose, without a doubt.

Opening half an eye the master said
You know what happens to my head
When my sleep is incomplete
The blasted migraine leaves me dead beat.

Sir! your migraine, all things said
Is surely better than waking up dead
Not just cold in hand and feet
But roasted, toasted and charred meat.

Aah, stop pestering me! I will awake
When it is time for me to take
Toothbrush to teeth, towel to face
Early risings are such a disgrace.

The old man neither stirred nor turned
While the ground floor burned
When the flames licked the windows on the right

The master turned left, avoiding the sight.
The servant tried once more to plead
With the master to heed
The urgent call of crumbling walls and blazing bed
Go away, you! Always and forever obedient, the servant fled.
(The children exit. The scene opens.

A train compartment with two passengers, both men, or one man [ONE] and one woman [TWO]. Both appear middle aged. They are not named. One of them has a headache.)

ONE

Aaahh...

TWO

Hmmm...

ONE

It is getting worse by the minute...Getting unbearable.

TWO

Which part of the head is hurting?

ONE

The right side...Excuse me, you are...?

TWO

Just asking, just asking. You seem to be in great distress.

ONE

An understatement, sir. The pain is killing me.

TWO

Hmmm...Right side, you say. Is it throbbing? *(One nods his head.)* Dhug dhug dhug dhug? *(One nods his head.)* Hmmm...

ONE

You can see how miserable I am, can't you?

TWO

Miserable, yes. Just what my brother had

ONE

Your brother...

TWO

My brother.

ONE

He has headaches just like this? Then you can –

TWO

Had.

ONE
Had? He got rid of them?

TWO
You could say that. He died.

ONE
He...

TWO
He is dead.

ONE
He died. Did he have –

TWO
Just like yours. In the last two days of his life he even looked just like you now.

ONE
Looked like me?

TWO
Sick. Really sick.

ONE
Sick? But my headache is just –

TWO
Throbbing! The pain going down the whole side, cramping the leg. How does your right leg feel? Ah, cramped, I can see...Tch tch tch tch! Your eyes, tired, yes? Partly opened lips, skin colour turned pale, looseness of arm joints...

ONE
I have all these? Why didn't anybody tell me? My friends, my family?

TWO
Everybody is busy with their own worlds nowadays. Who has the time to look at others closely anymore?

ONE
My doctor, he should have told me.

TWO
Doctor?! Do you believe in doctors?!

ONE
But they –

TWO
Utterly impossible people! Everything ulta-phulta in their work. When you have no problem at all, he gives you a dozen tests and twenty medications. When you are seriously sick he hardly has any time for you! Even on your deathbed –

ONE

Please! Please, sir, you are scaring me.

TWO

The doctor will attend to you only after your body has turned cold – to give your family a death certificate. And to collect fees for that.

ONE

Oh my, oh my, I am feeling really sick now! Aahh, my hands...are they turning cold, you think?

TWO

Hmmm...Let me ask you a few questions, if you don't mind. *(One nods in consent)*

At night do you sleep on your back or on your side?

ONE

On my back all the time. Why?

TWO

Just like my brother. He could not turn at all when he was lying on his back.

ONE

Ah, but I can turn. I can turn either side.

TWO

Ah, but you may not be able to in another two weeks.

ONE

Really?!

TWO

First there will be a pain there, on the right side of the rib cage. Then it will spread downwards, quickly. Within six days it will reach your toes. You will hear all the five toes cry out in pain. Then the arms. Then the swelling in the joints. Then the palpitation...

(He holds One's hands)

ONE

Stop! I am getting giddy!

TWO

You are palpitating.

ONE

I am not feeling good at all.

TWO

You are not looking good at all. You need serious attention.

ONE

I know, I know! But what should I do?

TWO
Are you by any chance on allopathic medicine?

ONE
Yes, of course.

TWO
Khatam! Allopaths are psychopaths! All their prescriptions are poisons, more dangerous than the illness itself! You should be more scared of the allopath than the disease.

ONE
Then what should I...? Should I change to homoeopathy?

TWO
Homoeopaths are sociopaths! Their medicines are nothing but tap water and chalk powder. The same tap water is given by different foreign sounding names.

ONE *(To himself)*
I think I will try Ayurveda...

TWO
If your body can't take a throbbing dhug dhug headache, how will it take Ayurveda? It is safer to take bhang with dhatura from a copper vessel.

ONE
Oh, my terrible fate! What am I to do now? You tell me, sir, what should I do?

TWO
Hmmm...

ONE
You will show me the way out, won't you?

TWO
There seems to be no way out.

ONE
But there must be –

TWO
It is just like my brother's case.

ONE
You are the one who has given me this scare. You must show me some way out!

TWO
What is there to be scared of? Our passage in this world is brief, although life itself is eternal. We come into this world, we stay awhile, we go. We must all go some time. We cannot take anything with us. Not even a throbbing headache. It will all be over soon.

ONE

I must remain cheerful! Look at the bright side of everything. Even my doctor says that to me... Oh! Do you think he knew?

TWO

Maybe. He is a doctor, after all. An allopath.

ONE

I want to get off the train!

TWO

The train is running.

ONE

I will get off at the next station. Yes, I will get off at Madhupur.

TWO

The train will not stop at Madhupur.

ONE

Why won't it stop there?

TWO

There is an outbreak of cholera there. The town is cut off. No train will stop there for another week.

ONE

I am scared! I am scared!

TWO

Scared of what?

ONE

I am scared I am dying.

TWO

According to scientists studying the subject of fear, those who are scared of dying have a greater probability of dying first.

ONE

Call the guard!

TWO

The guard got off at the last station. A new guard will get on at the next station.

ONE

Oh, my heart! My head! Call a doctor! There must be a doctor on the train!

TWO

Does it feel serious?

ONE

Yes, yes! Very serious! Please call a doctor! Quick!

TWO
Never trust a doctor when you are most in need!

ONE *(Collapsing in his seat)*
Please! I think I am dying!

TWO
Hmmm...Let's see... *(Putting his hand on One's head)*
Throbbing? The pain going down the whole side, cramping the leg. How does your right leg feel? Ah, cramped, I can see...Tch tch tch tch! Your eyes, tired, yes? Partly opened lips, skin colour turned pale, looseness of arm joints... *(Steps forward. A pause.)*
Just like my brother.

LINK – PROFIT AND LOSS

PROFIT AND LOSS

This short piece is inspired by Tagore's Riddle Plays, although not written by him. It was included in the play mainly for the children's group. This story-riddle is common in several cultures, probably originating in the Middle East. It is a tale of buying and selling around a horse. In the script below the horse is replaced by an ass.

Another version is included in the play THE COURT JESTER, but with a horse.

The Chowkidar enters and sits at the edge of the rostrum. He claps (or whistles or blows a pipe). The children enter clapping hands in glee and join him.

DEBLOO

You know what? When I get home I am going to ask my parents to buy me lots and lots of books about Robi-da.

CHILD 2 and 3

Me too!

CHILD 4

All his stories.

CHILD 5

All his plays.

CHOWKIDAR

You liked the stories played for you today, didn't you?

ALL

Of course!

PUPLI

I wish we could do a play too!

DEBLOO

You mean...

PUPLI

The actors have so many nice stories for us. Why can't we give them at least one story from our side?

CHILD 2

But this is their show!

CHILD 3

Their show, for us!

CHILD 4 *(To Chowkidar)*

What do you say? Can we?

CHILD 5

Can we? Can we?

CHOWKIDAR
Well, it all depends...

DEBLOO
Depends on what?

CHOWKIDAR
It depends on...

PUPLI
On time? We have enough time!

CHILD 4
Please!

CHILD 3
We want to give something in return!

CHILD 2 and 5
Please!

CHOWKIDAR
All right! You can do one story! Just one!

DEBLOO
Thank you!

CHOWKIDAR
And it had better be a short one. The actors are waiting to do their last two stories.

PUPLI *(To the other children)*
What should we perform?

DEBLOO
Something that's our own! For Robi-da!

CHOWKIDAR
Something short!

CHILD 2
A riddle!

CHILD 3 and 4
Yes!

CHILD 5
Robi-da wrote riddle plays, didn't he?

DEBLOO
I know! We will act a riddle!

PUPLI
The riddle of the ass!

ALL
Yes! The riddle of the ass!

CHOWKIDAR

And to think the actors are preparing a tiger story for you! Well, if you don't mind, I will just watch from this side.

(He starts to go)

CHILD 2

Wait! *(Chowkidar stops)*

We need you!

CHILD 3

We need you in the play.

CHOWKIDAR

Me? In this play? *(The children bring him to DC)*

CHILD 4

You can be the ass!

(By now Pupli has brought an ass mask and put it on Chowkidar. She and Debloo move to down-left corner to watch as Children 2 / 3 / 4 / 5 present the riddle-story.

Child 2 becomes Minister 1 and Child 4 becomes Minister 2 with a few add-on props from the stage. Children 3 and 5 narrate the riddle-story.)

CHILD 3

It was in the Kingdom of Hee-Haw. The asses in the kingdom were the very best. Strong, sturdy, hardworking, reliable.

CHILD 5

They came from a long line, sired by champion asses from all parts of the world.

CHILD 3

But the best of the best were the asses brought specially to the kingdom from faraway Bengaluru.

CHILD 5

Ah, but not everybody could own a Bengaluru ass, oh no. It was only the VVIPs who could get hold of a thoroughbred true-blue Bengaluru ass.

CHILD 3

Or...you knew a trick or two to get that ass without being either close to the king or holding a high rank.

(The first Minister enters. He goes up to Chowkidar in the ass mask — who kicks.)

CHILD 3

(To audience) This is the honourable Minister for Pots and Pans.

CHILD 5 *(To audience)*

You see, there were lots and lots of Ministers in this kingdom. It was to make sure that all the needs of the people were attended to properly.

CHILD 3
Some people have the need to be Ministers.

CHILD 5
One day we may have more ministers than people.

CHILD 5
Anyway, here we have the Minister for Pots and Pans.
(To Minister) Sir, if I may ask, where did you get this magnificent ass from?

MINISTER 1
(With pride, leading the ass to Child 3) He is Bengalurian.

CHILD 3
It is said that only His Highness, the King, may own a Bengalurian ass!

MINISTER 1
Chup! Impudent girl! This ass is mine! I have earned the right to own him! I don't suppose you know who I am in the king's court.

CHILD 5
An ass trader?

MINISTER 1
Hmmphh! Try again.

CHILD 5
I know, an ass doctor!

MINISTER 1 *(To audience)*
We will have to do something about text books for girls in our schools! *(Minister 2 walks on.)*
Ah, here he comes. I knew he was following me.

CHILD 5 *(To audience)*
Ah, the honourable Minister for Kettles and Cans.

MINISTER 2
A hundred salaams, ministerji!

MINISTER 1 *(To Child 3)*
Here it comes.

MINISTER 2
What a fine morning!

MINISTER 1
And...

MINISTER 2
Lovely blue sky!

MINISTER 1
And...

MINISTER 2
Birds singing in praise of this paradise on earth.

MINISTER 1
And...

MINISTER 2
What a magnificent horse!

MINISTER 1
Ah, you are referring to this ass, I believe.

MINISTER 2
Oh! It is.... Why, it is an ass from Bengaluru!

MINISTER 1
My ass!

CHILD 5 *(To audience)*
The Minister for Kettles and Cans wants that ass!

CHILD 3 *(To audience)*
We will have to help. You can take part too. Just listen carefully.
(Child 3 positions herself on the side of Minister 1 and Child 5 positions herself on the side of Minister 2. During the negotiation below the two Ministers "go along" with the game.)

CHILD 5
Oh ministerji, I have admired that ass of yours for a long time. I am wondering if you would care to sell him to me.

MINISTER 1
Perish the thought. He is too dear to me.

MINISTER 2
I can make it worth your while.

MINISTER 1
He is too precious. You can't buy him.

MINISTER 2
How about five thousand silver coins?

MINISTER 1
Well...no, sorry, he is –

MINISTER 2
Ten thousand!

MINISTER 1
Well, all right, since you insist!
(The ass crosses over from Minister 1's side to Minister 2.)

CHILD 5
A few days passed, and the Minister began to miss his ass. He decided to talk to the other Minister.

CHILD 3
Ahem...I say, my good fellow ministerji, I hope all is well with you... and my ass...
(Minister 2 raises his eyebrows)
I mean your ass. *(No response)*

MINISTER 1 *(Continuing)*
You know, I really miss that ass. He was so dear to me. I am wondering if you would consider giving him back to me...? *(No response)*
I can make it worth your while!
(Minister 2 looks at Minister1 at last) Say, twelve thousand silver coins?

MINISTER 2
Well, all right, since you insist!
(The ass crosses over from Minister 2 to Minister 1.)

CHILD 3
It was now the turn of Sri. Kettles and Cans to feel lost without the ass. He had to get him back.

CHILD 5
I say, my old friend, I was wondering...

MINISTER 1
Sorry, I am busy! Can't take your call just now.

MINISTER 2
I can make it worth you while! Say –

MINISTER 1
Sorry!

MINISTER 2
Fourteen thousand silver coins?

MINISTER 1
Well, all right, since you insist!
(The ass crosses over from Minister 1 to Minister 2.)

CHILD 5
What happened then?

CHILD 3
Right! Sri. Pots and Pans simply had to get his ass back.

CHILD 5
He pulled in his tummy, stuck out his chest, and approached the other Minister.

MINISTER 1
I say, old friend, I know we have been through all this before, but –

MINISTER 2
No!

MINISTER 1

But –

MINISTER 2

Sixteen thousand silvers?

(Minister 2 allows the ass to cross over to the other side.

CHILD 3 and CHILD 5 step DC with the ass in the middle. The two Ministers are on either side.)

CHILD 3

So, there we have it.

CHILD 5

The second Minister buys the ass from the first Minister for ten thousand silver coins.

CHILD 3

The first Minister buys the ass back for twelve thousand.

CHILD 5

The second Minister buys him once more for fourteen thousand.

CHILD 3

The first Minister buys him back once more for sixteen thousand.

CHOWKIDAR *(Taking off his mask)*

Now...at the end of all this buying and selling, who has ended making a profit?

(The Chowkidr puts on his mask again. The group engages the audience to give the answer. We see the two Ministers calculating frantically. The ass dances in glee and trots off. The children exit chasing the ass.

Pupli and Chowkidar take their positions DL to open the next story, Tiger Trails.)

TIGER TRAILS

This section of the play presents two parallel processes on the stage – a dialogue between Robi and his grand daughter and the enactment of a story by actors.

LINK

A spot comes on at the down-left corner. Pupli is seated, the Chowkidar is standing.

CHOWKIDAR
Robi-da's tiger tales!

PUPLI
What was it about the tiger that fascinated Robi? Did its ruthless power remind him of human upper caste arrogance? Or was it the beast's innocence and simplemindedness under the rough and tough exterior? The tiger found its way into a lot of Robi's writing, in both verse and prose.

CHOWKIDAR
Maybe it was his attraction to the character of the king in so much of his writing, and the natural parallel in this king of the Indian jungle. Maybe he was aware of his more than superficial fascination. Maybe that is why he transplanted his fascination on to his grand daughter, calling it her fascination.
(The Chowkidar withdraws. Pupli remains in the corner. Spot on armchair upstage.)

VOICE
Pupli went to a circus. Ever since she returned she thinks tigers, talks tigers, all the time. She asks me if I know any tiger stories. She asks if I can write tiger poems. Actually, she wants to tell me that there is a tiger that comes to visit her every night. Doesn't she get frightened? Will he not eat her up?

PUPLI *(With a knowing smile)*
Certainly not!

VOICE
What does the tiger do then?

PUPLI
In the middle of the night he appears at my window and scratches at the glass, calling me to open the window.

VOICE
Oh ma! And then?

PUPLI
And then, when I open the window he breaks into a giggle. *(She giggles)*

(The children's chorus joins Pupli to recite a Tiger poem.
In the opening shows it was recited by four children. In later productions
and in the Courtyard Theatre presentations it has been done by just two actors,
using the downstage stretch left to right.)

POEM
A black striped tiger wandering into a mansion saw
A servant preening himself before a mirror
Ah, dinner is served, he thought to himself
And moaned a half growl, half in jest.

The servant first shivered, then froze
The image of the beast in the glass growing at every step
The next moment he had fled the room
Wings sprouting in a flash on his heels.

When the beast leapt to the spot vacated
He saw an image unexpected.
The face was the same handsome beast
The body, horrors, had stripes of black.

He stormed out, all thought of dinner abandoned
To the river bank he rushed to scrub his skin clear
Rub, scrub, rub and scrub some more
The stripes looked darker than before.

PUPLI
On the bank opposite was our little Devi
Filling pots of water in her evening chore
In a flash he placed himself before her
Knocking a pot or two, spilling furor.
How dare you! Cried Devi. Those pots were full!
Do you know whose house they come from and go to?

Do you know who you are talking to, girl?
Asked the bundle of stripes and puffed whiskers.

Will you go on, or do you wish to hear
The crack of brass pot on hollow head?
Mr. Stripes, all things said, knew his priorities
Teaching Devi a lesson could wait.

His need now was a bar of detergent soap
Seen as his only hope of redemption

From the curse of brush strokes on his body
This impudence had to be tolerated.

Will you hand it over? Or will you make me do things
You will regret later or not live to tell?
Detergent soap? What was that? Devi confessed
She could never afford it, had not ever used it.

PUPLI
Lies! Cried the tiger. There she was
A spotless white stretch of cloth on a dark body
How could she not be in possession
Of the much needed bar?

Out with the soap! Or in you go as dinner!
Least ruffled, Devi cried Shameless beast!
Will you even in desperation of mind and body
Stoop to make a meal of one so low of birth?

You are doomed if you touch me
Doubly so if you taste the flesh on me
Your body defiled you will be cast out of your family
The heads of ancestors hung in shame.

PUPLI
Speechless, unbelieving, the beast retreated
As Devi, finding new courage, advanced upon him

Stay there! Not a step nearer! His growls turned to howls
As he bounded back where he came from.
(The chorus exits. The Chowkidar joins Pupli.)

CHOWKIDAR
We are ready for the next story, Pupli-di.

PUPLI
Do you have a good tiger story?

CHOWKIDAR
Oh, lots!

PUPLI
As good as the one in the poem?

CHOWKIDAR
All of Robi-da's tiger tales are fun.

PUPLI
Tell me, why are tigers always shown as mean and ruthless?

CHOWKIDAR

Oh, not at all! They are very religious and quite particular about their rituals.

PUPLI

Really?!

CHOWKIDAR

Everything they do is guided by their scriptures.

PUPLI

What do the scriptures say?

CHOWKIDAR

It is a great big book of wisdom in the Tiger Ashram. It is kept in the care of the Chief Pundit of the tiger tribe.

(The lights come on in the story area to reveal the old Chief Pundit of the tigers. Around him are apprentice pundits learning the Commandments from him, enjoying themselves. There is a flip chart board with the title AMAR SONAR COMMANDMENTS. The Chief Pundit opens the first chart: THOU SHALL NOT STEAL.)

CHIEF

Repeat after me: Thou shall not steal

ALL

Thou shall not steal.

CHIEF

What does that mean, can you tell?

ALL

What does that mean, can you tell?

CHIEF

I am asking you!

ALL

I am asking you!

CHIEF

Stop!

ALL

Stop!

(The Chief lets out a terrifying roar. The others are shaken out of their mirth and stand to attention. The Chief glares.)

CHIEF

Don't you dare!

(One of the tigers begins "Don't you ..." Another quickly cups his mouth.)

Now... What does it mean when the Good Book says Thou shall not steal?

A TIGER
It means thou are not allowed to steal.

ANOTHER TIGER
But we are allowed.

CHIEF (*A stifled roar, more in contempt*)
That is the way the stupid two-legged human creatures live their lives. Not Tigers. We are of superior stock. We never steal!

ALL
We never steal.

CHIEF
Neither do we covet the belongings of others. Every tiger hunts its own food, and hunts enough for the whole family.

A TIGER
No tiger steals another's food.

CHIEF
Never. And no tiger hunts more than what is actually needed.

ANOTHER TIGER
Ever seen an obese tiger?

A TIGER
Punditji, are there rules about what a tiger must not eat?

ANOTHER TIGER
Like garlic and onion?

CHIEF
A tiger must not eat or drink anything vegetarian. No artificial flesh or blood.

A TIGER
No tomato ketchup?

CHIEF
Absolutely forbidden. Listen.
(*He flips to the next chart: THE PARABLE OF TIGER LALU*)
One of our tribe once strayed into the house of a weaver at the edge of the village. In a corner of the loomshed was a tub of crimson dye.
(*He flips to the next chart: a tiger before a tub of dye*)
The tiger was delighted. "Aahh, how thoughtful of the man, he has kept a tub of fresh blood for me" Without another thought he thrust his face into the tub to start on the feast. It was like nothing he had ever drunk.
(*He flips to the next chart: a tiger with his face all red*)
It not only tasted odd, but it had turned his whole face dark red, cheeks, whiskers and all. He bounded out of the weaver's house and hid in the deepest part of the forest, hoping nobody would see him, and hoping it

would go away. It didn't go away. At last, angry with himself, and hungry as well, he came to seek advice from the pundits in the temple.

(Tiger Lal dashes in, his face completely red. The gathering of Pundits first roars in defence, then breaks into roars of laughter. The Chief brings order.)

CHIEF

Who are you?! And how did you acquire such an astonishingly splendid face?

LAL

I...was...I...I had an astonishing hunt, I made an extraordinary kill.
(Two tigers go up to Lal, interested, sniffing him all over.)

A TIGER

Tell us about it!

LAL

It was a great big rhino, you see. The largest ever seen this side of the Ganga.

CHIEF

I didn't think there were rhinos this side of the Ganga.

LAL

He thought he'd fix me in a charge. It was his last charge. There was a lot of blood. A lot of blood. I ripped his belly open in three quick strokes. Then I sank my face deep inside and drained him dry.

ANOTHER TIGER

His claws are clean. Not a trace of blood.

A TIGER

No smell of real blood on his face either.

CHIEF

Have you by any chance been indulging in vegetarian blood?

LAL

Well...You see...I was...

CHIEF

Disgraceful!

ALL

Disgraceful!

CHIEF

Stay there, your tail between your legs, while we decide what we must do with you.
(The pundit group goes into a huddle. Lal waits, as directed. The pundits turn.)

CHIEF

Guilty!

ALL

Guilty!

LAL

Please, sir, I am a simple soul. I was misled. It was my colour blindness. I swear I shall never again be deceived by anything vegetarian, no matter how craftily presented by those despicable humans.

CHIEF

Punishment!

ALL

Punishment!

LAL

I beg you, sir, have mercy. I have five daughters, all of marriageable age. Where will I find husbands for them if I am found guilty and punished. Their dowries will go up four times. They will start demanding twenty five or thirty buffalos for each daughter.

CHIEF

Too late!

ALL

Too late!

LAL

SIR !!!

(Cross fade to Pupli and Chowkidar Ddown-left)

PUPLI

And that is not all. If the tiger was found guilty by the council of pundits, no respectable priest would perform the last rites at his funeral. Imagine the shame on his family. They would have to get a lowly human from the city zoo to attend to the dead body. The shame would remain with the family for seven generations.

CHOWKIDAR

Is it so important to have funeral rites?

PUPLI

Of course! Without that there would be no food supply in the afterlife, and his ghost would starve to death.

CHOWKIDAR

But he would be dead already before the funeral.

PUPLI

Ohho! How can you understand all this? You see, death by starvation in this world is bad enough, but starvation after death is unthinkable!

CHOWKIDAR

You certainly know a lot about tigers, Pupli-di!

PUPLI

I do, don't I?
(Cross fade to pundits.)

CHIEF

Prepare to receive the judgement!

ALL

The judgement!

CHIEF *(Ponderous)*

Taking into consideration your past conduct as a conscientious member of the tribe, albeit muddled in thought and colourless in fashion, and also conceding the record of your acts of valour, leading by the nose, it is hereby decreed that the sentence for the verdict of guilt be reduced from the customary banishment to a solemn penance.

LAL

A penance?

ALL

A penance!

CHIEF

You will take a pilgrimage to the holy shrine of Our Lady of the Frame of Fearful Symmetry at the foothills of the Northern range. There, at the rear of the shrine will you stand three-legged through the length of an entire lunar month, from one amavasya night to the next, feeding only on the meat brought to you by either your maternal uncle's third daughter or the third son of the said uncle's cousin, thrice removed. Further, the food brought to you will be no more than once every seven days, and shall consist of nothing more than the meat from the thigh of a hyena.

(The sound of a temple bell struck once is heard. Lal is dumbstruck.)

LAL

Hyena?!

ALL

A concession for your good record.

LAL

(Whimpering) Hyena!

CHIEF

Further, you will be permitted to use only the paw of the leg that is off the ground to tear the flesh of the hyena's thigh.

LAL

Not even a squint-eyed wild dog? A woodcutter's thick-skinned ass?

ALL

Hyena!

LAL
I go...Hyena! I go. A toothless mongoose? I go...I go...
(Cross fade to Pupli and Chowkidar.)

PUPLI
Tigers are quite orthodox in their customs, are they not?

CHOWKIDAR
Of course! And they abide by them too, very strictly. Now, you know, the hyena is an untouchable beast for the tiger. It is detestable, its meat is unthinkable. But the hyenas hold the tiger in the greatest esteem. If they come across a tiger's half eaten meal, it is like prasad from the highest temple.

PUPLI
If tigers are so orthodox, why do they commit the sin of killing in the first place?

CHOWKIDAR
Ah, but the killing is sanctified. The tiger always has the right mantra before every kill. Well...sometimes after the kill.

PUPLI
Is the mantra chanted?

CHOWKIDAR
It is a deep growl, followed by a snarl.
(He exits. The spot on the armchair upstage comes on.)

PUPLI
And if the tiger forgets to growl the mantra?

VOICE
Oh, misery! The tiger will be reborn in the next life in the form of the animal killed!

PUPLI
Oh, ma! A tiger can be reborn as a human, then?!

VOICE
The one fate they dread most! That is why they are so particular about growling before killing a human. In the excitement it becomes a mighty roar.

PUPLI
What is so dreadful about being reborn as a human?

VOICE
What could be worse? The human body is hairless! No tail! How do they whisk flies off their backs? They need wives to do that for them! How ridiculous they look, standing on their hind legs all the time, covering up their undersides with clothing! The tiger scriptures have an explanation for all this madness. It says that Lord Vishwkarma had finished creating the whole universe and was about to take a much needed break. Just then a dog with a curly tail walked up to him and asked for a companion animal.

By then almost all the raw materials meant for creation had already been used up. Not wanting to disappoint the dog, looking up with a smile and a wagging tail, Lord Vishwakarma decided to make do with what was left. So, the human animal was created anyway. It turned out an odd creature, defective in many ways. A mistake, you could say. The rest of the earth is now stuck with them.

LINK – SHOES

THE BIRTH OF SHOES

LINK

Spot down-right on Debloo. He calls Pupli to his side. She crosses over.

PUPLI

Do you collect stamps? *(Debloo shakes his head)* Do you collect coins? *(Debloo shakes his head)*

(To audience) Some people collect stamps, some collect coins. What do you collect? *(Interaction)* And you? And you there?

Does anybody collect socks? No? Yes? Does anybody collect shoes? Why not? Well, here's something that may interest you. It is said that Imelda Marcos, wife of the past President of the Philippines, had a large collection of shoes.

DEBLOO

She was not the only one, was she? We have read about all kinds of other collections.

PUPLI

Pen collections, wine collections, crockery collections, cutlery connections, matchbox collections.

DEBLOO

Walking stick collections.

PUPLI

Lipstick collections?

DEBLOO

Wait! I know! I know what you are thinking. You know other people of great wealth and power who collect things like that. Saris, hand bags, ties, cell phones, even shoes. But you are afraid to take names. They might set the Inspector General of Police on you!

PUPLI

You and I, we will just have to be satisfied with stamps and coins. Maybe autographs.

DEBLOO

Back to shoes. The shoe collection of Imelda Marcos.

PUPLI

How many shoes? Can you guess?

DEBLOO

Actually, nobody knows the exact number, because the shoes were kept in different places – under the bed, in the bathroom, in the garage, on top of the fridge, as lampshades over her bed, as pots for her chrysanthemums, as salt and pepper shakers, as soup ladles, as ash trays, hidden in the crockery cupboard, in the cutlery drawer, rolled inside carpets, pinned on to hats, sewn on to gowns, tied up to door handles, dangled from ceiling fans, fitted to the twelve legs of the banquet table...Not to forget the garland of shoes on the front door on Christmas day.

PUPLI

Nobody knew the exact number of shoes owned. BUT in one place in the palace, where there was a shoe rack the length of a badminton court, they found...oh, about three followed by three zeroes, three thousand pairs of shoes. Plus or minus. More likely plus they thought.

DEBLOO

What sort of things did Robi have? He was part of a wealthy family, wasn't he? What was he pampered with in his childhood, I wonder.

(Spot on armchair upstage)

VOICE

I had very little direct contact with the outdoors. I suppose that is the reason I found endless joy in nature's charms whenever I had the chance. Too much material possession makes the mind dull and lethargic. We forget that our delight comes from what is inside, not what is out there. That really is the first lesson in growing up. A child's possessions may be few and seemingly trivial, but they need nothing more for that delight from inside. When we load a child with toys, we make them wretched and spoil their sense of play.

(Chowkidar joins Debloo and Pupli)

DEBLOO

It would be fun to have a collection of shoes.

CHOWKIDAR

Debloo-baba!

DEBLOO

Not for myself, silly! A collection, just like stamps, shoes from all parts of the world!

CHOWKIDAR

Aahh...That kind of collection!

PUPLI

I wonder what shoes they wear in Uzbekistan.

CHOWKIDAR

In Turkmenistan.

DEBLOO

In Kyrgyzstan.

CHOWKIDAR

I don't even know the spelling of that name. Do they wear shoes there?

PUPLI
Where were the first shoes made? Who invented them?

CHOWKIDAR
Oh, that is well known. It was in the land of Jootapalistan. In the reign of the good king Hobloo. You want to know how it happened? We can show!
(He signals to the action area and exits.
Cross fade to action area at centre stage. King Hobloo is on his throne, glum, frustrated with the dust on his feet. His chamcha ministers are perplexed.)

HOBLOO
Dust!

MINISTERS
>> Aah!
>> Dust!
>> Dhool!
>> On His Majesty's feet!
(They scramble for the dust on his feet for their foreheads.)

ALL
Aah...

HOBLOO
Aahchoo!
(The chamchas scramble to offer napkin, water, fan...)

HOBLOO
Chief Minister Gobloo!
(The chamchas make way. Gobloo approaches and pays respects.)

GOBLOO
Your Majesty!

HOBLOO
I have spent sleepless nights pondering about it...

GOBLOO
It is something in the air, Your Majesty.

HOBLOO
It is on my feet, Gobloo! There is dust on my feet!

GOBLOO
Aah, dust, Your Majesty. Your feet, Your Majesty.

ALL
>> Your majestic feet
>> Your Majesty

HOBLOO
I have noticed that my feet
Whenever they touch the street

Get soiled on the underside
With dust from the streetside.

GOBLOO

Feet...Dust...Underside...

ALL

Underside!

HOBLOO

Look closely at the brow of your king
You will see he is frowning.
(Cross fade to Chowkidar, Debloo and Pupli)

CHOWKIDAR

What was he keeping a council of ministers for, the king asked.
Was he not paying them enough? Were they not satisfied?
They bowed in embarrassment and moaned protestations.

DEBLOO

Did he make them stand in a corner, facing the wall?
Did he give them, what do they call it, a dressing down?

CHOWKIDAR

He certainly gave them an earful.

HOBLOO

So, am I not paying you enough? Check.
And are you happy with what you get? Double check.
Am I happy with what I get in return? Question mark.
Have you stopped dust getting to my feet? Exclamation mark!

GOBLOO

Ah, the dust, the dust
We must do something about the dust must we not?

HOBLOO

Must we not?!

ALL

We must, we must
*At a signal from the Chief Minister the chamchas and he carry the King
out of the scene ceremoniously. They chant "We must, we must, get rid of the
dust" as they carry him out. They return without him and pace about the
room, quite upset.*
   >> As they cross each other, they offer their handkerchiefs to the other.
   >> The hankies are accepted to wipe their perspiration.
   >> Soon all are wiping themselves.
   >> They pass on hankies as they cross each other.
   >> Soon all are wiping themselves with changed hankies.

GOBLOO
Stop!
(They all stop)
It is a dire circumstance, true, but no sweat!
We will do something about this yet.
You, no need to pale! And you, tummy in
Chest out, chin up, All our battles we are known to win.

MINISTERS
>> But my knees feel wobbly
>> My speech turns garbly
>> Butterflies in my tummily
>> A little lower it's rumbling.

GOBLOO
Rumbling?

CHAMCHA
I couldn't get it to rhyme with wobbly.
(Cross fade to Chowkidar, Debloo and Pupli)

DEBLOO
So, first the king had a sleepless night.
Now the ministers were sleepless too!

PUPLI
Tossing and turning and sweating through the night
Till at last a moment before break of day
Chief Minister Gobloo jumped out of bed to cry –

GOBLOO *(Voice in the dark)*
Eurekala-Avarekala-Dambola!!!
(Gobloo and the chamchas enter, carrying the king. They set him down. Gobloo pays his respects by the gesture of taking the dust off the king's feet and applying it to his head. The king looks pleased. He smiles. Gobloo grins.)

GOBLOO
Perhaps Your Majesty will consider ancient wisdom
Honoured through the entire wide kingdom
The King's feet we hold as most august
Partake of their dust we simply must.

ALL
We must! We must!
Foremost and first!

GOBLOO
Why deny the faithful
The honour of the dust?

HOBLOO

There is merit in acquired wisdom I admit
But by custom is the dust done away? Not a bit!
You neither touch the foot, nor wipe it clean
What thoughtless ministers you have been!
(Cross fade to Chowkidar, Debloo and Pupli)

PUPLI

The king's mood was clearly shifting in the downward direction.
From annoyance to anger, it was heading for a proper tantrum.

DEBLOO

He had a point, didn't he? What are ministers for anyway?
Shouldn't they serve king and country first?

PUPLI

King and country? Or country and king?

DEBLOO

It's the same thing!

PUPLI

Is it?

HOBLOO

A hundred and twenty ministers in this land
Committees, commissions working hand in hand
Scientists, godmen, magicians with robes so neat
Clueless about dust on my feet!
Take heed! It is Monday, the first day of this week
It is noon, the sun at its peak
Till noon of Sunday you have to toil
Find an answer! Or you boil in oil!

ALL

Sire!
(Hobloo marches off by himself. The others pick up the throne and rush after him. Too late.
The ministers get into a huddle.)

GOBLOO

Shinshinaki-Tambola!!!
(The huddle breaks. Gobloo announces grandly.)
An Enquiry Commission!
(A three-member Commission, convened by Gobloo takes its place. Several characters appear before the Commission one by one. We see Debloo and Pupli through the process.)

PUPLI

The experts came, the experts went.

The opinions and recommendations were piled higher and higher.

DEBLOO

Time was running out. It was Wednesday already!

PUPLI

A plenary session was called at the end.

(All the characters appear together. The king joins the group, chairing the session.)

DEBLOO

They were clearly divided into two opposite camps.

The first argued for farmers and agriculture

REPRESENTATIVE 1

(Vociferous)

You cannot remove the dust from the earth.

This is no matter of mirth.

Nothing will ever grow again, no grains, no herb, no fruit

With dust removed, the soil will hold no root.

HOBLOO

Bah! They think only of herbs and grains

My feet are dusty! Have they no brains?!

PUPLI

The king was not pleased. The other camp had engineers.

They had better come up with a solution. Or else!

REPRESENTATIVE 2

After due consideration of all data on hand

Giving corrections to bandwidth particles in sand

Other things being equal, assumptions x and y

Root mean square of area wet and dry

Extrapolated trajectory sine twice cosine

Area minus volume into mass turbine

HOBLOO

Where is this heading? What's the bottom line?

What do you have for these grimy feet of mine?

DEBLOO

They are all the same, the king is convinced

They must all be sacked, no words minced

PUPLI

Wait, the Chief Engineer has a conclusion.

REPRESENTATIVE 2

Brooms! Your Majesty, Brooms in fusion.

Exactly two million eighty three thousand brooms suffice

To cleanse the entire kingdom in a trice.

(The entire cast appears on stage with brooms, sweeping away.)

PUPLI

Every square inch of the kingdom was swept and scrubbed.
Where did it all go, the Kingdom's dust? Up in the air for a start
From up in the air to sideways with the breeze
From sideways to the insides of every room of every dwelling

(The king gets into a coughing and sneezing fit. The others have now covered their heads, but are still sweeping away. The king is shouting "STOP! STOP! But they can't hear him. The king finally snatches a broom and whacks a bottom or two. OW! OW!

All the hoods come off. They stare at the king...)

DEBLOO

Dust inside rooms, dust outside
Dust risen miles high filling the sky
Blanking out the sun and moon and stars
Dust all around, except on the ground!

HOBLOO

Blundering Dunderheads! Morons galore!
These are worse than the engineers of Bangalore!

REPRESENTATIVE 2

Sire! A minor error! A miscalculation!

REPRESENTATIVE 3

You must now try our recommendation, sire.

HOBLOO

It had better be better than the last bet
No time to waste, no time to regret

DEBLOO

What was the plan? What did they do?

PUPLI

Simple. Wet the earth and stamp out the dust!

DEBLOO

Do you think it might help if they stopped trying to speak in rhyme?

PUPLI

And concentrated on the task on hand? Maybe.

HOBLOO

Come here, all of you! Stop talking to me in riddles!
Enough of nursery rhymes! Tell me in plain words what your next preposterous plan is!

REPRESENTATIVE 3

Sire! The engineers have already completed the project of sweeping every square inch of the kingdom.

HOBLOO

Don't we know that!

REPRESENTATIVE 3

Thus, we know the exact area of land with dust. We propose that we work on the principle of prevention being the best cure.

HOBLOO

That being?

REPRESENTATIVE 3

We prevent the dust from becoming dust. We do this by dousing every square inch of the kingdom's land with water, and stamping the dust in.

HOBLOO

Stamping?

REPRESENTATIVE 3 *(Demonstrating)*

Stamp! Thus...All the dust will then be permanently restricted to remain where it belongs. On the earth. Not rising to soil the royal feet.

(All the characters mime watering the earth and stamping the spoil.)

PUPLI

They needed an army of one million to water the earth. And an equal number to stamp the earth as soon as the earth was watered. Every able bodied man and woman from every village was employed for the mission.

DEBLOO

A royal proclamation guaranteed employment for the rural poor so that they could be on the project through the year.

PUPLI

Volunteers by the lakhs poured into the recruitment offices. It was all to serve the good king, they said happily.

DEBLOO

Where did they get so much water?

PUPLI

Oh, there were the lakes, the rivers, the ponds. There were wells in every village.

DEBLOO

That was enough?

PUPLI

Just about. They were all drained to the last drop. Every, lake, pond, river and well.

DEBLOO

What happened to all the fish?

PUPLI

Well, they had to die. It was for a good cause, wasn't it? The water buffalos died too. All beasts around the water, actually. Of course, the boats could not sail anymore.

DEBLOO

With so much water poured into the city, it must have become a floating city.

PUPLI

A sinking city.

DEBLOO

Ten minutes of rain in Kolkata and you know what we have!

HOBLOO *(Roaring)*

A stinking city!

There's muddy water everywhere. My feet are free of dust, but they are now caked with clay!

REPRESENTATIVE 4

I know! I know!

We shall cover the entire land with cloth. It will bring employment for all the handloom weavers. Hessian cloth in villages, robust furnishing material in the cities, muslin in and around the royal palace. Since we have already calculated the exact area of land…

HOBLOO

Next!

REPRESENTATIVE 5

Sire! The problem as we see it is that your feet pick up dust when you step outside your royal chamber. Suppose you don't leave the royal chamber? Suppose we find a way to keep you within your royal chamber? Problem solved!

HOBLOO

Will you hold your tongue or do you prefer to have it surgically detached?

REPRESENTATIVE 5

All things considered, on balance, holding appears the better option, sire!

HOBLOO

Next!

REPRESENTATIVE 6

Sire! The problem of dust is the problem of its ascension, which is to say, its non-attachment to the earth. The problem defined thus, we need a solution by which dust is permanently attached to the earth, to be clung to like mother earth.

ALL

Aahh!

HOBLOO
Proceed.

REPRESENTATIVE 6
We shall locate the best cobbler in the kingdom. We shall commission to him the task of covering the entire land area of the kingdom in leather and sewing it tight. Not a speck of dust will be allowed to escape from beneath. The land shall be free of dust once and for all!

HOBLOO
Wah!

ALL
WAH!

HOBLOO
Go out and find the best cobbler in the land, and bring him here. He must appear before me immediately. No delay! Go!

REPRESENTATIVE 6
Sire! I have already found the man. He is waiting outside, awaiting your audience.
(A member of the group brings a cobbler in, bound. He is poor, emaciated, sparsely dressed. He carries a work bag. He is led to the king.)

REPRESENTATIVE 6
Kneel before His Royal Highness.
(The cobbler does so, his gaze fixed on the king's feet.)

REPRESENTATIVE 6
The king's feet –

COBBLER
They are dusty.

REPRESENTATIVE 6
Precisely. That is why you are called here.
(By now, the cobbler has taken out a cloth and is wiping the feet of the king.)

REPRESENTATIVE 1
You know that this is a vast kingdom.

REPRESENTATIVE 2
However, thanks to the caliber of our engineering science we know the exact area of the land, down to the last square foot.

OTHERS
>> The data are verified
>> And found correct
>> Other things being equal

REPRESENTATIVE 6
Your job...Cover up the land in leather and sew it tight.

COBBLER

Hobbe-na!

REPRESENTATIVE 6

What?

COBBLER

No can do!

REPRESENTATIVE 6

You are commanded to perform your task for His Royal Highness!

COBBLER

He has dusty feet.

HOBLOO

My good fellow, I don't think you know what you are saying. Nobody in this land can refuse a command given by the king!

COBBLER

Where will you find the leather? How many buffalos and cows and goats will you slaughter to make the skin to cover the earth?

REPRESENTATIVE 2

That can easily be computed…

REPRESENTATIVE 6

That is not our concern. That is what you have to find out. You have also to find a way to get all the leather needed.

HOBLOO

And it is your job to sew it all together and keep the dust trapped underneath.

(By now the Cobbler has taken out two pieces of leather that can be wrapped on the feet.)

COBBLER

It may be simpler to cover the royal feet with leather to prevent the dust getting to them.

(He slips on the makeshift footwear and ties them up.)

Your Majesty may walk a few steps to see how they fit.

(The king hesitates, then rises, takes a step or two tentatively…then walks about pleased!)

HOBLOO

And what do you call this…this thing on my feet?

SEVERAL

>> A foot coat!

>> From skin of goat!

>> A leg boat!

>> The feet afloat!

HOBLOO
Shoo!
(All quieten)
Yes, my good man, what do we call this marvelous covering for my feet?

COBBLER
Why not...shoo?

ALL
>> Aaah
>> A shoo
>> A shoo, a shoo

HOBLOO *(Pleased, but suddenly changing to worry)*
And I suppose the English will come along and find their own way to spell shoo!
(He recovers) Chief Minister Gobloo!
(Gobloo appears)
Chief Minister Gobloo, What is it you say when you have hit upon something good?

GOBLOO
Sire...Er...Eurekala...Avarekala...Dambola...

HOBLOO
That's it! All together now –

ALL
EUREKALA-AVAREKALA-DAMBOLA!!!
(All exit in grand procession.
The Chowkidar enters with his bag, sits at the foot of the rostrum. He claps [or whistles or blows a pipe] to get all the children in. They rush in cheerfully and sit around him, as at the start of the play.)

CHOWKIDAR
Where did you all disappear?

A CHILD
We followed the actors backstage!

ANOTHER
They gave us toffees!

ANOTHER
They were chocolate éclairs!

ANOTHER
Imported!

CHOWKIDAR
Real actors?

ANOTHER
Of course!

CHOWKIDAR
Real chocolate eclairs? Can I see?

ANOTHER
We ate them up!

CHOWKIDAR
Ah, yes! Ah, yes! It worked, did it not?
So you got something more than what I could give you from my bag!

PUPLI
Kabuliwala, nothing could be as wonderful as the treat you laid out
for us today!

DEBLOO
Thank you, Kabuliwala!
(The sound of a bus horn.)

CHOWKIDAR
Well, time up! And time to go! Let me leave you till the bus.

A CHILD
But we don't want to go yet!

ANOTHER
Can't we stay a bit longer?!

ANOTHER
Just one more story?!

ALL
Please!
(The sound of the bus horn again.)

CHOWKIDAR
That bus is real, you know! It will go away if you don't get into it in the
next minute.

DEBLOO
Can we see the actors once more, please?

A CHILD
Can't we say 'bye to them properly?

PUPLI
It's simple! You know what we must do?!
*(They stand in a tight huddle on the rostrum and close their eyes.
The Chowkidar signals off-stage.
The cast and crew enter once more in a procession with drums and pipes.
The children and the Chowkidar can't help joining them. The entire procession
weaves through the stage and auditorium and exits to a grand finale.)*

Close of play

A Little Bit of Lorca

A tribute to Federico Garcia Lorca
Including scenes from Blood Wedding,
The Shoemaker's Wonderful Wife, Yerma,
The Puppet Play of Don CRISTOBAL

Vijay Padaki

FOR
MADHU SMRITI SHUKLA

NOTES

Alliance Francaise de Bangalore came into being in 1970. Bangalore Little Theatre was already ten years old then and reasonably well established as a non-profit theatre organization which combined performance with outreach activity. It was only natural that BLT extended its hand to help AF set up its programmes in Bangalore. A long lasting cultural partnership gradually took shape.

In the 'nineties there was a marked increase in collaborative events, such as film screenings, training workshops and the occasional collaborative theatre production. BLT's annual Summer Project on Theatre (SPOT) began to be held at the AF premises.

With the success of the theatre events, it was decided to start a theatre club within Alliance Francaise with the assistance of BLT. It was called KATHAKAR. (The Storyteller.) The club would have an identity and a range of activities in keeping with its location in an Indo-French cultural centre. The main thrust of the theatre club would be to function as a forum for Theatre Appreciation. The thrust would be reflected in a variety of ways in the activities planned at the club:

- A Readers Theatre, presenting rehearsed play readings
- Training workshops in various aspects of drama
- Film screenings of theatre greats
- Lectures and lec-dems from theatre personalities
- Play festivals to encourage greater participation
- Indo-French adaptations of play scripts
- Hosting productions of visiting artists

The workshop production of SPOT 2001 was the first to be presented under the banner of Kathakar. The life and work of Federico Garcia Lorca was the subject of the production. The research by the workshop group included biographical essays, play scripts, critical analyses and the film on Lorca's life *The Disappearance of Garcia Lorca (1997)* starring Andy Garcia.

Roger Ebert's review of the film ends with the words:
"Do people read Garcia Lorca today? Or poetry in general? Not many, I suppose. I read some of his poems after seeing the movie, and felt the passion. But Garcia Lorca is perhaps more important today as a symbol than as a poet, and this film is really not so much about him as about memory and history – about how poets are given most of their power not by those who love them, but by those who fear them."

– Vijay Padaki

LANGUAGE NOTES

Naam:
> Name

Baap ka naam:
> Father's name

Ji hanh, Sigmund-ji, mere bachpan mein hi mujhe aisa lagta tha ki hamari saari zindagi bilkul maya jaal hai. Sirf do pal ka nightmare hai, our usmey hain hum butterly log – flutter flutter karke jeete hain, aur sutter futter karke marte hain:
> Yes, Sigmund sir, right in my childhood I had this feeling that the whole of life is an illusion. It is a nightmare of just two beats, and in that we are like butterflies. We go flutter flutter and stay alive, we flurry about and we die

Line maro:
> Flirting, a pick up line

FIRST PERFORMED

First performed by Bangalore Little Theatre in association with Alliance de Francaise October 2001

Characters in the Play

The ensemble of artists in the SPOT 2001 group played multiple parts from a selection of scenes of plays by Federico Garcia Lorca.
- Blood Wedding
- The Shoemaker's Wonderful Wife
- Yerma
- The Puppet Play of Don CRISTOBAL

The Ensemble .... ADITI BHAT, ARCHANA GK,
CARLOS GUIDO, DEEPAK MENON
PRAMODH BN, RAHUL JAIN,
RANJINI SRINIVASAN, SUJATA BALAKRISHNAN,
ARNAB MAJUMDAR, DIVYA GS, JAVED AMIR KHAN,
PRITHAM KUMAR, RAKESH MEHAR,
SAAD AHMED KHAN, SMITHA BHAT,
FAWAD BACKER, SABINA EM,
SANJEEV BALAKRISHNAN IYER

Trainer-Facilitators .... ALIYEH RIZVI, DEEPTHY SEKHAR,
RAJESH MEHAR, MADHU SMRITI SHUKLA

The play designed and directed by .... VIJAY PADAKI

I have a concept of Theatre which is, in a certain way, personal and strong. The theatre is poetry, which rises up from the stage and is made human. And when this happens it talks and shouts, cries and despairs. The theatre requires that the characters who appear on stage are dressed in poetry and, at the same time, we should see their bones, their blood.

1936

A LITTLE BIT OF LORCA

*The characters shown in the play script are the actors in the workshop group
Rahul, Deepak, Rakesh, Sanjeev, Javed, Saad, Pritham, Arnab, Aliyeh,
Pramodh, Carlos, Sabina, Divya, Aditi, Sujatha, Ranjini, Archana, Madhu
Empty stage.*

*A tight spot comes on at one corner. The first stanzas of the poem 'At Five in
the Afternoon' are heard over the sound system.*

*[Readings from Lorca's poetry over a spot on the floor recur through the play.
The Bangalore workshop group chose At Five in the Afternoon. A performing
group may choose any other poem.]*

At five in the afternoon.
It was exactly five in the afternoon.
A boy brought the white sheet
at five in the afternoon.
A friar of lime ready prepared
at five in the afternoon.
The rest was death, and death alone
at five in the afternoon.
(The sound and the spot fade out.
Enter a lone balladeer singing a Lorca poem set to music.)

*[Two poems are chosen: Ditty of First Desire and Memento. Both are given
below. The actor may choose either. In the Bangalore production they were sung
in alternate performances.]*

Ditty of First Desire

In the green morning
I wanted to be a heart.
A heart.
And in the ripe evening
I wanted to be a nightingale.
A nightingale.
   Soul, turn orange-colored.
   Soul, turn the color of love.
In the vivid morning
I wanted to be myself.
A heart.
And at the evening's end
I wanted to be my voice.
A nightingale.
   Soul, turn orange-colored.
   Soul, turn the color of love.

Memento

Whenever I die
bury me with my guitar
beneath the sand.
Whenever I die
among orange trees
and mint plants.
Whenever I die
bury me, if you would
inside a weather vane.
Whenever I die.
(The balladeer continues.

Enter SPOT group. Two or three go up to him to listen. The others busy themselves setting up the stage and warming up, including a folk dance. Some stand aside holding scripts and discussing them.

They look at the balladeer and their colleagues as they work.)

ACTOR 1
Sounds familiar, doesn't it?

ACTOR 2
It does. Where have we heard it before?

ACTOR 1
Not the tune so much, but the words.

ACTOR 2
The words, the words...

BALLADEER
From a poet in a distant land.

ACTOR 1
Which land?

ACTOR 2
How distant?

BALLADEER
Have you heard of the land of Iberia?

ACTOR 2
You mean...

ACTOR 1
That part of Europe sticking out into the Mediterranean.

ACTOR 2
You mean Spain. Portugal and Spain together.

ACTOR 1
Like a boxing glove – the Iberian peninsula.

ACTOR 2
OK, OK, you went to the right school and read the right books!

ACTOR 1
And went to drama classes too.

BALLADEER
Then you know something about Spanish art and culture.

ACTOR 2
Ole! Ole!
(Actor 2 rushes off to one corner and becomes a bull, and charges at Actor 1 who becomes a bull fighter. They fool around a bit.)

BALLADEER
There is a lot more to Spain than bulls, you know.

ACTOR 2
Yeah, the bullshitting.

ACTOR 1
You must excuse my friend. He gets a bit –

ACTOR 2
He's like that only. Country type. Wrong school. Overdue for overhauling.

ACTOR 1
Tell us about the song.

ACTOR 2
Yeah, the song.

BALLADEER
A poet, musician, writer – a well rounded artist.

ACTOR 2
Sounds like...

ACTOR 1
Could it be...

BALLADEER
Have you heard the name of Lorca?

ACTORS 1 AND 2 *(Together)*
Lorca!

ACTOR 2 *(To the others)*
Hey! Guess what? He's playing Lorca!

BALLADEER
Do you know Lorca?

ACTOR 1
We think we do.

ACTOR 2
Do we know Lorca? Of course, we do!
(By now a few others have joined in.)

ACTOR 3
Naam – Garcia Lorca. Baap ka naam – Federico Lorca.
(Actor 4, a self appointed Director steps forward.)

BALLADEER
Do you know Lorca?

ACTOR 1
We think we do.

ACTOR 4
Best known outside Spain for his classic tragedies, Lorca was nevertheless drawn to writing for the theatre rather late in his life. It is said –
(Two other actors gently but firmly shut him up and take him off to a side.)

BALLADEER
Not quite so.

ACTOR 1
It is said that playacting came naturally to him, very early – even in his childhood.

ACTOR 5
Like in his Upper KG.

ACTOR 6
Like he was chosen to play the lead part in Jack and the Beanstalk.

ACTOR 5
He played the tree?

ACTOR 1
He certainly had an indulgent family and home surrounding.

ACTOR 7
Guess what his favourite toy was? A toy playhouse – a little playhouse in which he could arrange characters and create his own plays. Like a puppeteer.

BALLADEER
What he did as a child might not have been drama in his mind. Not the way we use the Word today. He was simply a very imaginative child.
(Actor 7 begins to assemble a small group and direct them as little Lorca.)

BALLADEER
The servants in the household were always ready to go along with his games.

ACTOR 7
Maria! Rosita! Here, put these on. You will be Mama. And you, of course, will be my Papa. And I will be... hmm... I won't tell you. You will have to find out.

ACTOR 8
What shall we play today?

ACTOR 9
Tell us, Sweetie, what shall we play today?

ACTOR 1
There is the story of Lorca enacting a funeral scene.

ACTORS
A funeral scene!

BALLADEER
The death of an insect.
(The actors mime the insect funeral scene.)

ACTOR 5
The funeral – scripted and directed by Garcia Lorca, Upper KG.

ACTOR 6
Stage management, Garcia Lorca. Costumes, Garcia Lorca. And starring...

ACTOR 8
Do we know it is only a bee?

ACTOR 9
Do we know if he knows?
(The scene ends)

ACTOR 7
He took his playacting seriously, didn't he?

BALLADEER
He took himself seriously.

ACTOR 5
I wonder if he knew he was going to become a famous personality in the theatre.

ACTOR 6
I wonder if people referred to themselves as "theatre personality" in those days.

ACTOR 8
Every croaking froggie in the well thinks so today, doesn't he?

ACTOR 9
He or she.

ACTOR 8
Correction. Thanks.

ACTOR 7
He can then say in a Times of India interview that oh, he has been doing plays from as long as he can remember. From the kindergarten maybe. *(Actor 9 glares)* He or she.

BALLADEER
His first play...

ACTOR 3
The Butterfly's Evil Spell!

ACTOR 2
Presenting... The Butterfly's Evil Spell... Characters in the play...
Dona Beetle, Witch Beetle, Dona Proud Beetle, Boy Beetle, First Field Beetle, Second Field Beetle, Other Field Beetles, Two Girl Beetles, Guard Beetles...

ACTOR 8
Some fireflies...

ACTOR 9

And a scorpion.

ACTOR 3

Do you think there was some connection? Some carry over from his childhood?

ACTOR 1

He might have been a lonely child. There was a serious illness in his infancy. Because of that he was not sent to school till much later.

ACTOR 7

But it did not come in the way of his having the very best of private tuition at home.

ACTOR 10

Couch! *(Lying down on an imaginary couch)* Ji hanh, Sigmund-ji, mere bachpan mein hi mujhe aisa lagta tha ki hamari saari zindagi bilkul maya jaal hai. Sirf do pal ka nightmare hai, our usmey hain hum butterly log – flutter flutter karke jeete hain, aur sutter futter karke marte hain.

BALLADEER

Maybe. Who knows – maybe there was. But you mustn't forget that first and foremost Lorca was really a poet.

(The balladeer strums his guitar and repeats the last stanza of the poem-song. [Or sings a fresh piece.] The Actors sit down to join in. Actor 10 accompanies him on a dhol.

After a while Actor 11 takes over and renders the same poem-song in Hindi. At the end, there is much good feeling in the group.)

ACTOR 5 *(To the balladeer)*

You know, it will be nice if you can join us for a while.

ACTOR 6

Yes, we can do a little bit of Lorca together, you and us.

BALLADEER

Well, I can spend this day with you. And then I must go my way.

ACTOR 2

Go where?

BALLADEER

Wherever my guitar takes me. Wherever the doors are opened to a song brought in by the wind.

ACTOR 2

Before the pizza delivery gets in.

ACTOR 4 *(Stepping in to take charge)*

This is what I think we should do.

(A small group of actors begins to form a semi-circle around him.)

We will write a prologue, a sort of curtain raiser, to introduce the work of Garcia Lorca to the audience. It will lead up to the opening scene of...
(The group has closed in menacingly)
What do you say we begin with... *(The group has picked him up)*
I think we should begin with one of his classics...
(The group carries him off, plants him at the back.)

ACTOR 11
Is that what we are going to do? A Lorca classic?

ACTOR 5
One of the biggies. Blood Wedding!

ACTOR 6
Yerma, Dona Rosita the Spinster.

ACTOR 11
The House of Bernarda Alba.

ACTOR 10
An all-woman play about being women – long before it was fashionable to talk about that sort of thing.

ACTOR 11
Is there a women's college anywhere that hasn't done The House of Bernarda Alba?

ACTOR 3
And discovered Lorca in the process?

ACTOR 10
And discovered themselves in the process.

ACTOR 3
Is there any drama group anywhere that has not done a Lorca?

ACTOR 10
Anywhere, any language.

ACTOR 2
Even the NSD must have done a Lorca or two. I think.

ACTOR 10
What about the great silicon anthill called Bangalore?

ACTOR 7
You know, if we are to perform in this city I'd be careful about choosing a Lorca.

ACTOR 11
Not sure they can take it, hunh?

ACTOR 7
Not sure we have what it takes.

ACTOR 2 *(Teasing, to 11)*

He means he's not sure we have the actresses...

ACTOR 11

Oh yeah? *(Calling the actors by name)* Ranjini! Aliyeh, Archana! Get in here! OK, Rakesh *(Actor 4)*, you too.

(Actor 4 steps forward. She shoves a playbook into his hand. The chosen actors form a scene grouping. The others step back and sit as an outer circle.)

1. BLOOD WEDDING

ACTOR 4

Blood Wedding. Act Two. The wedding celebration. Only the bride knows that it is not going to be consummated. She awaits her lover, Leonardo, a married man from a rival clan, to carry her off from her room, even as the wedding celebrations are on. The bridegroom's home. The groom's mother and the bride's father are waiting for the dancing to begin. It is learnt that Leonardo and his wife have arrived. A strained cordiality is raised – before the impending violence between two feuding families.

ACTOR 7 *(Joining)*

Act 2, Scene 2. The bride's home. The maid is clearing up things and singing.

[EXTRACT ENACTED FROM ACT 2, SCENE 2.]

> Lover, lover of the earth.
> Watch the water passing as your wedding day arrives.
> Gather up your skirts beneath your husband's wing,
> And go from your house.
> For the bridegroom is a dove with his breast on fire
> And the fields await the news of blood being shed.
> Turning the wheel, turning and the water passing by.
> Now the wedding day arrives, let the water glow!

MOTHER *(Entering)*

At last!

FATHER

Are we the first to return?

MOTHER

No. Leonardo arrived a few minutes ago with his wife. He drove like a demon. His wife nearly died of fright. He travelled the road as though he was galloping it on horseback.

FATHER

He's looking for trouble. Only bad blood there.

MOTHER

What kind of blood do you expect? His whole family has it. It's from his great-grandfather, who began their murderous ways, and the rest of the evil race inherited it, with their knives and their false smiles.

FATHER

Forget about all that!

MAID

How can she forget about it?

MOTHER

I grieve to the depths of my being. When I'm confronted with them, I only see the hand that murdered my loved ones. Do you see me? Am I mad? Well, it is madness not to have screamed out all that my heart should utter. There's a cry in my heart every moment, against the ones who should be punished, and wrapped in their shrouds. But they leave me with my dead and I have to be silent. Then people criticize. *(She takes off her shawl)*

FATHER

This isn't the day to raise such things.

MOTHER

When the conversation runs that way, I have to speak out. And today above all. Because now there'll be no one left in the house but me.

FATHER

Hoping for fresh company.

MOTHER

That's my dream. Grandchildren. *(They sit down)*

FATHER

I hope they have plenty. This land needs unpaid labour. They must wage war on the weeds, the thistles, the stones that emerge from nowhere. And that labour must come from the owners, to punish and tame it, and sow the seed. They need a host of sons.

MOTHER

And daughters! Men are creatures who pass on the wind! They're forced always to deal with weapons. Girls need never set foot in the street.

FATHER *(Cheerfully)*

I'm sure they'll have both.

MOTHER

My son will do well by her. He's from good stock. My father could have had many sons with me.

FATHER

What I wish is that the thing could be done in a day. That they could produce two or three full-grown men straight away.

MOTHER

But it's not like that. It's so slow. That's why it's so terrible to see the blood of a single one spilt on the ground. A fountain that spurts for a moment and has cost years of our life. When I reached my son, he was lying in the middle of the street. I moistened my hand with blood, and tasted it with my tongue. Because it was mine. You don't know what that means. In a monstrance, of crystal and topaz, I would place that earth soaked with blood.

FATHER
Well, we must wait. My daughter is broad-hipped and your son is strong.

MOTHER
I trust so. *(They rise)*

FATHER
Prepare the trays of food.

MAID
It is done.
(Leonardo and his wife enter.)

LEONARDO'S WIFE
I hope all will go well!

MOTHER
Thank you.

LEONARDO
Are you having a feast?

FATHER
Not much of one. People can't stay long.

MAID
Here they come now!
(The newly-weds enter arm in arm. Leonardo leaves.)

BRIDEGROOM
I've never seen so many people at a wedding.

BRIDE *(Sombre)*
Never.

FATHER
It's splendid.

MOTHER
Entire families have come.

BRIDEGROOM
People who never leave their homes.

MOTHER
Your father sowed, and you are reaping the harvest.

BRIDEGROOM
There are cousins of mine I've never met before.

MOTHER
All the ones from the coast.

BRIDEGROOM
They were nervous at handling the horses.

MOTHER *(To the bride)*
What are you thinking about?

BRIDE
I'm not thinking of anything.

MOTHER
So many blessings can weigh heavy.
(Guitars are heard.)

MOTHER *(Forcefully)*
Ignore their weight. You should be light as a dove.

BRIDE
Will you stay here tonight?

MOTHER
No. My house is empty.

BRIDE
You should stay.

FATHER *(To the Mother)*
Look at the dance they're performing. A dance from the shores of the sea.
(Leonardo appears and sits down. His wife stands behind him, looking tense.)

MOTHER
They're my husband's cousins. Good for ever when there's dancing.

FATHER
It's good to see them. Something new for this house!
(He goes out.
Leonardo exits silently in another direction.)

FIRST GIRL
Let's go and unpin your veil.

BRIDE *(To the bridegroom)*
I'll be back soon.
(She leaves with the girl.)

WIFE
May you be happy with my cousin!

BRIDEGROOM
I'm sure I will.

WIFE
Just the two of you, here, not going far, creating a home. If only I too
lived out here.

BRIDEGROOM
Why not buy some fields? Hill land is cheap, and it's healthier for
raising children.

WIFE
We've no money. And the way we're going!

BRIDEGROOM
Your husband is a good worker.

WIFE
Yes, but he likes to chop and change too much. Flitting from one thing to another. He's not steady.

MAID
You're not eating? I'll go and wrap some wine-cakes for your mother, she loves them.

BRIDEGROOM
Give her three dozen.

WIFE
No, no. A few will be enough.

BRIDEGROOM
It's a special day.

WIFE *(To the maid)*
And Leonardo?

MAID
I've not seen him.

BRIDEGROOM
He must be with the rest, outside.

WIFE
I'll go and see. *(She leaves)*

MAID
It's all beautiful.

BRIDEGROOM
You're not dancing?

MAID
No one has asked me.

BRIDEGROOM *(Cheerfully)*
They don't know any better. Lively elders dance better than the young.

MAID
So, you're full of compliments, young man! What a family yours is! Men amongst men! When I was a little girl I was at your grandfather's wedding. What a presence! It was as if a mountain was getting married!

BRIDEGROOM
I haven't quite the same build.

MAID
But you've the same gleam in your eye. Where's the little one?

BRIDEGROOM
Taking off her veil.

MAID
Oh, Look! Since you won't be asleep by midnight, I've prepared some ham and a couple of glasses of good wine. On the lower shelf of the larder. If you need them.

BRIDEGROOM *(Smiling)*
I never eat late at night.

MAID *(Mischievously)*
If not you, then the bride. *(She leaves)*

FIRST BOY *(Entering)*
Come and drink with us!

BRIDEGROOM
I'm waiting for the bride.

SECOND BOY
She'll still be here at dawn.

FIRST BOY
Which is when it's nicest.

SECOND BOY
Just one, now.

BRIDEGROOM
Let's go.
(They leave. Sounds of merriment. The bride enters. Two girls run from the opposite side to greet her.
The bridegroom reappears and slowly embraces the bride from behind.)

BRIDE *(Startled)*
Don't do that!

BRIDEGROOM
Are you frightened of me?

BRIDE
Ay! It's you.

BRIDEGROOM
Who else would it be? Your father, or me.

BRIDE
That's true!

BRIDEGROOM
Except that your father would have embraced you more gently.

BRIDE *(Gravely)*
That's for certain!

BRIDEGROOM
Because he's old. *(He embraces her firmly and a little roughly)*

BRIDE *(Curtly)*
Don't!

BRIDEGROOM
Why not? *(He releases her)*

BRIDE
Because... of all the guests. Someone might come in.

BRIDEGROOM
Why not? It is accepted.

BRIDE
Yes. But wait... later.

BRIDEGROOM
What's wrong? You seem troubled!

BRIDE
It's nothing. Don't leave me.
(Leonardo's wife appears.)

WIFE
I didn't mean to interrupt...

BRIDEGROOM
Yes?

WIFE
Has my husband been here?

BRIDEGROOM
No.

WIFE
It's just that I can't find him and his horse is not in the stable.

BRIDEGROOM *(Cheerfully)*
He'll have taken it for a gallop.
(The Wife leaves, looking anxious. The Maid enters.)

MAID
Are you happy with it all?

BRIDEGROOM
I wish it was over. The bride is a little tired.

MAID
What is it, child?

BRIDE

It's like a throbbing in my head.

MAID

A bride from these hills needs to be tougher than that. *(To the Bridegroom)* You're the one to cure it, now she's yours. *(She hurries out)*

BRIDEGROOM *(Embracing the bride)*

Let's go and dance. *(He kisses her)*

BRIDE *(Distressed)*

No. I want to lie down for a while.

BRIDEGROOM

I'll keep you company.

BRIDE

What! With all the guests still here? What would they say? Let me just be quiet for a while.

BRIDEGROOM

Whatever you wish! But don't let it take all night!

BRIDE *(From the doorway)*

I'll be fine later. *(She leaves)*

BRIDEGROOM *(Calling after her)*

I hope so!
(The Mother enters.)

MOTHER

My son.

BRIDEGROOM

Where have you been?

MOTHER

Wandering about here and there? Are you pleased?

BRIDEGROOM

Yes.

MOTHER

And your wife?

BRIDEGROOM

A bit upset. It's a difficult day for brides!

MOTHER

A difficult day? It's the best one of all. For me it was like coming into an inheritance. It's like ploughing the fresh earth, and planting new crops.

BRIDEGROOM

You are leaving?

MOTHER
Yes. I need to be home.

BRIDEGROOM
Alone?

MOTHER
Alone. No, my head is full of thoughts: of men and conflict.

BRIDEGROOM
Conflict that is no longer conflict, though.

MOTHER
That's what life is, conflict.

BRIDEGROOM
Whatever you say!

MOTHER
Try to be affectionate towards your wife. But if she gets a bit above herself, or turns awkward, give her a caress that hurts a little, a bite, and then follow it with a gentle kiss. She won't be upset, because she'll know you're a man, her master, who gives the orders. I learned that from your father. And as he's no longer here, I must teach you how to be firm with her.

BRIDEGROOM
I'll do just as you say.

FATHER *(Entering)*
Where's my daughter?

BRIDEGROOM
She went in.

FATHER
She's not there!

BRIDEGROOM
No?

FATHER
She must have gone up to the verandah.

BRIDEGROOM
I'll go and see.
(He exits. The sound of guitars and merriment.)

BRIDEGROOM *(Returning)*
She's not there.

MOTHER *(Anxiously)*
No?

FATHER
Where can she have gone?

MAID *(Entering)*
The little one. Where is she?

MOTHER *(Gravely)*
We don't know.

FATHER *(Dramatically)*
She's not dancing?

MAID
There's no sign of her there.

FATHER *(Excitedly)*
There's a crowd in there. Go and look hard!

MAID
I have looked hard!

FATHER *(Tragically)*
Where can she be?

BRIDEGROOM *(Returning)*
Nothing. She's nowhere to be found.

MOTHER *(To the Father)*
What is all this? Where is your daughter?
(Leonardo's wife enters.)

WIFE
They've fled! They've fled, she and Leonardo! On his horse. She was holding him tight: they went past like the wind.

FATHER
That's not true! No! Not my daughter!

MOTHER
Yes, your daughter! Child of a suspect mother, and he, he's the same. Yet she's my son's wife!

BRIDEGROOM
We'll hunt them down! Find me a horse!

MOTHER
A horse, quick, bring me a horse! I'd give what I have for one, my eyes my tongue even...

A VOICE
Here!

MOTHER *(To the Bridegroom)*
Go, go! *(He starts to leave with two of the guests)* No... Wait! That family are so swift to kill, so certain...and yet...hurry, and I must follow!

FATHER
It can't have been her. She'd rather drown herself in the well.

MOTHER
Someone honest and pure would run to drown themselves; but, no! Yet she's my son's wife now. There are two lots of kinfolk here. *(Everyone enters)* My family, and yours. All of you... hunt them down! Shake the dust from your shoes. Go, help my son! For he has family, here; his cousins from the coast, and you who've come from miles around. Hunt them! Take every road. The hour of blood is here once more. Both lots of kinfolk. You and yours, I and mine. Go! Go!
(The actors freeze. They get out of character slowly.)

ACTOR 10
And that was written in 1932?!

ACTOR 2
Opened in Madrid in March, 1933. Took a good fifty years for it to be given decent renditions in the English language.

BALLADEER
It is well known that Lorca's inspiration for the play came from a newspaper account of an actual event a few years earlier.

ACTOR 7
It had remained with him.

ACTOR 1
The childhood contact with the Andalusian countryside, its people and their customs – they must have left strong impressions.

ACTOR 3
What were the reactions to Blood Wedding?

ACTOR 5
There was great excitement.

ACTOR 6
They were bold strokes on a large canvas.

ACTOR 5
There was also great anxiety.
(The corner spot comes on as at the start of the play. This time there are two men in the spot. Their hats have their faces in shadow. A stanza of the poem come on over the sound system. This happens several times through the play.)
A coffin on wheels is his bed
at five in the afternoon.
Bones and flutes resound in his ears
at five in the afternoon.

The wounds were burning like suns
at five in the afternoon.
At five in the afternoon.

Ah, that fatal five in the afternoon!
It was five by all the clocks!
It was five in the shade of the afternoon!
(The spot fades out.)

ACTOR 7

It could not have been easy – writing about things like that.

BALLADEER

Like what things?

ACTOR 3

Blasphemous things.

ACTOR 1

He was only expressing as best as he could – as only a poet could – the inevitable conflict between the path of instinct and the forces of tradition.

ACTOR 10

He was just being realistic.

BALLADEER

In content, not in form. In form it was always the poetic imagery that stood out.

ACTOR 4 *(Stepping forward)*

In his stage directions, for instance, there is a lot of deliberate stylization – especially in the colours suggested for the sets and stage props.

(Two actors set up a piano stool. Actor 7 sits on the stool and mimes striking chords on the piano while talking to a small group.)

ACTOR 8

He played the piano.

ACTOR 9

Did he! He was an accomplished player.

ACTOR 8

He often composed poems as he played.

ACTOR 9

He thought up stories to tell as he played.

ACTOR 8

There were always people around him as he played.

ACTOR 9

And he played to them.

ACTOR 11

So different from the violence and agony and pain in his plays.

BALLADEER

Some of his plays.

ACTOR 11

Like Blood Wedding.

ACTOR 1

Blood Wedding is really a very poetic play.

ACTOR 7

It remains so till the very end.

ACTOR 4

The denouement. The violence unleashed takes its tragic course. There is no place to retreat except into themselves. Act Three, Scene Two. The scene suggests a convent-like space. The mother is led in by a neighbor.

(The voices of two girls are heard over the audio system.)

Crushed flowers their eyes, their teeth
Like two fists of hardened snow.
Both of them fell, the bride returned
Her hair, her dress dyed with blood.
Covered with blankets they come
On the shoulders of handsome lads.
It is so; that's all. It was just.
On the golden flower, black sand.
Black sand.
On the golden flower.
Beneath the flower of gold
They carry them from the river.
Dark-haired the one,
Dark-haired the other.
Let the nightingale of shadow
Fly, and call to the flower of gold!
(The next extract is enacted: Act 3, Scene 2.)

MOTHER

Hush.

NEIGHBOUR

I can't.

MOTHER

Hush, I said. *(In the doorway)*
Is there no one here? *(She raises her hands to her face)*
My son should have been here. But now my son is an armful of withered flowers. Now my son is a dark voice behind the mountains. *(Angrily, to the neighbour)*
Will you be quiet? I'll have no tears in this house. Your tears are tears from your eyes, nothing more, but mine will flow when I'm alone, from the soles of my feet, from the root, and they'll flow hot as blood.

NEIGHBOUR

Come home with me; you can't want to stay here.

MOTHER

Here. Here, where I am. And in peace. They're all dead now. I'll be able to sleep at night, sleep free of the fear of guns and knives. Other women will lean sleepless from their windows, drenched by the rain, to catch sight of their sons' faces. Not I. My dreams will be of a cold dove of marble carrying flowers of frost to a graveyard. But no; not a graveyard, no grave; it's a couch of earth, a bed to cradle them, and rock them under the sky.

(A woman dressed in black enters, and kneels down at stage left.)

(To the neighbour) Take your hands from your face. The days to come will be terrible days. We wish for no one. The earth and I. My grief and I. And these four walls. Ay! Ay! *(She sits down, grief-stricken)*

NEIGHBOUR

Have pity on yourself.

MOTHER *(Smoothing her hair back with her hands)*

I must be calm. *(She remains seated)* Because the neighbours will come, and I don't wish them to see me so wretched. So poverty-stricken! A woman without a single son to clasp to her breast.

(The Bride appears.
Her orange blossom has vanished and she is wearing a black shawl.)

NEIGHBOUR *(Approaching her angrily)*

Where are you going?

BRIDE

I have come.

MOTHER *(To the neighbour)*

Who is it?

NEIGHBOUR

Don't you see?

MOTHER

That is why I ask who she is? To pretend I don't know, to avoid sinking my teeth in her throat. Viper!

(She rushes at the Bride as if to strike her, but stops short. She the neighbour)

Do you see her? Here she is, and she weeps, and I halt here, and I fail to tear out her eyes. I don't understand it myself. Did I not love my son enough? Well; and her honour? Where is her precious honour now?

(She strikes the Bride, who falls to the ground.)

NEIGHBOUR

For God's sake! *(She tries to separate them)*

BRIDE *(To the neighbour)*

Let her go; I came here so that she could kill me, so that they could take me with them. *(To the Mother)* But not with your bare hands; with shears, with a sickle, with whatever force might break my bones. Let her be! I want her to know, in her anger, I am pure, and that they'll bury me without any man having gazed on the whiteness of my breasts.

MOTHER

Be silent; what does that matter to me?

BRIDE

Because I ran with another, I ran! *(Anguished)* You too, you would have gone. I was a woman on fire, wounded inside and out, and your son was a stream of water that could give me sons, land, health; but the other was a dark river, filled with branches, that brought me the murmur of its reeds, and its song between clenched teeth. And I went with your son who was like a child born of water, cold, while the other sent flocks of birds that prevented me walking, and sent frost into the wounds of a poor withered woman, a girl scorched by the flames. I did not want it. Listen to me! I did not want it. Do you hear? I did not want it. Your son was my goal, and I did not betray him, but the other seized me in his arms like a wave of the sea, struck me like the kick of a mule, and I must be dragged along forever, forever, forever, forever, even if I had been old and all your son's sons had held me back by the hair!

(Another neighbour enters)

MOTHER

She's not to blame. Nor I! *(Sarcastically)* Who is then? A fine whore, a light sleeper it is, who throws away her orange blossom to seek a corner of the bed warmed by another woman!

BRIDE

No more. No more! Take your revenge; here I am! Look how tender my throat is; it would cost you less effort to cut it than to cull a dahlia in your garden. But what you say is not so! I'm as chaste and pure as a new-born babe. And with the power to prove it. Light a fire. Let's put our hands into its flames; you for your son, I, for my body. You'll be the first to withdraw.

(Another neighbour enters.)

MOTHER

What does your purity matter to me? What does your death matter? What does nullity after nullity matter to me? Blessed are the crops, because my sons lie beneath them; blessed is the rain, because it moistens their faces. Blessed is God, who unites us in rest.

(Another neighbour enters.)

BRIDE

Let me weep with you.

MOTHER
Weep, but over there, stand in the doorway.
(The young girl enters. The Bride stands in the doorway, the Mother centre-stage.)

WIFE *(Entering and moving to the left)*
He was the finest of horsemen
who now is a mound of snow.
Through the fairs and mountains,
and women's arms he rode.
Now the mosses of midnight
offer a crown for his brow.

MOTHER
Sunflower of your mother, mirror of all the earth.
Set a cross on his breast of bitter oleander;
a sheet now to cover him, a sheet of gleaming silk,
and water there to weep between his quiet hands.

WIFE
Ay! Let four boys lift him on their weary shoulders!

BRIDE
Ay! Let four young men carry death through the air!

MOTHER
Neighbours.

YOUNG GIRL *(In the doorway)*
They're bringing them now.

MOTHER
It's no matter.
The Cross. The Cross.

WOMEN
Sweet are the nails, Sweet is the Cross,
Sweet is the name of Jesus.

BRIDE
May the Cross shelter the dead and the living.

MOTHER
Neighbours: with a knife, with a little knife,
on a fatal day between two and three,
two men killed for love. With a knife.
With a little knife that barely sits in the hand,
but penetrates deep through the startled flesh
to reach the point where trembles enmeshed
the dark root of a cry.

BRIDE

And this is a knife, a little knife
that barely sits in the hand;
a fish without scales, or the river,
so that one fine day, between two and three,
with this knife were quenched two strong men
whose lips turn yellow.

MOTHER

It scarcely sits in the hand.
But penetrates, chill, through the startled flesh
to reach the point where trembles enmeshed
the dark root of a cry.
(The actors freeze. They get out of character slowly.
The actress playing the Bride begins to weep. The Mother joins her, and then
the Neighbour. They form a huddle.)

MOTHER

So beautiful.

NEIGHBOUR

He makes death so beautiful.

BRIDE

So inviting

BALLADEER

He played with death all the time. In very many ways. He loved to stare
death in the face.
(The corner spot comes on, revealing the two men. Stanzas of the poem come
on over the sound system. They fade out with the spot.)
But now he sleeps without end.
Now the moss and the grass
open with sure fingers
the flower of his skull.
And now his blood comes out singing;
singing along marshes and meadows,
sliden on frozen horns,
faltering soulless in the mist
stumbling over a thousand hoofs
like a long, dark, sad tongue,
to form a pool of agony
close to the starry river long.
Oh, white wall of Spain!
Oh, black bull of sorrow!
(The actors continue.)

ACTOR 1
On the one hand was the sensitivity of a poet.

ACTOR 2
On the other hand was a macho Spanish society.

ACTOR 5
On one side was insight.

ACTOR 6
On the other was a mass myopia.
(A pause. The actors look at each other.)

ACTOR 7
The subject of Lorca's sexuality has remained controversial.

ACTOR 6
But undisputed

ACTOR 1
By contemporary norms he would be considered gay.

ACTOR 6
And acceptable.

ACTOR 7
As some in his inner circle did.

ACTOR 1
But the times were different. There were many who found his relationships difficult to explain.

ACTOR 6
Or acceptable.

ACTOR 2
Was Salvador Dali a lover?

ACTOR 3
The sculptor Emilio Aladren?

ACTOR 7
Or was he just himself? As with many other things in his life, did he simply dare to find a path for human relationships all his own?

ACTOR 8
The sense of isolation in this journey of self discovery is evident in his first volume of poetry.

ACTOR 9
On one side a tenderness and a hand extended.

ACTOR 10
On the other the vivid portrayal of masculinity in so much of his writing.

ACTOR 6

A fascination for masculinity some would say.

ACTOR 2

And a hostility from an unfeeling social order....

BALLADEER

But there was not the faintest doubt that Lorca had an aesthetic core to his soul.

ACTOR 11

The vibrant cultural environment in Granada attracted the greatest artists from within Spain.

ACTOR 10

Musicians, writers, artists and scholars – Juan Cristobal, the sculptor, Andres Segovia, the guitarist, Manuel Falla, the composer, with whom there was a lasting friendship.

ACTOR 11

The bohemian air in places like Café Alameda also permitted a great deal of creative exploration.

BALLADEER *(Striking a chord on his guitar)*

The musician in Lorca soaked it all in.

(The balladeer leads a song. The group joins in. Soon it transforms into a gypsy ballad with a distinct fusion sound. The song ends on a high.)

[In the Bangalore production the workshop group adapted a gypsy tune of Manitas de Plata.]

ACTOR 9

What would you call a play like The Shoemaker's Wonderful Wife?

ACTOR 10

A musical?

ACTOR 1

A farce.

ACTOR 9

A farce?

ACTOR 2

A farce from Lorca?

ACTOR 7

Wait a minute. *(He produces a book)* Look at what it says here. The Shoemaker's Prodigious Wife – "a violent farce in two acts".

ACTOR 2

How does that help, what it says there? *(Taking the book from him)* Look at this other play. The Love of Don Perlimpin and Belisa in the Garden – "an erotic print in four scenes".

ACTOR 1

Let me show you. *(Taking the book)* Act Two. The henpecked cobbler has left his wife.

The gossipy neighbourhood –

ACTOR 10

The randy neighbourhood –

ACTOR 1

The meddlesome neighbourhood is all set to make inroads into her life. When the scene opens, the wife is seen in her home with Don Blackbird and a Young Man.

Many of the characters in Act Two are of course set to line maro the woman. The Young Man wears a broad rimmed hat and a sash. He is awkward. His arms hang listlessly as he looks at the wife longingly. Come on, give us this scene.

(Three actors quickly set up the scene.)

All right now, give it a go.

ACTOR 10

A comic line maro scene.

(The actor playing the Young Man makes a comic start. Actor 4 steps forward to direct them. He is rolled away by two other actors. The Young Man tries again. Actor 7 takes the book from 1, goes up to the Young Man and gives him a whack on the head.)

ACTOR

What was that in aid of?

ACTOR 1

That's what it says. Here – *(Reading)* If the actor who plays the part indulges in the slightest exaggeration, the director should hit him on the head. Nobody should exaggerate. Farce requires the actors to be even more natural. The dramatist has drawn the character. All the actor has to do…

ACTOR 7

… Is to look within himself to see how stupid we really are – without trying too hard.

ACTOR 11

Tell you what – let's do a couple of bits from The Shoemaker's Wife.

ACTORS CHORUS

Yeah… Let's… Great idea… Super… etc.

(A small group quickly sets up the opening scene.)

ACTOR 4 *(Stepping forward)*

What we must do at the start of the play –

ACTOR 5

You know what you can do?

ACTOR 6

You can play the Director.

ACTOR 4

I can?

ACTOR 5

It says so in the script.

ACTOR 6

Here. The play opens with the Director addressing the audience.

2. THE SHOEMAKER'S WONDERFUL WIFE

EXTRACT from Act 1 is played.
An actor playing the DRAMATIST enters quickly. He holds a letter.

DRAMATIST
Distinguished ladies and gentleman... *(Pause)* Or rather, ladies and gentlemen, which is not to say the writer doesn't think you are distinguished. In fact, the opposite. But the word contains the tiniest him of fear, a kind of plea for the audience to be kind to the actors' performance and the writer's brilliance. The writer doesn't ask for kindness; just for attention once he's leapt that barbed and dreadful barrier of fear that writers have of writing for the theatre. Because of this, which is quite absurd, and because the theatre is often simply a business, poetry has disappeared from the stage in search of other places.
(The SHOEMAKER'S WIFE is beard shouting.)

SHOEMAKER'S WIFE *(off)*
I want to make my entrance!

DRAMATIST
All right, all right! Don't be so impatient! It's not a gown with a train or fantastic feathers you're about to appear in. It's just a rag, do you hear? The dress of a shoemaker's wife!

SHOEMAKER'S WIFE *(off)*
Let me make my entrance!

DRAMATIST *(Describing the empty stage in great detail)*
The SHOEMAKER's house. A bench and tools. A completely white room. A large window and door. Upstage a white street with some small grey doors and windows. Doors stage-left and stage-right. The setting has an air of optimism and exuberant joy down to the tiniest details. A soft mid-afternoon orange light fills the stage.
(When the curtain rises the SHOEMAKER'S WIFE enters furiously from the street and stops in the doorway. She wears a dress of strident green and her hair, displaying two large roses, is tightly drawn. Her manner is aggressive but simultaneously sweet.)

WIFE
Shut up, loud mouth! You think you're the cat's whiskers! But if I did it, it's because I wanted to. You rotten little snake!.
If anyone had said to me... me with this fair hair and these dark eyes... you see how attractive they are... and this waist, and these ever-so-pretty colours... That I'd go and get married to... I'd have pulled my hair out. *(She starts to cry. Knock at the door.)* Who's there? *(No answer. A second knock, furiously.)* Who's there?

BOY *(timidly)*
A friend.

WIFE
What do you want? And why are you so sullen?

BOY *(pouting)*
Don't get angry. It isn't my fault. And I do learn my grammar properly every day.

WIFE *(sweetly)*
Child, child. Of course I'm not angry with you. *(She kisses him)*

BOY
All right... because I know you'll never have children and...

WIFE
Who told you that?

BOY
My mother said it the other day. She said: 'the shoemaker's wife won't have any children; and my sisters laughed and so did Aunty Rafaela.

WIFE *(nervously)*
Children? I'll have children one day... prettier than any of theirs; and they'll be more lively, and more respectable. As for your mother, there's something you ought to...

BOY
Goodbye, Mrs. Shoemaker. And the very best of luck... And God protect you from all harm...
(The BOY runs out into the street.)

WIFE
Goodbye, child. If you'd only been strangled at birth, I wouldn't be suffering these trials and tribulations now! Money, money! Whoever invented money deserves to have his hands cut off, and be struck blind.

SHOEMAKER *(at the bench)*
What are you talking about, woman?

WIFE
Nothing that concerns you.

SHOEMAKER
Oh no, there's nothing that concerns me. Oh, no, Nothing at all. My duty is to suffer.

WIFE
I have to suffer too...and I'm only eighteen.

SHOEMAKER
And I'm fifty-three... which is why I hold my tongue, and my temper. I know too many things...I work to provide for you and...God's will be done!

(The WIFE has her back to the SHOEMAKER. She turns and moves towards him tenderly.)

WIFE
Not that again, my sweet, Not that!

SHOEMAKER
If I could only be forty again, or even forty five...
(He wallops a shoe with his hammer.)

WIFE *(Forcefully)*
You'd have me under you thumb. You think a girl can't be good of her own accord... You think I'm worthless.

SHOEMAKER
Woman...control yourself.

WIFE
But my youth and looks are worth a fortune.

SHOEMAKER
Woman...the neighbours will hear you!

WIFE
I curse the day I listened to friend Manuel. I Curse the day! *(Hitting herself on the forehead)* Fool! Fool! Fool! I've had so many wonderful admirers.

SHOEMAKER *(wanting to calm her)*
So people say.

WIFE
So people say? The whole world knows it. The best young men throughout these parts. But the one I liked best was Emiliano... you saw him for yourself... the one who rode on a black mare, covered with tassels and tiny bits of glass, and he carried a whip of willow and spurs of gleaming copper on his feet. And what a cloak he wore in winter-time! Such fine blue cloth, and trimmed in silk!

SHOEMAKER
I had one once...a really splendid cape!

WIFE
Oh, yes I'm sure you did! Stop dreaming! What shoemaker's ever worn anything as good as that?

SHOEMAKER
Woman, don't you see...?

WIFE *(interrupting)*
Then there was the other one...
(The SHOEMAKER hammers the shoe furiously.)
Such a fine young gentleman...he must have been eighteen or so...you can say it so quickly! Eighteen!

SHOEMAKER

I was eighteen once.

WIFE

You've never been eighteen in all your life... But he was. And he used to say such lovely things to me...like this...

SHOEMAKER (*hammering furiously*)

Be quiet! You are my wife, like it or not, and I'm your husband. You were starving. Nothing to wear. Nowhere to live. Why did you have to choose me? You and all your whims and fanciest!

WIFE (*getting up*)

Be quiet! Don't make me say what I shouldn't. And do your duty by me. I don't believe all this!

(*Two NEIGHBOURS wearing mantillas pass the window. They are smiling.*)

Who'd have said you'd treat me like this, you drunk old man? Go on! Hit me if you want to. Hit me with the hammer!

SHOEMAKER

Don't make such a fuss, woman! The people are coming Oh, my God!

(*The two NEIGHBOURS pass the window again.*)

WIFE

I've lowered myself, that's what I've done. Fool! Fool! Fool! A curse on good friend Manuel! A curse on all the neighbours! Fool! Fool! Fool!

(*She leaves, hitting herself on the forehead.*)

SHOEMAKER (*gazing into a mirror counting his lines*)

I should have known, from reading all those books, that men are fond of all women. But women are fond of only some men. I was perfectly fine as I was. My sister's to blame for this. She would insist, my sister: 'If you're all on your own, who's to know what will come of you?' And this is what has come of me! Let lightning strike my sister down! God rest her soul!

(*He goes to his bench. Through the main door the MAYOR appears. He is dressed in blue, wears a long cloak, and carries a long staff of office with silver decorations. He speaks slowly and mockingly.*)

MAYOR

At work, I see.

SHOEMAKER

At work, Mr. Mayor.

MAYOR

Doing nicely?

SHOEMAKER

Can't complain.

(*The SHOEMAKER carries on working. The MAYOR looks around.*)

MAYOR

But something's wrong.

SHOEMAKER *(without looking up)*

Yes.

MAYOR

Wife?

SHOEMAKER *(nodding)*

Wife

MAYOR *(sitting down)*

That's what comes of marrying at your age... a man of your age should be a widower... one wife dead at least. I've had four: Rosa, Manuela, Visitacion, and Enriqueta Gomez was the last. Fine girls all of them, extremely fond of dancing and clean water. Many's the time they felt this stick, without exception. That's how I ran the household... nose to the grindstone!

SHOEMAKER

You can see the kind of life I have. My wife... she doesn't love me. She talks from the window to everyone, even Don Blackbird. It makes my blood boil.

MAYOR

You need to hug a woman, stamp on her and let hear the sound of your voice. And if she still tries to be cock-of-the-walk, take a stick to her. It's the only way. Rosa, Manuela, Visitacion, and Enriqueta Gomez, the last of my wives, they'll all bear witness to that from the other side, if that's where they are.

SHOEMAKER

The fact is there's something I haven't told you. *(Looking around fearfully)*

MAYOR *(with authority)*

Then tell me!

SHOEMAKER

It's a terrible thing to say, but... I don't love my wife.

MAYOR

God forbid!

SHOEMAKER

Yes, sir, God forbid!

MAYOR

So why, you idiot, did you marry her?

SHOEMAKER

That's it precisely. I don't know why. My sister's to blame, my sister: 'If you're all on your own, who's to know what will become of you?' Over and over again! I had money and health, so I said 'all right '. Oh blessed solitary life! Let lightning strike my sister down, God rest her soul!

(The WIFE enters, powdering her face from a compact, smoothening out her eyebrows.)

WIFE
Good afternoon!

MAYOR
A very good afternoon to you! *(To the Shoemaker)* Good looking girl. A very good looking girl!
(The WIFE sits by the window, looks at the street, flirts.)

SHOEMAKER
See that?

MAYOR
A little sharp... but a fine-looking girl. Such a perfect waist!

SHOEMAKER
You don't know her.

MAYOR
Pssch! *(As he exits)* Let's hope your head is clearer. *(To WIFE)* Take things easy, my child! What a waste of a fine figure! *(He goes out looking at the girl)* Such splendid hair!
(He leaves.
A YOUNG MAN wearing a sash stops outside the window. A flat hat is pulled down over his eyes and he seems very sad.)

YOUNG MAN
Enjoying the fresh air, Mrs. Shoemaker?

WIFE
The same as you.

YOUNG MAN
And always alone... so sad!

WIFE *(sharply)*
What do you mean... so sad?

YOUNG MAN
A woman like you, with such fine hair, such a lovely bosom...

WIFE *(more sharply)*
What do you mean sad?

YOUNG MAN
Because you deserve to have your portrait painted on post-cards... and not be stuck in a room like this.

WIFE

Do you really think so? I do love post-cards, especially those from suitors on some distant journey...

YOUNG MAN

Oh, little shoemaker's wife, I am on fire!
(They continue talking.)

SHOEMAKER *(to audience)*

She talks to everyone! And at this late hour! What will they say in church as they count their beads? What will they say at the casino? They'll be discussing every little detail... down to my underwear! *(The WIFE Laughs)* My God! I've every reason to leave! I wish I could hear the sacristan's wife. And the priests. What can they be saying? That's what I'd really like to know.
(He leaves, very agitated.)

YOUNG MAN

How shall I put it? I love you, I love thee truly, as if...

WIFE

Oh, I truly like that 'I love you, I love thee'. It's got a sound to it, as if someone were ticking me behind the ear with a feather. 'I love you, I love thee'.

YOUNG MAN

How many seeds does a sunflower have?

WIFE

I don't know.

YOUNG MAN

As many as the sighs I sigh every moment of the day for you, for thee...
(He comes very close.)

WIFE *(sharply)*

I think you'd better keep your distance. I don't mind listening to nice, pretty things. But nothing more, do you understand?

YOUNG MAN

I refuse to move until you promise me, my dear little shoemaker's wife, promise me you will...
(He attempts to embrace her. She slams the window shut.)

WIFE

The cheek of it! He must be mad! If you suffer on my account, you'll have to put up with it... As if I'm here just to... Can't a girl speak to anyone in this town? As far as I can see, there's no alternative: a nun or a dish-cloth. That's all I need!
(Sniffing the air, running) The dinner's burning! Stupid woman!
(It is getting dark. The SHOEMAKER appears. He is wearing a great cloak and carrying a bundle of clothes.)

SHOEMAKER

I'm either someone else or I don't know myself! My little house! My little bench! Wax, nails, Calf-skins! One topic of conversation throughout the village... me her, all those young men. Let lightning strike my sister down, God rest her soul! I'd rather be alone than pointed at by others!

(He goes out quickly, leaving the door ajar. The WIFE enters stage-left.)

WIFE

Supper's ready... do you hear? *(Going to the exit)* Do you hear? Has he had the nerve to go to the inn... to leave the door wide open and the boots not finished? Just wait till he gets back. I'll have something to say to him. What do they think they are, men! Have you ever seen such... If his not back in two minutes, I'll eat by myself, make no mistake! The trouble I took to prepare white bread, a lean piece of bacon, and pumpkin with syrup and lemon-peel on top... The things I do for him! The lengths I go to take care of him!

(For the whole of this speech she reveals great energy, moving around arranging the chairs, trimming the oil-lamp, removing bits of fluff from her dress.

The BOY appears.)

BOY

Are you still angry? *(She seats him on her lap.)*

WIFE.

Why are you so sweet?

BOY

I came to tell you something no one else wants to tell you. 'You, go, you go, you go' they all kept saying and then they said 'the child can go'... because it was something no one else wanted to tell you.

WIFE

So tell me quickly. What is it?

BOY

Don't be frightened, No one's died.

WIFE

Go on!

BOY

It's this, Mrs Shoemaker... Ah, look, a butterfly... a beautiful butterfly... *(The BOY gets up and begins to chase it.)*

A butterfly, a butterfly... We need a hat... Look, it's yellow with red and blue spots... it's lovely...

WIFE

BUT child, you were going to...

BOY *(strongly)*

Be quiet, talk quietly. You'll frighten it. Quick give me your handkerchief.

WIFE *(involved in the pursuit)*
Here!

BOY
Shhh... move quietly.

WIFE
You'll let it get away... NOW! NOW!

BOY *(full of delight, chasing it with the handkerchief)*
Stay! Stay! Don't try to fly again!

WIFE *(running in another direction)*
It's getting away. It's getting away from us!
(The BOY runs out through the door in pursuit of the butterfly.)

WIFE *(shouting)*
Where are you going?

BOY *(stopping)*
It's true... But don't blame me!

WIFE
Come on. Tell me what's happened. Quickly!

BOY
It's just that... well... it's just that your husband, the shoemaker, has gone away... forever.

WIFE *(shocked)*
What?!

BOY
That's what he said... at our house, before getting into the coach. I saw him... and he told us to tell you, and now the whole town knows it.

WIFE *(Sitting down)*
It isn't possible. It isn't possible.

BOY
It's true. Please don't scold me.
(The BOY runs out. NEIGHBOURS appear at the window and the doors. The WIFE gets up. She stamps furiously.)

WIFE
Is this how he pays me? Is this how he pays me?

MAYOR
Be quiet, woman. If your husband's left, it's because you didn't love him and he couldn't stand it anymore.

WIFE
I suppose you think you know better than me. Of course I loved him, of course I did! So many rich and handsome suitors, and I never said 'yes' to one of them! My poor husband! The things they must have told you!

(The actors freeze briefly. Two Actors narrate the scene as it unfolds. It is a whirling choreography of an assortment of neighbours, criss-crossing each other as they 'take over' the house of the Shoemaker's wife, attending to her, solicitous.)

ACTOR

The neighbourhood rushes in

ACTOR 2

Lorca has them dressed in different colours...

ACTOR

Yellow, red, green, black, purple....

ACTOR

They take over the house.

ACTOR

We have dashes of colour darting through the stage in all directions.

ACTOR

They take over the house.

ACTOR

Attending to the Shoemaker's wife.

ACTOR

Being nice to her.

(The actors freeze, the neighbours forming a semi-circle around the Shoemaker's wife. The Mayor and the Boy join the tableau.

The actors get out of character.)

ACTOR 11

So... he goes off.

ACTOR 10

So... the field is open.

ACTOR 2

You have a procession of visitors of all kinds – nosey ones, gossipy ones, randy ones, snickering ones, all finding some excuse or the other to just drop in and look her up.

BALLADEER

The shoemaker returns, of course.

ACTOR 8

He can't do without her.

ACTOR 9

She begins to miss him too.

ACTOR 8

The shoemaker returns, but in disguise – to test the waters once again, so to speak.

ACTOR 9

They meet. They confide in each other.

(The group sets up the closing scene for act 2. The extract is enacted.
The Tableau remains frozen. The Shoemaker enters. He is disguised. He
places his things on a table or bench, preferably Down-left or Down-right.
There is a story roll and a bag of puppets. He waits. The tableau breaks up.
The neighbours and the Shoemaker's wife position themselves at points upstage.
The Mayor and the Boy move to the Shoemaker.)

MAYOR

So... you are a puppeteer, are you?

SHOEMAKER

A storyteller with puppets.

MAYOR

And these are...

SHOEMAKER

Let them be, Mr. Mayor... I take it you are the mayor... they are my
bread and butter.

BOY

I'm sure I've heard that voice somewhere before.

(Throughout the scene the BOY looks at the SHOEMAKER with a sense
of puzzlement.)

Let's see the puppets!

SHOEMAKER

As soon as I've had a glass of wine.

MAYOR

Do you live far from here?

SHOEMAKER

Oh, yes. Extremely far.

MAYOR

Seville perhaps?

SHOEMAKER

No

MAYOR

France then?

SHOEMAKER

And a few more.

MAYOR

It must be England.

SHOEMAKER

I'm form the Philippines.

(The Neighbours gasp in wonder. The WIFE is ecstatic.)

MAYOR
You must have seen the rebels then.

SHOEMAKER
Just like I'm seeing you now.

BOY
What are they like? Do they have horns?

SHOEMAKER
Impossible people. Almost all of them are shoemakers.
(The NEIGHBOURS stare at the WIFE)

WIFE *(angrily)*
Aren't there any other professions?

SHOEMAKER
Not a single one. In the Philippines it's all cobblers.

WIFE
I expect they'll all be stupid. Ours are extremely clever.

MAYOR
Shh! What does your show consist of?

SHOEMAKER *(emptying his glass, clicking his tongue and looking at the wife)*
Not much show, but lots of substance. I reveal the inner self. I enact the tales of the hen-pecked shoemaker and the cruel giantess of Alexandria, the adventures of Don Diego Corrientes, the escapades of the dashing Francisco Esteban, and especially the art of shutting-up chattering and upstart women.

WIFE
My poor husband knew all of that!

SHOEMAKER
God forgive him!

WIFE
Now you listen...
(The NEIGHBOURS laugh)

BOY
Be quiet, please.

MAYOR *(authoritatively)*
Be quiet! These tales have something to teach us all. The stage is yours, sir.
(The SHOEMAKER unrolls the scroll on which the story is painted, divided into small squares, painted in red ochre and strong colours. The NEIGHBOURS gather around. The WIFE sits the BOY on her knee.)

SHOEMAKER
Attention, please!

BOY

Oh, this is exciting!
(He hugs the wife. The audience murmurs excitedly.)

WIFE *(to the BOY)*

Now pay attention in case I don't understand it all.

BOY

It can't be as hard as the Bible.

SHOEMAKER

Distinguished audience... Listen to the true and edifying tale of the fiery wife and the poor hen-pecked husband, and let it be a warning and example to you all. *(In a dark tone)* Open up your ears. Sharpen your minds!

(The NEIGHBOURS crane their necks and some of the women hold each other's hands tightly.)

BOY *(to the WIFE)*

When the puppet master speaks, he sounds exactly like your husband. Don't you think so?

WIFE

His voice was much more gentle.

SHOEMAKER

Are you ready then?

WIFE

It's sending shivers up my spine.

BOY

Me too!

SHOEMAKER *(pointing with his stick)*

There was a farm in Cordoba
Amongst the oleander trees,
And there good Mr. Tanner lived,
And took a wife for company.
(The neighbours are expectant.)
She proved extremely sharp with him, He treated her most patiently,
Her age, in truth, was twenty years,
And his was more like fifty.
My God, you should have seen them fight!
Look here, behold this monster shrill.
She mocked, she stung, she tortured him.
If looks and words could only kill!
*(We see on the scroll a woman of child-like and weary appearance.
The onlookers murmur.)*

WIFE

What a horrible woman!

SHOEMAKER

Now Mrs. Tanner had such hair,
An empress would have envied her.
Her skin was smooth and soft and clear,
As clear as Lucena's river.
(The NEIGHBOURS laugh.)
See now how young men courted her,
Such dark and strong and handsome chaps,
While tassels of the finest silk
Adorned their horses gleaming backs.
See how she flirts with one of them
Her hair, her dress, none handsomer,
While there her poor husband toils
And vents his anger on his leather.
(Very dramatically now)
Oh, husband old in years and good,
And with a wife so immature.
These scoundrels riding past the house,
Will have her for themselves, I fear.
(The WIFE has been sighing deeply and now begins to cry.)

SHOEMAKER *(turning)*

What is it?

MAYOR

My dear child! *(He beats his stick on the floor)*

RED NEIGHBOUR

A woman who cries always has something to hide!

PURPLE NEIGHBOUR

Please go on!
(The NEIGHBOURS murmur and shush.)

WIFE

It's just that the story makes me sad. I can't help it, you see. I can't help it.
(She tries to control herself, hiccuping in the most comic manner.)

MAYOR

We must have silence!

BOY

Come on!

SHOEMAKER

Please don't interrupt! You can't imagine how hard it is to remember
the piece by heart.

BOY *(sighing)*

Oh yes, that's very true.

SHOEMAKER *(in a bad temper)*
  Riding on a Cordoban mare
  Came one of her boldest suitors.
  'My sweet,' he said, `if you really want,
  Tomorrow we'll eat together,
  The two of us at your place,
  And I'll love you forever.'
  `But what if my husband comes?' she said,
  To which he replied, 'Oh, no.'
  `But what if he does?' she carried on.
  `Then I'll kill the so-and-so.'
  `He's very quick,' she answered him,
  `You'd better get a revolver.'
  `I'll do better than that,' he said to her,
  `He can feel the edge of this razor.'
  `Is it sharp?' she asked. 'Like ice,' he said,
  `And it's never been used before.'
  `Are you telling the truth?' I swear I am.
  Your husband's dead for sure.'
  (The WIFE covers her eyes and holds the BOY tight.
  The NEIGHBOURS' sense of high expectation is mirrored in their faces.)
  `Ten times this blade shall strike him down,
  Each blow is planned with utmost care:
  Four in the back, two in the chest,
  And two in either side, just there.'
  `And will you do it soon?' she said.
  `Tonight when he's coming back,
  When he's bringing leather and horse-hair home,
  He shall die on the river bank.'
  (On the last line a loud and anguished cry is suddenly heard off-stage. The
NEIGHBOURS *get up. Another cry much nearer.*
  The SHOEMAKER drops the scroll and the rod.
  Everyone trembles in a comic manner.)

BLACK NEIGHBOUR *(at the window)*
  They've got their knives out!

WIFE
  My God!

RED NEIGHBOUR
  Holy Mary!

SHOEMAKER
  This is terrible!

BLACK NEIGHBOUR
They are killing each other! Carving each other up... and *(pointing to the WIFE)* all because of her.

MAYOR *(nervously)*
We'd better go and see.

BOY
I'm scared, I'm scared!

GREEN NEIGHBOUR
Quickly, quickly!
(They begin to leave.)

VOICE *(off)*
She's a bad lot! It's all her fault.

SHOEMAKER
Keep calm, my dear. Is your husband there in the street?

WIFE *(bursting into tears)*
My husband? Oh, Mr. Puppet Master!

SHOEMAKER
What is it?

WIFE
My husband left me because of them! And now I'm alone and no one to comfort me.

SHOEMAKER
You poor girl!

WIFE
I loved him so much! I worshipped him!

SHOEMAKER
That's not true!

WIFE *(suddenly stops crying)*
What?

SHOEMAKER
I mean... it's all so strange, it seems impossible. *(He is shaken.)*

WIFE
I know. And ever since then I haven't been able to eat, or sleep, or breathe. He was my happiness, my protection.

SHOEMAKER
You loved him as much as that and he still left? As far as I can see, your husband must have been a blockhead.

WIFE
I'll ask you to hold your tongue No one's asked for your opinion.

SHOEMAKER

I'm sorry. I didn't mean to...

WIFE

The thing is... he was very clever.

SHOEMAKER *(jokingly)*

He was?

WIFE *(strongly)*

Oh yes! those ballads and all that stuff you sing and recite in the villages. That's nothing compared with what he used to know. He used to know three times as much as that!

SHOEMAKER *(gravely)*

Impossible.

WIFE *(strongly)*

I mean four times as much. He used to recite them to me in bed... ancient stories you've never even heard of... *(Sweetly)* And I used to get frightened... and he'd say to me: 'But my dearest darling, it's only a story.'

SHOEMAKER *(indignant)*

A pack of lies!

WIFE *(startled)*

What? Are you mad?

SHOEMAKER

All lies!

WIFE *(angrily)*

What on earth do you mean, Puppet Master?

SHOEMAKER *(standing, angrily)*

Your husband was quite right. Those stories are nothing but lies! Pure fantasy!

WIFE *(sharply)*

Of course they are. Do you think I'm a fool? But you can't deny they do make a strong impression.

SHOEMAKER

They make an impression on impressionable people.

WIFE

You are talking about me!

SHOEMAKER *(meekly)*

My dear, I don't know what you mean. I don't even know you, and I've done you no harm. Why treat me like this? It must be my fate. *(He is almost weeping)*

WIFE *(strongly, but moved)*

My good man, try to understand. I said that because I'm always on edge. Everyone attacks me, criticizes... so I have to defend myself at the least provocation. You see, I'm on my own, I'm a young woman, and only memories to cling to... *(She weeps)*

SHOEMAKER *(weeping)*

My dear girl, I understand. I understand much better than anyone can imagine... because... I'm going to tell you this in confidence... your situation is... oh yes... it really is... identical to mine.

WIFE *(fascinated)*

Really?

SHOEMAKER *(slumps on the table)*

My wife... my wife abandoned me!

WIFE

A woman like that deserves to drop down dead!

SHOEMAKER

She used to dream of a world I couldn't share. She was full of whims, and bossy too, and far too fond of chat, and sweets I couldn't afford. And then one wild and stormy day she left me... forever.

WIFE

So what are you doing on the road?

SHOEMAKER

I'm trying to find her, to tell her she's forgiven, and to spend what's left of my life with her. No one my age wants to spend his life in inns.

WIFE *(quickly)*

I will get you some hot coffee. It'll do you good after all this hullabaloo. *(She goes to the counter to pour some coffee and stands with her back to the SHOEMAKER.)*

SHOEMAKER *(crossing himself exaggeratedly and wide-eyed)*

May God reward you, my pretty pink carnation! *(She brings him the coffee.)*

SHOEMAKER *(draining the cup)*

I really envy your husband.

WIFE

Why?

SHOEMAKER *(gallantly)*

Because he married the best wife in the world.

WIFE *(softening)*

The things you say!

SHOEMAKER

I'll be glad to be on my way again... I mean you alone, me alone, you so pretty, me so free with my tongue... I might say something...

WIFE *(reacting)*

For heaven's sake! What are you thinking of? My heart belongs to the man who's out there, wherever he is, the man I must be faithful to. My husband!

SHOEMAKER *(overjoyed, throwing his hat on the floor)*

Wonderful! Wonderful! Spoken like a true woman!

WIFE *(surprised, somewhat ironic)*

I think you must be a bit... She points a finger to her head.

SHOEMAKER

If you say so. But I have to tell you that I love my wife, my lawful wedded wife, and no one else.

WIFE

And I my husband, and no one but my husband. I've said it often enough, you'd think the deaf would have heard by now. *(Placing her hands across her breast)*

My dearest darling shoemaker!

SHOEMAKER *(aside)*

My dearest darling wife!
(There is knocking at the door.)

WIFE

Lord! One crisis on top of another! Who is it?

BOY

Open the door.

WIFE

What can it be? Why have you come?

BOY

I've run all the way to tell you...

WIFE

What's happened?

BOY *(panting and hot)*

They've stabbed each other... two or three young men... and they say it's your fault. There's blood everywhere. All the women have gone to see the judge, so he'll force you to leave the village.

WIFE *(to the SHOEMAKER)*

You see?

BOY

The square is full of groups... as if it's a holiday... and everyone's against you!

WIFE (*quickly*)
I'm going. I want to see this wickedness for myself.
(*She leaves quickly.*)

SHOEMAKER
Oh... little house of mine! Such lovely warmth from all your doors and windows! Oh, what wretched inns, what awful food, what rough and dirty sheets along the highways of the world! I must have been stupid not to know my wife was pure gold, the purest gold there is! It makes me weep!
(*The WIFE enters.*)

WIFE (*boldly*)
If they dare come here, I'll be waiting... with the courage that comes from people who've always ridden the steepest mountains bareback.

SHOEMAKER
Don't you think your courage might fail one day?

WIFE
The woman sustained by love and honour never fails. I know I'm capable of going on until my hair turns white.

SHOEMAKER
I'll say goodbye then... we may not meet again... at my age...

WIFE (*responding*)
I don't want to say goodbye like this. I'm a happy person. (*In a firm, clear voice*)
My good friend, may God help you find your wife and enjoy the care and respect you used to have. (*She is moved*)

SHOEMAKER
I wish you the same concerning your husband. You know, it's a small world. If I happen to meet him on my travels, is there anything you'd like me to tell him?

WIFE
Tell him I worship him.

SHOEMAKER (*coming closer*)
Anything else?

WIFE
And although he's fifty and a bit, bless him, he's much more handsome and brave than any other man on earth.

SHOEMAKER
My child, that's wonderful! You love him as much as I love my wife.

WIFE
Oh, much more than that!

SHOEMAKER
Impossible! I'm a little dog and I bark to my wife's command. But so I should. She's got more brains than me! *He is close to her, an adoring expression on his face.*

WIFE
And don't forget to tell him I'm waiting, and the winter nights are long.

SHOEMAKER
You'll welcome him back then?

WIFE
As if he were the King and Queen in one.

SHOEMAKER *(trembling)*
So what if he happened to be here now?

WIFE
I'd be beside myself with joy!

SHOEMAKER
You'd forgive his foolishness?

WIFE
I forgave him long ago.

SHOEMAKER
Would you want him to come this very moment?

WIFE
If only he would!

SHOEMAKER *(shouting)*
Well, he's here!

WIFE
What?

SHOEMAKER *(removing his glasses and his disguise)*
I can't wait any more! My dear little wife!
(The WIFE is as if transported, her arms away from her body.
The SHOEMAKER embraces her and she stares at him throughout this climactic moment. Off-stage (or on the audio system) there is poem recited.)

VOICE
Do you know young Mrs. Shoemaker,
The one whose husband ran away?
She went and opened up an inn,
And there the gentry come to stay.

WIFE *(responding)*
Rogue, scoundrel, blackguard, liar! Do you hear that? It's all your fault! *She throws chairs.*

SHOEMAKER *(emotionally, going to his bench)*
My dear wife!

WIFE
You vagabond! Oh, I'm glad you've decided to come back! I'm going to lead you such a dance! You'd be better off with the Inquisition or the Templars of Rome!

SHOEMAKER *(at his bench)*
My true happiness is here!
(The poem is heard nearer still, the NEIGHBOURS appear at the window.)

VOICES
Please tell us, Mrs Shoemaker,
Who buys you all those lovely things?
Those blouses made with fine, soft silk,
Embroidered with a fancy fringe.
We know the Mayor fancies her,
Don Blackbird too, he's really keen.
Oh, silly Mrs Shoemaker,
The like of it we've never seen!

WIFE
Such rotten luck! To have to put up with a man like this! *(Going to the door)*
Shut up, loud mouths! Obscene creatures! Come on, come on! There are two of us now to defend the house! Two of us! Myself and my husband!
(Turning to the SHOEMAKER) This wretch, this good-for-nothing!
(The poem fills the stage. A bell begins to ring furiously in the distance. The actors get out of character.)

BALLADEER
Do you believe me now that Lorca's work was not all dark and tragic?

ACTOR 1
In the face of the greatest tragedy overtaking Spanish society Lorca maintained his cheerful disposition.
(The corner spot comes on, revealing two men. Stanzas of the poem come on over the sound system. They fade out with the spot.)
Autumn will come with its seashells,
its misty grapes, its gathering of hills,
but no one will want to look in your eyes
because you have died forever.
Because you have died forever
like all the dead of the earth,
like all the dead who are forgotten
under a mound of darkened dogs.
No one knows you. No. But I sing to you.

I sing for the future your profile and your grace.
The ripe gleam of your wisdom.
Your appetite for death and the taste of its mouth.
The sadness borne in your valiant joy.

ACTOR 11 *(Continuing)*
Why are there so many strong women characters in Lorca's plays?

ACTOR 10
He wrote them for you maybe.

ACTOR 11
No, seriously, just look at the scripts we have been reading.

ACTOR 2
More psychoanalysis, what?

BALLADEER
Have you read Yerma?

ACTORS
Ah, Yerma!

ACTOR 8
That's a part I'd love to play.

ACTOR 9
That's a part I must play.

ACTOR 10
That's a part even the men would love to play some day.

ACTOR 2
You will one day – the rate at which our actresses are getting spliced and moving out.

ACTOR 10
And adding to the population tally.

ACTOR 7
Not Yerma.

ACTOR 1
That was her tragedy. Not having a child.

BALLADEER
That's what the name Yerma means – wasteland or barren land.

ACTOR 8
Lorca did that with many characters in his plays, didn't he?

ACTOR 9
Giving them names that said something.

ACTOR 10
Do we have time to do something from Yerma?

ACTOR 11

What do you mean "do something from Yerma"? How can we do anything except the whole play?

ACTOR 8

The whole play? Here? Now?

ACTOR 2

To this audience?

ACTORS CHORUS

>> Let's do a scene...
>> Or two...
>> Just a little bit...
>> We must...
>> How can we not...
Etc. ending with the question to Actor 4
>> What do you say, Mr. Director, sir?

3. YERMA

EXCERPT. The group plays a scene from Act 1, Scene 1.

JUAN
There's nothing the matter with me. It's just your imagination. I work hard. Every year I grow a little older.

YERMA
Every year...You and I will stay on here year after year...

JUAN *(Smiling)*
Naturally. And peacefully, too. The work is going well, we've no children to worry about.

YERMA
No children... Juan!

JUAN
What is it?

YERMA
Is it because I don't love you enough?

JUAN
You love me.

YERMA
I know girls who've trembled and wept before they climbed into bed with their husbands. Did I cry the first time I slept with you? Didn't I sing as I turned back the fine linen? Didn't I say: 'What a scent of apples these sheets hold?'

JUAN
That's what you said!

YERMA
My mother wept because I wasn't sorry to leave her. And it was true! No one was ever happier at being married. And yet...

JUAN
Hush.

YERMA
I will hush. And yet...

JUAN
It's too much, having to listen to it all the time...

YERMA
No. Don't tell me what they say. I see with my own eyes it's not true... the force of the rain falling on stone makes it crumble to soil, and weeds

grow that people say are fit for nothing. Weeds may be fit for nothing, yet I still see their yellow flowers blowing in the breeze.

JUAN

We must hope!

YERMA

Yes, and love each other!

(Yerma, taking the initiative, kisses and embraces her husband.)

JUAN

If you need anything tell me and I'll get it for you. You know I don't like you going out.

YERMA

I never go out.

JUAN

You're better off here.

YERMA

Yes.

JUAN

The streets are for idlers.

YERMA *(Darkly)*

Of course.

(The husband leaves and Yerma goes back to her sewing. She passes her hand over her belly, lifts her arms in a beautiful sigh, and sits down to sew. She sings.)

Where do you come from, my child?

'From heights that are icy cold.'

(She threads the needle)

What do you need, my love?

'The warm feel of your robe.'

Let branches stir in the light

and fountains leap in the air!

(As if she is speaking to her child)

A dog barks in the yard,

A breeze sings in the trees.

The ox lows for the herdsman

And the moon ruffles my hair.

What do you wish, child, far away?

(She pauses)

'The white hills of your breast'

Let branches stir in the light

And fountains leap in the air!

(Sewing)

I can only say yes, my child.

I'll be broken and torn for you.
What a grief it is to me now,
Your first cradle, this womb!
When, my child, will you come?
(Pause)
'When it smells of jasmine, your flesh.'
Let branches stir in the light
and fountains leap in the air!
(Yerma continues humming. Maria enters through the doorway carrying a bundle of clothes.)

YERMA

Where have you come from?

MARIA

From the store.

YERMA

From the store, so early?

MARIA

I'd have waited at the door till they opened to get what I wanted. Can you guess what I bought?

YERMA

I'd imagine coffee for breakfast, sugar, bread.

MARIA

No. I bought lace, three lengths of cloth, ribbons and coloured wool to make tassels. My husband had money and he gave it to me.

YERMA

You're going to make a blouse.

MARIA

No, it's for... you know?

YERMA

What?

MARIA

Because it's arrived! *(She lowers her head)*
(Yerma rises and looks at her admiringly.)

YERMA

In only five months!

MARIA

Yes!

YERMA

You can tell it's there?

MARIA

Of course.

YERMA *(With curiosity)*

And how do you feel?

MARIA

I don't know. *(Pause)* Worried.

YERMA

Worried. *(She takes hold of her)* But...when did it come? Tell me...You weren't expecting it?

MARIA

No, I wasn't...

YERMA

You could have been singing, couldn't you? I'm singing. You must... tell me about it.

MARIA

Don't ask. Have you ever held a live bird cupped in your hands?

YERMA

Yes.

MARIA

It's the same... but deep inside you.

YERMA

How beautiful! *(She gazes at her, at a loss)*

MARIA

I'm anxious. I don't know a thing.

YERMA

About what?

MARIA

About what I should do. I'll ask my mother.

YERMA

Why her? She's old and she's forgotten about all that. Don't walk too much, and when you breathe, breathe as softly as if you had a rose between your teeth.

MARIA

Listen, they say that later he kicks you gently with his little legs.

YERMA

And that makes you love him more, when you can say 'My son!'

MARIA

In the midst of it all I feel embarrassed.

YERMA
What did your husband say?

MARIA
Nothing.

YERMA
He loves you deeply?

MARIA
He doesn't say, but he clasps me and his eyelids quiver like green leaves.

YERMA
Did he know that...?

MARIA
Yes.

YERMA
And how did he know?

MARIA
I don't know. But on our wedding night he kept saying it to me with his mouth pressed against my cheek, so my child seems like a dove of light he set free in my ear.

YERMA
What joy!

MARIA
But you know more about this than I do.

YERMA
What use is it to me?

MARIA
It's true! Why that should be? Of all the brides of your year you are the only one...

YERMA
That's how it is. Of course there's still time. Helena took three years, and others in my mother's day even longer, but five years and twenty days, like me, is too long to wait. I don't think it is right for me to wear away my life here. Many a night I go out in the yard barefoot to walk about, I don't know why. If I go on like this, I'll end badly.

MARIA
See here, you foolish creature! You're talking like an old woman. What are you saying! No one should worry about these things. One of my mother's sisters had one after fourteen years, and you should have seen how beautiful a child it was!

YERMA (*Eagerly*)
What was he like?

MARIA
He bellowed like a little bull, with the energy of a thousand cicadas all buzzing at once, and he peed on us, and tugged our plaits, and when he was four months old he covered our faces with scratches.

YERMA *(Laughing)*
But it doesn't hurt.

MARIA
I tell you...

YERMA
Bah! I've seen my sister feed her child, and her breasts covered with scratches, and it hurt a lot, but it was a new pain, a good one, essential to health.

MARIA
They say you suffer a lot with children.

YERMA
It's a lie. That's what weak, complaining mothers say. Why do they have them? Having a child is no bouquet of roses. We must suffer if they're to grow. I sometimes think we must give half our blood to them. But that's good; healthy, beautiful. Every woman has enough blood for four or five children, and when she doesn't have them it sours her... as it shall me.

MARIA
I don't know what's wrong with me.

YERMA
I've heard the first time always makes you fearful.

MARIA *(Timidly)*
We'll see... How well you sew...

YERMA *(Taking Maria's bundle)*
Give that to me. I'll cut you out two little dresses. And this?

MARIA
For diapers.

YERMA
Good.
(She sits down.)

MARIA
Well then... till later.
(As she comes near Yerma presses her belly lovingly)

YERMA
Don't go running over the cobblestones.

MARIA
Bye. *(She kisses her and exits)*

YERMA

Come again soon.

(Yerma is in the same position as at the start of the scene. She takes her scissors and begins cutting out.

The actors get out of character.)

ACTOR 1

Where shall we take it from here?

ACTOR 8

She tries everything.

ACTOR 1

But it doesn't seem to help.

(The Actors are preparing the next scene as they talk.)

ACTOR 8

Nothing helps.

YERMA

How far will Yerma go in seeking her heart's desire?

MARIA

Yerma decides to join the pagan festivities in a fertility fair.

ACTOR 1

It is in a hermitage in the mountains, a place to which many barren women make a pilgrimage.

ACTOR 8

There are young there, hoping to father a child or to win a woman away from her husband.

ACTOR 1

Drunken young men and women are in revelry, and copulate in fields.

ACTOR 8

Even Juan attends, letting his hair down, drinking with his companions.

ACTOR 1

Yerma does not join in the debauchery.

ACTOR 8

An Old Pagan Woman tries to get her to see things differently.

ACTOR 1

She suggests that the problem might be with Juan, that he is infertile.

ACTOR 8

She offers Yerma her son as an alternative husband with whom to try for a baby.

YERMA

Yerma refuses the Old Woman's offer.

MARIA *(Now to play the Old Woman)*
The Old Woman then turns on Yerma and declares her as barren.

ACTOR 1
Yerma appears resigned to her fate as a childless wife.

ACTOR 8 *(Indicating that the scene is ready)*
Let them take it from there.

EXCERPT: The actors play the scene: Act 3, Scene 2.
Two traditional Masks appear: one male and the other female. The masks they carry are large. The Male carries a bull's horn in his hand. They are not in any way grotesque, but rather beautiful and with a suggestion of earthly purity. The Female shakes a ring of large bells. The stage darkens.
The opening verses of a poem appear on the audio system.

In a stream along the mountain
The sorrowing wife was bathing.
All about her body creeping
Little snails through the water.
The sands all along the shore
And all the breezes of morning
Brought a flame to her laughter
And made her shoulders shiver.
Ay, nakedly she stood there
Lovely lady of the water!

The lights come on to reveal the two masks continuing the prologue to the scene. They are joined by a Chorus and are surrounding Yerma and the Old Woman. The two women can either remain still or have choreographed moves.

FEMALE MASK
When the darkness falls I'll tell you
When the glittering night is falling.
When it gleams above our wandering
I'll rip the seams of my clothing.
Ay, now how white
The sorrowful wife!
Ay, how she sighs in the branches!
You'll be red poppies, carnations,
When the man spreads his mantle.

MALE MASK *(shaking the horn)*
If you come here wandering
Begging for your womb to flower
Don't you wear a mourning veil,

But a fine gown of soft linen.
Walk alone along the walls where
The fig-trees grow thickest,
And support my mortal body
Till the white dawn moans.
Ay, how she shines there!
Ay, how she was shining there!
Ay, how the woman quivers!

FEMALE MASK

Ay let love wreathe her
With coronets and garlands,
Arrows of brightest gold
Through her breasts be darted!

MALE MASK

Seven times she wept there,
Nine times rose again.
Fifteen times they joined
Orange-tree with jasmine.

FEMALE MASK

Come and see the splendour
Of she who is bathing!
Like a reed she bends.
Like a flower she bows.

MALE MASK

Let the dance flare high
And the shining body
Of the spotless wife!
(The Old Woman speaks to Yerma. She is cheerful at the start of the scene.)

OLD WOMAN

Let's see if you'll let us sleep now. But there'll be something else later. *(Seeing Yerma downcast and silent)* Why did you come here? Tell me.

YERMA

I don't know.

OLD WOMAN

You're not convinced? And your husband?
(Yerma shows signs of fatigue, someone whose mind is oppressed.)

YERMA

He's over there.

OLD WOMAN

What's he doing?

YERMA

Drinking. *(Pause. Putting her hands to her forehead.)* Ay!

OLD WOMAN

Ay, ay. Less of that: show more spirit. I couldn't tell you before but now I can.

YERMA

What can you tell me that I don't know already?

OLD WOMAN

What can no longer be silenced. What shouts itself from the rooftops. The fault is your husband's, do you hear? Not you. It is your husband. Let him cut off my hands if it isn't. Neither his father, nor his grandfather conducted themselves like men who breed well. For them to have a child heaven and earth had to be joined. They're just balls of spit. But your family are not. You have brothers and cousins for miles around. See what a curse has fallen on your beauty!

YERMA

A curse. A blight of venom on the crop.

OLD WOMAN

But you have feet on which you can leave his house.

YERMA

Leave?

OLD WOMAN

When I saw you in the procession my heart leapt. Women come here to find new men, and the Saint performs miracles. My son is waiting for me behind the chapel. My house needs a woman. Mate with him and the three of us can live together. My son is strong. Like me. If you enter my household, there'll be the smell of babies again. The ashes of your coverlet will turn to bread and salt for your children. Come. Take no notice of others. And as for your husband, in my house there are strong hearts and weapons to prevent him even crossing the street.

YERMA

Hush, hush! It's not like that! I can't take another. I can't go seeking men out. Do you think I could know another man? Where would my honour be then? Water can't run uphill or the full moon rise at noon. No. I'll keep to the path I'm on. Did you really think I could yield to another man? That I could go and beg for what is mine, like a slave? Understand me, so you never say it to me again. I am not seeking any other.

OLD WOMAN

When one is thirsty, one is grateful for water.

YERMA

I'm like a parched field where a thousand pairs of oxen should drive the plough, and what you offer me is a little glass of water from the well. My grief is one that's already beyond the flesh.

OLD WOMAN *(Firmly)*

Then stay that way. Since you wish to. Like a thistle in a wasteland. Pinched and barren.

YERMA *(Firmly)*

Barren, yes, I know that! Barren! You don't need to hurl it in my face. Don't come and pleasure yourself, as children do, with the sufferings of some small creature. Ever since I married I've been avoiding that word and this is the first time I've heard it said to my face. The first time I recognize that it's true.

OLD WOMAN

You rouse no sympathy in me, none. I'll go look for another wife for my son.

(She exits. A large choir of pilgrims is heard singing in the distance. Yerma starts to leave. Her husband appears from behind her.)

YERMA

Were you there all along?

JUAN

I was there.

YERMA

Spying on me?

JUAN

It may be called that.

YERMA

You heard what I said?

JUAN

Yes.

YERMA

So? Leave me and go and join the singing. *(She sits again)*

JUAN

It's time I spoke too.

YERMA

Speak, then!

JUAN

And time I complained.

YERMA

About what?

JUAN

That I have a bitterness in my throat.

YERMA

And I in my bones.

JUAN

This is your last chance to resist this continual lament for shadowy things, outside existence, for things that are lost in the breeze.

YERMA *(With dramatic astonishment)*

Outside existence you say? Lost in the breeze, you say?

JUAN

Things which haven't happened and neither you nor I can control.

YERMA *(Violently)*

Go on, go on!

JUAN

For things that don't' matter. Do you hear? That have no importance to me. That's what I had to say to you. What matters to me is what I can hold in my hands, what I can see with my eyes.

YERMA *(Rising to her knees, desperately)*

That's it. That's it! That's what I wanted to hear from your mouth. Truth is not felt when it's inside oneself, but how vast it is, how loud it cries, when it emerges, and raises its arms! IT'S DOESN'T MATTER! Now, I've heard you!

JUAN *(Approaching her)*

Think that it had to be so. Listen to me. *(He embraces her to help her rise.)* Many women would be happy to live your life. Life is sweeter without children. I'm happy without them. It's not your fault.

YERMA

What did you seek in me, then?

JUAN

Yourself.

YERMA *(Excitedly)*

That's it! You wanted a home, tranquillity and a woman. But nothing more. Is that true?

JUAN

It's true. As everyone else does.

YERMA

And the rest? Your son?

JUAN *(Firmly)*

Didn't you hear, it doesn't matter! Don't ask me again! Do I have to shout it in your ear so you can understand, and live peacefully for once!

YERMA

And you've never thought about it even when you could see I wanted one?

JUAN

Never. *(They are both on the ground)*

YERMA

And I'm not to hope for one?

JUAN

No.

YERMA

Nor you?

JUAN

Nor I, likewise. Resign yourself!

YERMA

Barren!

JUAN

But living peacefully. Both of us: in gentleness and friendship. Embrace me! *(He embraces her)*

YERMA

What do you want?

JUAN

I want you. In the moonlight you are beautiful.

YERMA

You want me as if you were wanting a pigeon to eat.

JUAN

Kiss me... like this.

YERMA

That, never. Never!

(Yerma gives a cry and grasps her husband by the throat. He falls backward. She chokes him until he is dead. The choir of pilgrims starts up.)

Barren, barren, but I'm certain at last. Now I know for certain. And alone.

(She rises. People begin to gather.)

I'll sleep, without waking with a start to see if my blood announces new blood. With a body barren forever. What do you want? Don't come near me: because I've murdered my child! I've killed my own son.

(The group that remained in the background gathers. We hear the sound of the choir of pilgrims.

The scene ends. The actors get out of character.)

ACTOR 1

It was not an easy play to put across.

ACTOR 7

It was not the best of times to put it across.

(The corner spot comes on, revealing two men. Stanzas of the poem come on over the sound system.

The men step out of the spot and walk up to the group. The scene of a midnight knock is enacted in silence. An actor is dragged aside and taken away.)

ACTOR 1

By the beginning of 1936 the hopes reposed in the Second Spanish Republic were clearly dashed.

ACTOR 2

Franco's military set the Civil War in Motion.

ACTOR 3

Lorca was in Granada.

ACTOR 4 *(Still directing)*

At this point we should tell them about the persecution.

ACTOR 5

The rebels trooped into the city and took control.

ACTOR 6

They had their fascist supporters.

ACTOR 7

They began to clean up the city.

ACTOR 8

Locate, pick up and put away the radicals, the intelligentia.

ACTOR 9

Pick up the troublemakers. Put them away. If necessary, put them to sleep.

ACTOR 10

Lorca's brother-in-law was a staunch Republican.

ACTOR 11

He was also the Mayor of Granada.

ACTOR 10

No go. He was among the first to be shot.

BALLADEER

Lorca was forced to take refuge in the home of a poet friend. Through all of these traumatic events Lorca's spirit remained undaunted.

ACTOR 1

He looked death in the eye.

ACTOR 7

Taunted death.

ACTOR 11

Invited death?

ACTOR 4

Break! OK, enough of the gloom. We must remember Lorca also by the fun he put into our lives.

ACTORS CHORUS

>> Agreed...

>> That's right...

>> Salute...

>> Yeah, his fun plays...

Etc.

BALLADEER

Have you heard of Lorca's puppet plays?

ACTOR 1

He was a puppeteer himself, wasn't he?

ACTOR 7

Puppeteers appear as characters in some of his plays.

ACTOR 1

We saw that in The Shoemaker story.

ACTOR 3

Aren't puppet plays country stuff?

ACTOR 11

What kind of people really relate to them?

ACTOR 8

Low brow anyway.

ACTOR 11

Look who's talking? Who was the lead temptress in the tamasha production last season, may I ask?

ACTOR 8

That was different!

ACTOR 7

It's always different when we do it, right?

ACTOR 1

An age old problem. Lorca knew how to make good drama out of down to earth stuff – country stuff, as you call it.

ACTOR 7

He knew how to take good drama to country folks.

BALLADEER

And vice versa.

ACTOR 1

And still give them an evening of entertainment.

(By now a part of the group has set up the scene for the puppet play. The group picks up Actor 4, carries him to down centre and plants him there.)

ACTOR 4 *(As Director)*

Ladies and Gentlemen ! Presenting...

4. THE PUPPET PLAY OF DON CRISTOBAL

Ladies and Gentlemen:

The poet who has taken and shaped this puppet farce from the lips of the common people has every reason to believe that tonight's sophisticated audience will accept, with understanding and good will, the delightful and rough language of the puppets.

The traditional puppet-show has the rhythm, the magic and , the wonderful freedom that the poet has preserved in the dialogue. The puppet-show is the expression of the people's imagination, the touchstone of its grace and innocence.

Because of this, the poet who knows the audience will respond with sheer joy to words and expressions that come fresh from the earth, that serve as a model of purity at a time when evil and confusion and dark feelings enter our very homes.

(The POET appears.)

POET

Men and women, listen. Child, shut up, will you! I want there to be perfect silence... so perfect we can hear the glug-glug-glug of running water; or the sound of a bird as it opens its wing; or an ant as it moves its tiny feet; or even a sudden heart-beat that sounds like a hand as it parts the rushes on the river bank. The older girls will need to close their fans... the younger ones will need their little handkerchiefs of lace to listen to and observe the affairs of Dona Rosita, married to Don Cristobal, not to mention affairs of Don Cristobal, married to Dona Rosita. Listen. The sound of the drum. Laugh cry, do as you like. I'm off to get myself a piece of bread, the tiniest bit of bread the birds have left for me, and then to iron the company's costumes. *(He looks to see if anyone is watching)* I want to tell you I know how roses are born, and how the starfish develops and grows...

DIRECTOR

Do put a sock in it! The prologue ends where it says: 'I'm going to iron the company's costumes.

POET

Of course, sir.

DIRECTOR

A writer must remain a writer. You have no right to reveal our secrets.

POET

No, sir.

DIRECTOR

Don't I pay you?

POET

Yes, Yes, sir. It's just that deep down I feel that Don Cristobal is good.

DIRECTOR

Fool! You won't shut up. I'll come over and smash that lily-white milk-sop face of yours. Who are you to put an end to his trade-mark?

POET

I've said my piece. I'll say no more.

DIRECTOR

No, sir. You'll say what's required, and what the audience knows to be true.

POET

Distinguished audience. As the writer, it's my duty to tell you that Don Cristobal is bad.

DIRECTOR

And can't be good.

POET

And can't be good.

DIRECTOR

Carry on.

POET

All right, Mr. Director. And can never ever be good.

DIRECTOR

Fine. How much do I owe you?

POET

Five guineas.

DIRECTOR

There we are.

POET

I'd rather it wasn't in gold. Gold reminds me of fire, which doesn't suit a poet of the night like me. I'd much prefer silver. I always fancy a silver coin's been lit by the moon.

DIRECTOR

Ha ha ha. No wonder I make a profit. Let's make a start.

POET

Open your window, Rosita.
The play's about to begin.
A little death's in store for you,
And a husband who's always snoring.
(*Music.*)

DIRECTOR

Cristobal.

CRISTOBAL
What?

DIRECTOR
Get on stage. The people are waiting.

CRISTOBAL
I'm coming.

DIRECTOR
Dona Rosita.

ROSITA
I'm putting my shoes on.
(Sound of snoring.)

DIRECTOR
Is that Cristobal snoring?

CRISTOBAL
I'm coming, Mr. Director, when I've finished peeing.

DIRECTOR
Shut up. And don't be crude.
(CRISTOBAL enters.)

CRISTOBAL
Good evening, gentlemen.

DIRECTOR
Get on with it, Don Cristobal. We have to get the play started. You're a doctor.

CRISTOBAL
Me a doctor? I'm going to the bullfight.

DIRECTOR
Remember, Don Cristobal. You need money to get married.

CRISTOBAL
I know I do.

DIRECTOR
Then get it quick.

CRISTOBAL
I'll get my club.

DIRECTOR
Excellent. I can see you understand me.
(The PATIENT enters.)

PATIENT
Good, day to you.

CRISTOBAL
I fancy you mean good night.

PATIENT
In that case I'll say good evening.

CRISTOBAL
Good night! Good night!

PATIENT *(timidly)*
I think I might manage good right.

CRISTOBAL
You'd better manage good night.

PATIENT
I can see from all you say you're a very fine doctor.
I'm sure you'll cure me. *(Loudly)* Good day to you.

CRISTOBAL *(loudly)*
I've told you once. Good night. Good night.

PATIENT
All right. I'm ready when you are.

CRISTOBAL
What's the trouble with you?

PATIENT
A sharp pain here,
Where my head comes out of my collar.
I hadn't really considered it
Till cousin John suggested it.

CRISTOBAL
The sure cure for that's to pull your head off. *(He seizes him)*

PATIENT
Ouch! Ouch! Ouch! Don Cristobal!

CRISTOBAL
Be so good as to stick your neck out. I want to examine your jugular.

PATIENT
I can't move it. I can't.

CRISTOBAL
I'm telling you. Stretch your neck.

PATIENT
Ouch, ouch! I can't.

CRISTOBAL
Use your fingers. Ease your neck out.

PATIENT
If I could, I would. But I can't. *(Aggressively)* I bid you good day, good day, good day, good day.

CRISTOBAL
I'll be back in a minute. Don't go away.
(CRISTOBAL leaves. The PATIENT complains.)

PATIENT
Oh, ah, oh, ah! My neck hurts. Perhaps I've got jugularitis!

CRISTOBAL *(entering with a stick)*
Now then.

PATIENT
What's that, Don Cristobal?

CRISTOBAL
Just my brandy flask.

PATIENT
But what's it for?

CRISTOBAL
To warm your neck up.

PATIENT
Try not to hurt me.

CRISTOBAL
Since when did force hurt anybody? I hope you've brought some money for me.

PATIENT
Of course, of course. There's twenty here
And twenty there...so that makes forty.
Inside my coat another nine...
Makes almost fifty. And for emergency
Another twenty; I keep it up
My arse for safety.

CRISTOBAL
Believe me, I know how to cure you,
But don't tell anybody.

PATIENT *(aggressively)*
I bid you good day, good day, good day, good day, good day.

CRISTOBAL *(hitting him with the stick)*
Good night.
Now stick your neck out.

PATIENT
I can't, Don Cristobal.

CRISTOBAL *(hitting him with stick)*
Good night.
Now stick your neck out.

PATIENT
I can't, Don Cristobal.

CRISTOBAL *(hitting him)*
Stick your neck out.

PATIENT
Oh, my poor neck!

CRISTOBAL
Stick it out further.

PATIENT
Oh, my neck!

CRISTOBAL
Further. *(Hitting him.)* Further, further, further.
(The PATIENT sticks out his neck.)

PATIENT
Oooooooohhhh!
(He sticks out his neck all the way.
He gets up, but DON CRISTOBAL knocks him down again.)

CRISTOBAL
Take that, take that, you little swine.
Didn't I promise you'd soon feel fine?
He's dead. Best get the corpse away.
A thud is heard.
Ole, ole, ole, ole.

DIRECTOR
Did he have any money?

CRISTOBAL
Yes.

DIRECTOR
You can get married now.

CRISTOBAL
I shall get married.

DIRECTOR
Here comes Dona Rosita's mother. You have to speak to her.

MOTHER.
I'm Dona Rosita's mother.
I want to recommend her
To anyone who'll have her.

Her two little titties are ever so pretty,
Her little bottom sits on her neatly,
And a bird in a cage sings to her sweetly.
But what she needs most is a man to marry.
I'll find her two if I possibly can.

CRISTOBAL
Good lady.

MOTHER
Ah, good gentleman.
A man of pen and ink, I think.

CRISTOBAL
I'd take my hat off if I had
One on, good lady. You probably know
I intend to marry.

MOTHER
I do have a daughter.
Depends how much you'll give me for her.

CRISTOBAL
Well, what about an ounce of gold,
The kind the Moor, it's said,
Once shat in times of old?
An ounce of silver too, perhaps,
The kind, it's said, the cat
In times of old once crapped?
And these small grubby coins,
The kind your mother spent
Some centuries ago,
To have some fun, when she was young.

MOTHER
If I could have a mule, good sir,
You'd see how grateful I could be
To you. I'd like to ride to Lisbon
Soon, you see. By moonlight hopefully.

CRISTOBAL
A mule's too much for me, madam.

MOTHER
Oh, do come on, good Don Cristobal.
You've plenty of money. And my
Rosita — you know how lovely she is,
And you so old, and with a belly
Flabby as a wineskin.

CRISTOBAL
You, good lady, are a hag.
Sorry. I meant to say an old bag.
I expect you wipe your backside with an old rag.

MOTHER
How dare you, you filthy drunken sot.

CRISTOBAL
All right. I'll give you what I've got.
The mule is yours. Now where's Rosita?

MOTHER
You'll find her in her bedroom.
She's only got a petticoat on,
And she's quite alone.

CRISTOBAL
My excitement is mounting.

MOTHER
I expect it is. It's not surprising.

CRISTOBAL
Show me her picture.

MOTHER
After you've signed this contract...here.

CRISTOBAL
To see the tips of your toes,
Rosita, I promise I'll do
Whatever I'm required to.

MOTHER
Just give her a kick if she disobeys.
Pay me enough and she'll do what I say.
(Music, singing off.)

ROSITA *(off)*
Longing, longing, longing,
Longing and desire.
More and more, my darling,
I can feel love's fire.
(Enter ROSITA.)
On such a night the stars shine bright
Up there above the houses.
On such a night the kids count stars
While old men sleep on horses.
But, as for me, I'd like to be:
On the divan with Juan,

On the settee with Pepe,
On the sofa with Saldivar,
Across a chair with fair Enrique,
Upon the floor with Antonito
Against the wall with strong Pascual,
On the chaise longue with Juan, Ramon,
Arturo, Pepe, Antonito.
Oh yes, oh yes, I want to marry.
Do you hear me? Marry.
A sweet young boy,
A good-looking soldier,
A man of the church,
A lover bold as brass and tall.
Or twenty lads from Portugal.

CRISTOBAL

Are we agreed?

MOTHER

Agreed.

CRISTOBAL

If we aren't, I've got my stick. You know what it's for.

MOTHER

Oh! What have I done?

CRISTOBAL

Are you afraid?

MOTHER *(trembling)*

Oh!

CRISTOBAL

Say: 'I'm afraid'.

MOTHER

I'm afraid.

CRISTOBAL

Say: 'Don Cristobal has tamed me'.

MOTHER

Don Cristobal has tamed me.

CRISTOBAL

As I shall tame your daughter.

MOTHER

In that case...

CRISTOBAL

I'll give you the ounce of gold shat by the Moor in times of old, and you'll give me your daughter Rosita. You should be grateful to me for not being over fussy about her age.

MOTHER

She's only twenty.

CRISTOBAL

I said I'm not too fussy about her age.
Though I do admit she is quite pretty...

MOTHER

Her two little titties are ever so pretty.
Her little bottom sits on her neatly.
And a bird...

CRISTOBAL

Oooooeeeeeeee!

MOTHER

...in a cage sings to her sweetly.

CRISTOBAL

And I shall marry because Rosita's a true `boccato di cardinali'.

MOTHER

Does your excellency speak Italian?

CRISTOBAL

No. But when I was young I spent some time in France and Italy, in the service of a certain Mr Pantaloon. But my life is none of your business. You should be trembling. Everyone who meets me has to tremble... do you understand? Has to tremble.

MOTHER

I'm all of a tremble.

CRISTOBAL

Summon Rosita.

MOTHER

Rositaaaaa.

ROSITA

What is it, mother?
I want to marry
An unborn calf, a crocodile,
A general, a little donkey,
I don't care what, I'm not really fussy,
It's all the same, whatever I marry.

CRISTOBAL

What juicy ham to the front and back of her!

MOTHER

Do you want to get married?

ROSITA

I want to get married.

MOTHER

Do you want to get married?

CRISTOBAL

I want to get married.

MOTHER *(weeping)*

Oh, please don't treat her badly! My poor little daughter!

CRISTOBAL

Inform the priest.

(The MOTHER leaves, wailing. CRISTOBAL draws near and they leave for the church. The bells ring out.)

POET

Do you see? We are expected to laugh. The moon can be a hen that lays its eggs. The moon can be a piece of bread to a poor man and a stool of pure linen to the man who's rich. But... the owner of the theatre is something Don Cristobal and Miss Rosita never see. But the owner has the characters kept in an iron box and only lets them be seen by ladies with silk bosoms and stupid noses and gentlemen with beards who belong to a club and are always saying 'Jolly good'! But Don Cristobal and Miss Rosita are not like that.

DIRECTOR

Who is it saying such things?

POET

I was saying they're about to get married.

DIRECTOR

Stop poking you nose in. If I had any sense, I'd boot you into the street.

CRISTOBAL

Oh, Rosita!

ROSITA

Have you had too much to drink?

CRISTOBAL

I'd like to be made of wine so I could drink myself and my belly a great pie, an enormous pie with plums and sweet potato. Rosita, sing me something.

ROSITA

What shall I sing? Goicoechea's `Can-can' or Gil Robles's `Marseillaise'?
Oh, Cristobal, I'm frightened! What are you going to do to me?

CRISTOBAL

I'm going to mmmmmmmmmm...

ROSITA

Oh no, don't frighten me.
At twelve o'clock tonight, what are you going to do to me?

CRISTOBAL

I'm going to aaaaaaaa....

ROSITA

Oh, don't frighten me.
At three in the morning, what are you going to do to me?

CRISTOBAL

I'm going to piiiiiiii...

ROSITA

And then you'll see how my little bird will fly!
(They embrace.)

CRISTOBAL

Oh, Rosita!

ROSITA

Are you really a very heavy drinker?
I think you need a short siesta.

CRISTOBAL

Wake me up a little later.
See if my canary's perkier.

ROSITA

Oh, yes, yes, yes.
(CRISTOBAL snores.
CURRITO enters and embraces ROSITA.
Sound of great big kisses. CRISTOBAL wakes up.)

CRISTOBAL

Rosita, what was that?

ROSITA

Oh, dear, oh, dear. Can't you see how big the moon is? How bright it
is? It was just my shadow. Shadow! Away with you!

CRISTOBAL

Shadow! Shoo!

ROSITA

What a great big nuisance the moon is, Cristobal! Why don't you have another short siesta?

CRISTOBAL

Wake me up a little later.
See if my pecker's any livelier.

ROSITA

Oh, yes, yes, yes.
(The POET enters and begins to kiss ROSITA.)

CRISTOBAL

Rosita, what was that?

ROSITA

There's not much light. You can't see properly. It's only the sewing machine. Listen.
(Sound of kisses.)

CRISTOBAL

It's very loud.

ROSITA

I'll have it moved, sweet Cristobita.
Why not take another siesta?

CRISTOBAL

I shall. A wife's advice is always best.
My poor pecker needs a rest.
(The PATIENT appears and ROSITA kisses him.)

CRISTOBAL

I heard another noise.

ROSITA

The sound of the sun beginning to set.

CRISTOBAL

A kind of brrr. I thought it was you.

ROSITA

Don't be like that. The frogs perhaps, croaking in the pond.

CRISTOBAL

Ah, yes. Quite probably. It does sound likely. Brrr...

ROSITA

Not so loudly. It could be the lions in the circus, or cuckolded husbands in the street.

MOTHER

Rositaaaaa! The doctor's here.

ROSITA

Oh dear. The doctor. Oh, oh, oh! My poor little belly's hurting me!

MOTHER

You wicked man. It's all your fault. Now you'll have to give us all your money.

ROSITA

All your money. Oh! Oh! Oh! *(They leave.)*

DIRECTOR

Cristobal.

CRISTOBAL

What is it?

DIRECTOR

Come at once, Dona Rosita's ill.

CRISTOBAL

What's wrong with her?

DIRECTOR

She's giving birth.

CRISTOBAL

Giving birth?

DIRECTOR

She's already had four.

CRISTOBAL

Oh, Rosita! You'll answer for this. You bad, bad woman! You've cost me a fortune already. Pim! Pam! Brrrr.

(ROSITA's cries off.)

CRISTOBAL

Who's the father?

MOTHER

You are, you are.

CRISTOBAL *(striking her)*

Who's the father?

MOTHER

You are, you are. *(CRISTOBAL strikes her again. ROSITA cries off.)*

DIRECTOR

She's having the fifth.

CRISTOBAL

Whose is the fifth?

MOTHER

Yours. *(He strikes her)*

CRISTOBAL

Whose?

MOTHER

Yours. No one else's. (He strikes her) Yours, yours, yours.
(She dies and slumps across the rail.)

CRISTOBAL

I've killed you! I've killed you! Damn! I'll find out who the father is.
(He begins to go out.)

MOTHER *(rising)*

Yours, yours, yours.
(CRISTOBAL strikes her, goes off, comes back with DONA ROSITA.)

CRISTOBAL

Take that, take that... for... for...
(The DIRECTOR's great head appears on the stage.)

DIRECTOR

Enough! *(He picks up the puppets and shows them to the audience)*
Ladies and gentlemen: The peasants of Andalusia often watch this kind
of play beneath the grey branches of the olive trees, or in the darkness of
abandoned stables. Amongst the eyes of mules, as hard as fists, embroidered
leather harnesses from Cordoba and heaps of damp and tender ears of corn,
the words we wouldn't tolerate in cities where the air is thick with alcohol
and games of cards explode, with joy and charming innocence. Those bad
and vulgar words take on a fresh simplicity when spoken by the puppets
as they recreate the magic of this ancient rural farce. So let us fill the
theatre with fresh and pure wheat and hear upon the stage vulgarities that
overwhelm the tedious triviality to which it is condemned. Let us honour
today in the puppet show the Andalusian Don Cristobal, cousin to the
Galician Buluhl and brother-in-law to Aunt Norica from Cadiz; brother of
Monsieur Guinol from Paris, and uncle to Don Arlechino from Bergamo.
He is a character in whom the pure ancient spirit of the theatre still survives.

(The actors get out of character.

*The actors indulge in a bit of post-performance horse-play, packing up. The
lights dim as the group troops out. A smaller group joins the balladeer. They
speak to the audience.)*

VOICE 1

It was the afternoon of August 16, nineteen hundred and thirty six.

VOICE 2

Lorca was arrested and taken away to the government's headquarters.

VOICE 3

He was held there for two days. That's what they said. Supposedly two days.

VOICE 4

From there he was driven away to an unnamed destination, probably in the early hours of August 19.

VOICE 5

It is not clearly established where he was taken.

BALLADEER

Most likely it was the countryside outside a village.

(Rapid fade out. A shot is heard, followed by two others. The smaller group of actors leaves.

The corner spot comes on again. There is nobody in it. The last two stanzas of the poem are heard over the sound system.)

Every afternoon in Granada,
Every afternoon, a boy dies.
Every afternoon, the water sits down
To speak with his friends.
The dead wear moss wings.
The clouded wind and the cleaned wind
Are two pheasants that fly through towers
And the day is a wounded little boy.
Left in the air not a lark wisp
When I found you by the wine caves.
Not left anywhere on the earth a cloud crumb
When you choked yourself with the river.
A water colossus fell over the mountains
And the valley went turning with stray dogs and lilies.
Your body, in the violet shadow of my hands,
Was, cold on the bank, an indifferent archangel.

(The lights come on. The balladeer strums his guitar and sings the last stanza of the opening poem. There is a slow fade out.)

Close of play

Wormwood

by Amlin Gray

*Suggested by material from **August Strindberg's** memoir-novels collectively titled **The Son of a Servant***

*From: **ZONES OF THE SPIRIT,** Two Short Plays*

The play published in this volume includes a curtain raiser on August Strindberg developed at Bangalore Little Theatre as part of the workshop production.

FOR
KUMUDA RAO

CHARACTERS IN THE PLAY

MARIKA BORG .... *25. Blond and fair skinned, with incongruously dark eyes. A reformed painter in danger of recidivism.*

JOHAN EKDAHL .... *25. A somewhat feckless young former fellow student of Marika, now a waiter at The Snout.*

MALACHI .... *A malicious old man in his seventies, proprietor of The Snout. Muse and evil angel of Ossian.*

OSSIAN BORG .... *29, but looking older. Marika's husband. A broad high forehead and a great mane of hair he can never quite tame. Himself a former artist, not a painter but a writer, and also insecurely reformed.*

Excerpts from the Prefatory Notes to Zones of the Spirit

During a time when he was much influenced by Nietzsche, August Strindberg wrote that the philosopher's seed had fallen into his brain pan. To adopt Strindberg's characteristically discomforting metaphor: Strindberg's seed has fallen into my brain pan. These plays are the result.

. . . .

The second of the pair of plays, which plays in about seventy minutes, is *Wormwood*. Its characters and story... were suggested by ideas I have about Strindberg's addiction to writing, which he often felt degraded and disgraced him. Several passages incorporate images from Strindberg's memoir-novels called collectively *The Son of a Servant*. For the rest, Ossian Borg is not August Strindberg... (although) the latter did, for example, frequent a Berlin tavern called "At the Black Pig" and, at a later period, wrote with a feather from the hat of his (third) wife, Harriet Bosse.

. . . .

Strindberg wrote the First Part of *The Dance of Death*, one of his harshest and most despairing visions, during the same three-week period as *Easter*, perhaps his most confident testament to the possibility of redemption. One man may be many men. No two imaginary worlds, incompatible though they may be, invalidate each other.

Amlin Gray

NOTES

The play Wormwood should need no further introduction after the prefatory notes provided by the author, Amlin Gray. The curtain raiser would benefit from an explanation.

The curtain raiser was developed as part of the workshop process, bringing together the research by the team and their understanding of the literature scanned. It became evident early that the real value of the curtain raiser might be in sharing an important insight gained. It conforms and contributes to the core concept in the design of *Wormwood* in the production by Bangalore Little Theatre: *transformation*. The play depicts transformations in individual personalities, relationships and equations.

The curtain raiser aims at establishing other transformations:
* a performance space into a scene
* an Indian time-space ambience into a European one
* a group of artists into characters.

There was one principal objective for the curtain raiser. It had to provide just that much information about Strindberg – his life, work and times – to help appreciate *Wormwood*. This may not be necessary for Western audiences who will have, perhaps, a greater familiarity with Strindberg. It should help in an Indian performance, especially in a less evolved public appreciation of the theatre arts.

It appeared important to strike the right balance among the main elements in the curtain raiser: biography, personality, drama. This balance had to be struck in both the written content and in the delivery. Most important, although it is "performed" on stage, the curtain raiser should be viewed as a facilitator to *Wormwood*, rather than as a play in itself.

Following from the above, the construction in the curtain raiser is deliberately non-conversational. This must make some demands on the actors playing it. It might not help to deliver the lines either as a poetry reading or as a string of declamations. Since the actors are actually working on stage, setting it up, helping each other, it might be useful to experiment with a mix which has body states that are conversational, here-and-now, and a speech that is semi-stylized, sounding academically elegant. The sub-text for the actors might be an aspiration to look and sound good as actors, having done their own research on Strindberg! The actors from the main play, in contrast, are more relaxed and genuinely conversational, providing the supplementary remarks on Strindberg from their own research.

Most of the stage area is bare. All the hard props for *Wormwood* – a long table, chairs, stools, chest, etc. – are stacked on one side. Through the curtain raiser the actors set up the stage for the main play.

The actors in the curtain raiser are four stage hands. They are named One, Two, Three and Four here. They enter at different times, going about their business, but also helping each other out. Their specific moves and businesses are not all indicated in the script. They talk to one another and to the audience as they work.

The actors from the main play enter and become part of the curtain raiser, but are not too deeply involved. They are putting finishing touches to their costumes and make-up. Ossian Borg sits with his back to the audience throughout, and speaks only one line, just before his exit. We see Malachi's character make-up being done through the curtain raiser.

- Vijay Padaki

FIRST PERFORMED

First performed in Bangalore as a workshop production by
Bangalore Little Theatre in January 1993

Part 1: The Curtain Raiser
The production crew working on the play:
One (Lights) .... DEEPAK PADAKI
Two (Make up) .... MALLIKA PRASAD
Three (Costumes) .... KUMUDA RAO
Four (Props) .... D. VENKATESH

Part 2: The Play
Marika Borg .... VANI KRISHNASWAMY
Johan Ekdahl .... VIKRAMJIT RAM
Malachi .... M BHASKAR
Ossian Borg .... VIVEK SHAH

Technical resource .... SANJEEV JAIN, PRAKASH BELAWADI,
                                                          SUJATHA BELAWADI
Asst. Director .... ABHAY TOSHNIWAL
Front of House .... CHANDRA MOULI,
                                                  SHIVAKUMAR BELAWADI

Play designed and directed by .... VIJAY PADAKI

PART I: A STRINDBERG CURTAIN RAISER

by Vijay Padaki

The stage is almost dark. A single tight spot, held very low, reveals One (Lights) entering, going up to the chest, opening the lock, taking out a clipboard with a checklist on it. He flashes a torch light over the audience to the lights cabin.

ONE
Workers, please.
(The stage has work lights. One sets up a prop or two, decides to wait for others. He takes out a leather bound book from the chest, sits, and starts to read.)
ONE
The Son of a Servant
(Two enters. Make up)
TWO *(Entering and setting up a make up kit)*
The fourth of twelve children. The mother a servant and, after her death, when he was thirteen, a stepmother who was a housekeeper in the same family.
ONE
A collection of novels and stories. A collection of acute observations – escaping the eye of artists and writers crowded around him.
TWO
Escaping their pens even if passed by the eye. *(A pause)*

....

ONE
Autobiographical. Writers great and small have started down the road with autobiographical displays.
TWO
Retreated there in predictable cycles of pilgrimage.
ONE
How easily is the substance of life experiences rejected as unsatisfactory.
TWO
Unsafe.
ONE
Unsuitable for literature.
TWO
Not for the son of a servant. For him, observation of the self transformed to a proud literary craft. He gave it legitimacy. He expanded its territory at a pace so terrifying it frightened the writer himself at times.

ONE *(At the book again. Reading.)*
"However life shaped itself, I always became aware of connections and repetitions. I saw in one situation the result of another earlier one. Or meeting this person I was reminded of that one whom I had met in the past." *(Closes the book)* The Stranger, in the play After the Fire.

(One starts on other chores. Malachi enters, sits at stool at one end of the table set by now. Two starts on his make-up.)

....

TWO
Connections. Not tripped and trapped under layers of subconscious carpeting, but allowed free run of the land – in all directions, all formations.

ONE
And through it all, the same acute observation. The mental vivisection of the self.

TWO
The same methodical thoroughness of a scientist in a laboratory, nursing an experiment through to its beatific conclusion.

ONE
And what a terrible price to be paid for the gift of keenness in observation.

TWO
The ominous signs in galloping thought trains. The line crossed from literary self flagellation to persecutory visions. The crowding of the brain could not continue forever. *(A pause)*

ONE
The first breakdown came in 1891. The first marriage, too, had soured.

TWO
There would be two more breakdowns later in life. And two more marriages – also breaking up. As if to help the cause of medical science and art history.

ONE
The image of the dead mother who recognized his precocious intelligence, but never gave the love he longed for was like a Madonna that beckoned with a clawed hand.
They call it the double bind.

TWO
Of each tragic marriage he was to say in the end that it had stayed physical, while his search remained spiritual.

ONE
Each an artist. Actress, writer, painter. None extraordinary in talent, not a candle to his towering brilliance, but an artist nevertheless, with individual sensitivity. Any recognition of that in the marketplace was like a rejection of oneself.

TWO
Opening phantom wounds, breeding fears upon suspicions.
ONE
And through it all, the same acute observation, the same ruthless dissemination.
TWO
Dementia Praecox they called it in his time. A paranoid schizophrenia.
ONE
Popularly but incorrectly called persecution mania. Hallucinations following intense bouts of delusion are not uncommon in the state.
TWO
He turned to science, spending long hours in his own laboratory, experimenting with innumerable combinatorial reactions, seeking proof for the hypothesis that Sulphur was a compound that could be split further.
ONE
Retreating to England after his first marriage had run aground, he feared all the beggars in London had conspired a plot against him, and then saw them all in a horde, grown to monstrous sizes and chasing him down the street.
TWO
His own fear of his condition made him want more, much more, from a wife. He needed an intensity of attachment that was beyond definition, beyond reach. And when it was not forthcoming, the wife, too, was sucked into the vortex of delusory detail.
ONE
He suspected her friends, men and women.
TWO
He suspected her dog.
ONE
He was driven to a morbid fear of losing out artistically. The beckoning Madonna was declared the sex enemy.
TWO
He drove his wife to the comforting arms of friends. The sex war continued through life. *(A pause)*

....

Three enters (Costumes), followed by the three other actors. They are partially costumed, the base make-up on. They speak very little in the following passage, busying themselves with the final details of readying and getting into character. Ossian Borg has his back to the audience throughout.
THREE
What makes the raincloud that makes the lakes?

ONE
Circumstances. A sickness precipitated by a peculiar, most unfortunate and tragic configuration of life experiences.

TWO
Constitution. The sickness precipitating tragic life experiences.

THREE
Nowhere was the dialectic manifest more convincingly than on the stage. It opened up a new dramatic form, a new realism.

ONE
A tortured, violent, realism.

THREE
His best known play, The Father, is often interpreted as the vehicle for his obsession with the question of birth legitimacy – his own and his children's. Put alongside the next play, Comrades, a larger thesis emerges on the nature of woman.

TWO
Carried further in Miss Julie and with even more devastating effect in Creditors.

THREE
The atmosphere of feminine power. The character on stage representing a monstrous regiment of women.

ONE
The inevitability of an abject humiliation of men, their inherent strength and reason sapped, their esteem debased.

THREE
Woman as predator. *(A pause)*

....

Four enters. (Props)

FOUR
Not all his writing came out of a punishing introspection. Following every menacing tide of dark pessimism there stood revealed another view of the world, another understanding.

THREE
There were historical plays.

JOHAN
The chamber plays for a specially created intimate theatre.

TWO
The mystical plays, the dream plays.

FOUR
Giving each return to realism a bolder abstraction, a daring texture.

ONE
The Dream Play. Generations ahead of its time. The first theatre of surrealism.

MALACHI
To be rediscovered and reinvented several times over.

TWO
The course clearly set by the turn of the century in the first dream play.

MARIKA
When realism is spent, is it the end of reality?

JOHAN
Or are the eyes then opened to new realities?

ONE *(Reading)*
"... to imitate the disconnected but seemingly logical form of the dream... a medley of memories, experiences, free fancies, absurdities and improvisations... no judgement, no exoneration, merely narration... one consciousness reigns above them all – that of the dreamer".

FOUR *(Taking the book from One and continuing.)*
"... not characters who sit asking foolish questions in order to elicit smart replies... let people's brains work irregularly – as they do in actual life..."

JOHAN *(Continuing, but without the book.)*
"... where no topic is drained to the dregs, but one brain receives haphazard from the other a cog to engage with..." *(A pause)*

....

FOUR
His capacity for tenderness.

MARIKA
A quality even artists close to him could not quite fathom.

FOUR
It was no secret that the characters in his writing were direct transcripts of real people around him.

TWO
The character of Eleanora in Easter, his most tender play, was written for his third wife.

THREE
There was no trace of the sex enemy in Eleanora, the play itself celebrating expiation and forgiveness.

ONE
The shepherds' hymn of thanksgiving after the storm. He was moving, at last, from a long held gloom into a warm sunlight.

JOHAN
But the very next play was Dance of Death, a tale set in an isolated fort, where a man and his wife have lived, for twenty five years, hating each other with a deadly venom.

MALACHI
Each wishing the other's death.

THREE
Many regard the play his greatest work.

MARIKA
Understandably.

FOUR
Fitting the dominant image of the man.

MARIKA
The image upheld.

ONE
He, himself, was convinced that A Dream Play was his best.

JOHAN
Indra's daughter, coming down to earth to look into men's complaints.

MARIKA
Happiness at the surface.

MALACHI
Misery and suffering at the heart of things.

ONE
Always. *(A pause)*

TWO
Opinions, analysis, hypotheses....

JOHAN
Theories.

TWO
The writing defying all conjectures.

FOUR
Save one.

THREE
He wrote, therefore he was.

ONE
To compare and contrast.

TWO
A natural literary pastime.

FOUR
Above them all, a power unmatched in nineteenth century drama.

ONE
Henrik Ibsen... *(Pause. Awkward moment for all.)*

MARIKA
Quote.

JOHAN
Not a trifle dull and dowdy. Adolescent, facile.

MALACHI
Lacking in deep passion.

MARIKA
Unquote.

ONE
The one comparison he detested was with Ibsen.

OSSIAN *(Rises)*
"That famous Norwegian blue-stocking" *(Exits)*

TWO
Who, on the other hand, admired him openly.

JOHAN
Predicting that he would become the greater writer of the two. *(Exits)*

....

THREE *(Final touches on Marika)*
Children.

FOUR
A devotion that never flagged.

MARIKA
The child in him.

ONE
His first daughter from his first wife.

FOUR
And his last daughter.

TWO
The closest companions in the evening of his life.

THREE
His first wife... *(Pause)*

TWO
The news of her death, four weeks before his own.

FOUR
In his grief, the admission...at last.

ONE
She was the woman he had loved most of all.

MALACHI *(Takes a feather, fixes it on Marika's hat, gives it to her.)*
Quote. Unbroken by scene divisions.

MARIKA
One unified action from start to finish with all stress upon the passions.
(Exits with Malachi.)

THREE
The world of spirit.

TWO
Action of the soul, not the body.

FOUR
All stress upon the passions. Unquote.

ONE
Test run, please!
(The lights come on and go off in each of the acting areas on stage, while One finishes the last touch up chores on stage. He moves down at the end.)

ONE
In his later years he sometimes wrote with a feather from his wife's hat.
(He exits on a fade out. A beat.
The play Wormwood begins. The first lines of the play are heard in the dark.)

PART 2
WORMWOOD

The setting, very dimly visible at first, is a windowless storeroom off the main room of a low tavern in Stockholm. The tavern might be imagined as a cut or two below the one depicted in Munch's "Christiania Bohemians" etchings. Much of the room is occupied by a long table littered with crates, broken furniture and assorted junk. A good deal of the floor is similarly taken up. Over all lies a thick layer of dust. On the walls, somewhat incongruously, hang a couple of undistinguished expressionistic paintings — dim, muddy landscapes and one murky study of the room itself. A door to Stage Right is the room's only exit and entrance.

A key is heard in the lock. The door is opened. Marika Borg steps into the doorway. We can hardly see her yet, but her voice is full and musical.

MARIKA

This is it?

JOHAN *(Behind her, not yet visible at all; a fresh, direct voice)*

That's it.

MARIKA

I can't see a thing.

JOHAN

Go on in.

MARIKA

Can't you go in first and light a lamp?

JOHAN *(Squeezing past her)*

I'll go ahead of you, but we'll have to shut the door before we can have any light. The old spider's still in his quarters upstairs, but there'll be customers for supper soon. It's as good as my job if he catches us.

(He shuts the door behind them. The room is again in almost total darkness.)

MARIKA

This room smells like the inside of an old shoe.

JOHAN

I'm not allowed in here myself unless he sends me to fetch liquor for behind the bar. Excuse me once more, the gas lamp is there, where you're standing.

(He strikes a match on the wall and lights a lamp to the U side of the door. We see now that he is a pleasant-looking man of 25. His threadbare suit would just pass muster, given a few points for effort, at a fairly formal afternoon occasion. Marika, the same age, is a fair-haired woman of fine bearing. Of her superbly clear features, the most notable are her incongruously dark eyes, set deep in her face. Her clothes are as formal as Johan's but less worn and more imaginative. She surveys the room with great interest.)

MARIKA

So this is the famous Back Room.

JOHAN

It's just a storeroom now.

MARIKA

When Ossian was living here, it can't have been this dark. Ah, there's another lamp. Let's light that one too.

JOHAN

We don't want too much light in case it shows under the door. You don't know Malachi. He's got the eyes of a snake.

MARIKA

I thought he was a spider.

JOHAN

He's the worst of both combined.

MARIKA

If he does come in, then, I'll want to be able to see him. May I have the matches, Johan? *(Reluctantly, he allows her to take them.)* Thank you. *(Moving to the lamp on the center of the back wall and lighting it.)* The odor is less overwhelming with light in the room. Still it's enough to turn your lungs to mummy.

JOHAN

No one's lived here since your husband left, and that's almost four years ago.

MARIKA

Where did Ossian sleep?

JOHAN *(Pointing to a pile of boxes, rungless chairs, etc., to L)*

There's a roll of blankets there under the cobwebs. They say he laid those on the table for a mattress.

MARIKA *(Trying to picture it)*

And he slept here every night, a whole year?

JOHAN

Not at night. He just slept in the daytime. He loved the night.

MARIKA

My husband hates the night.

JOHAN

He didn't always.

MARIKA

Is that something else that "they" say?

JOHAN

He said that. *(Quoting)* "The nighttime, even in a closed room like the prison where I die away my life, is as fertile as the mucky soil where worms nest. The day is as barren as glass."

MARIKA

Do you know his books by heart?

JOHAN

Just sections.

MARIKA

Which book is that from?

JOHAN

The Snout.

MARIKA

I've read The Snout. I've never read the other book.

JOHAN

You've never read The Orphan?

MARIKA

Ossian asked me not to. I'd read The Snout already, back when you and I were students at the Institute. All the budding artists had to read about the scandalous writer's Bohemian life.

JOHAN

They're both extraordinary books. They're not like anything else ever written.

MARIKA

And a good thing – that's what Ossian would say.

JOHAN

I read them all the time. It's like nibbling on food that's so rich you can hardly keep it down. I sometimes come in here to read The Snout. Your husband wrote it at this table. This is where he sat. These blue stains might be spills from his pen. In the preface to The Snout, he says he wrote the book in ink instead of blood because he really should have written it in – *(quickly editing)* – in matter.

MARIKA

"Matter"?

JOHAN

Well, the word he used was "pus."

MARIKA

That sounds like what a tenant of this room would write with.

JOHAN
I'd move in here and paint in...matter if I thought that it would help me paint the way he wrote.

MARIKA
You're still painting, then?

JOHAN
Oh, I'm still painting, absolutely.

MARIKA
Then why do you wipe tables for this Malachi?

JOHAN
I have to make a living.

MARIKA
But don't people buy your work?

JOHAN
I don't try to sell it.

MARIKA
Why not?

JOHAN
It isn't very good.

MARIKA
Well, but it must have gotten better since the Institute.

JOHAN
It can't have gotten worse, you mean?

MARIKA
I suppose it could have stayed the same –

JOHAN
I'm afraid it has.

MARIKA
Are your figures still out of proportion?

JOHAN
I don't try figures anymore. Trouble with figures is, you have to use a model. When you're done, the model wants to look.

MARIKA
What do you paint then? Still life?

JOHAN
Painting indoors is depressing. You begin with a perfect white canvas, then you mark it, and it's ruined forever. Of course you do the same outdoors, but there are more distractions. So what I paint is mostly landscapes. Painting landscapes is like fishing. You don't really go to catch

fish. The line in the water is just an excuse to let you sit out in the scenery. I do enjoy my painting. I just don't need to bother other people with it.

MARIKA

What did you think of Gustav's exhibition today?

JOHAN

What a surprise to meet you there! I go to all the openings, but this was the first time I'd seen you at one.

MARIKA

I don't go to the galleries. But with all the hoopla in the papers about Gustav – I thought that that was why I went, but now I'm here I wonder...

JOHAN

Gustav's made a lot of progress, don't you think?

MARIKA

His career is right on schedule. He had it all mapped out while we were still at school. He'd start off doing portraits of the wives of senior clerks. Their husbands would give dinners to unveil the portraits, and he'd work up new commissions there. He's progressed to the middle range bureaucrats. With this current exhibition, he'll soon be painting presidents and chairmen. In five years he'll have painted the King and then the world will be his oyster.

JOHAN

Do you envy him?

MARIKA

His work's not worth a whistle, but I am fond of oysters. And of sourgrapes, you're thinking?

JOHAN

I'm not thinking.

MARIKA

No woman who had any kind of station to protect could ever work up a career like Gustav's. She wouldn't have the freedom of the private homes, or of the public places either. *(With a gesture, she has cited The Snout as an example of the last.)*

JOHAN

I have the freedom. I could never do what he's done, though. The Countess of Wherever would taker one look at her left eye halfway down her cheek and have here butler throw me out. But I'm really quite content with what I am doing now. Maybe when I'm old and looking back I'll think I should have been dissatisfied, but I'm perfectly fine for the present. In fact, if I'm to keep my job we'd better go now.

(Marika is still looking around the room. She's never really stopped since she arrived.)

MARIKA

I still can't see it.

JOHAN

See what?

MARIKA

Ossian here, in this room. I can't picture it. But then, I can't imagine him writing those books. Who's still here that knew him?

JOHAN

There's just Malachi.

MARIKA

Would your snake-eyed spider talk to me?

JOHAN

He loves to talk about your husband. He's been trying to get him back here ever since he left.

MARIKA

Oh, has he? How?

JOHAN

When I started at The Snout, I was the errand boy. One of my jobs was to run messages from Malachi to Mr. Borg, inviting him to come and have a drink.

MARIKA

You could have saved your shoes. Ossian made a vow. He swore he'd never set foot in The Snout again. If he ever came back here, he told me, he'd stay for the rest of his life.

JOHAN

Oh, Malachi would like that even better. Your husband's reputation brought in tourists. If he were living here again –

MARIKA

This place was a tourist attraction?

JOHAN

Yes. That's pretty much dropped off by now. They used to come, though. Swedes, Norwegians, Germans, even French and English. They'd sit down, muss their hair and tear their shirtfronts open, and order an "Ossian Borg."

MARIKA

Is that something you drink?

JOHAN

Straight absinthe, like he drank when he was here. The funny thing is, we can't serve that to the tourists. It's been outlawed.

MARIKA

Outlawed? People still drink absinthe.

JOHAN
Not the real stuff, though. The distillers still make something they call absinthe, but it doesn't have the principal ingredient.

MARIKA
What was that?

JOHAN
Wormwood. The government found out that it was poison. It caused fever and myopia and persecution mania. What we sell now is just anisette.

MARIKA
And your employer thought that, if he lured my husband here, he wouldn't notice that the offered drink was counterfeit?

JOHAN
The difference in flavor is subtle, they say.

MARIKA
Ossian has a subtle palate, such as only men whom food and drink almost disgust can have. An almost squeamish sensitivity. If your Malachi believes that he could fool my husband with a substitute, hedoesn't know him.

JOHAN
He likes to say he knows him very well.

MARIKA
These notes he sends — they never come to Ossian at home. They must go to his office.

JOHAN
Yes.

MARIKA
Does Ossian accept them?

JOHAN
Not in person, but his secretary takes them.

MARIKA
Does Ossian send back answers?

JOHAN
He never did while I was running them.

MARIKA
Who runs them now?

JOHAN
Axel's the new errand boy.

MARIKA
Is Axel here?

JOHAN
He should be here by now.

MARIKA
Let's have him in.

JOHAN
He'd tell on us. He's terrified of MALACHI.

MARIKA
Then let's have Malachi himself. It's time that we two met.

JOHAN
You mean call Malachi in here? I've told you —

MARIKA
I can't talk to him out front. There are windows. Very small ones and with filthy glass, but still the world outside is passing by. *(Starting for the door)*
Let's see if Malachi's come down yet.

JOHAN
Marika, this isn't fair. You wanted to see the Back Room so I smuggled you in. You can't let me lose my job for it.

MARIKA
I don't see why you want this job. If waiting tables is your goal in life, you're even-tempered and presentable, any cafe in Stockholm would hire you.

JOHAN
I like it here.

MARIKA
Why?

JOHAN
It has a history. People gathered in the front room to argue ideas. They started trends and they formed schools and movements. Your husband was the catalyst. He wouldn't let the others back here very often, They'd knock and knock and, most times, he'd just sit here with the door locked. But then, other times he'd throw it open and have everybody in. Painters, sculptors, novelists, poets and playwrights, philosophers and students on a spree, all rubbing shoulders with the routine drunkards.

MARIKA *(Pointing to the painting of the Back Room on the wall.)*
Was one of them responsible for this?

JOHAN
All the paintings are by men who drank here.

MARIKA *(Examining the painting)*
This must be a version of the Chamber of Debauchery itself. It's signed "Jansen."

JOHAN
Karl Jansen, yes.

MARIKA
Should I have heard of him?

JOHAN
I don't suppose so. He died two years ago out in the front room, in a fit of delirium tremens.

MARIKA *(Dismissing the painting)*
No loss to his movement. How would you paint this room?

JOHAN
Who, I? No particular way. *(Swimming)* In browns and grays with — I don't know, perspective, so it looked like three dimensions...
How would you?

MARIKA
I wouldn't.

JOHAN
I mean if you hadn't stopped painting.

MARIKA
I have stopped painting.

JOHAN
So you told me at the gallery. You didn't tell me why. Was it because a woman couldn't build up a career – what you said before?

MARIKA
That might have stopped me if I hadn't had another reason.

JOHAN
What?

MARIKA
The night that Ossian proposed to me, he said we'd have to make a bargain. I'd stop painting and he wouldn't start writing again.

JOHAN
Did you want him to stop writing?

MARIKA
He'd already stopped before we met.

JOHAN
What kind of bargain was he offering then?

MARIKA
One I found acceptable.

JOHAN
But, Marika, your work was brilliant.

MARIKA
You all thought so at the Institute.

JOHAN
No one was even close to you. You knew how good you were.

MARIKA

I had a strong suspicion. I didn't really know until Ossian asked me to stop. He only saw my paintings once. He'd been working for my father for a year. One night he came to supper and we met. After that he called quite often. He was gracious and polite and very charming. One evening he came back to my studio next to my room. He looked at my self portraits and the series I'd done of the storms on the skerries.

JOHAN

I remember those.

MARIKA

Ossian stared at the self portraits. A look came on his face I'd never seen before. He was terrified. Two days later he proposed to me and asked me if I'd give up painting. At first I thought that he was testing me to see how much I cared for him. He wasn't testing. I'd really have to stop, as he'd stopped writing. If his books hadn't had their terrible corrosive power, he could have peacefully continued writing, just as you've continued painting. But he'd had to stop and so would I. That's when I knew that my painting was good.

JOHAN

And that's when you renounced it.

MARIKA

Yes.

JOHAN

Marika — excuse me if I make a little speech. You've probably guessed that I spend more time in the museums and the galleries than standing at my easel....

MARIKA *(Picking up a small mauve vase that is lying on the table)*
Was this Ossian's, do you suppose?

JOHAN

I don't know. What I'm saying is, I love to look at paintings that I couldn't do myself. I'm glad they're in the world. I feel it as a loss — I feel it as a loss to me — that you're not painting anymore. That's all.

MARIKA

That's a very generous sentiment. But it's really not my problem, is it?

JOHAN

Don't you miss painting?

MARIKA

I don't actually know. I might be here to find out some part of the answer. *(Still examining the vase)* Ossian likes to gather mountain violets for our parlor. I wouldn't think that flowers could survive in here.

JOHAN
Have you found out the answer?

MARIKA
Not yet. *(Deliberately, she drops the vase, which smashes loudly)*

JOHAN
Marika!

MARIKA
Butterfingers.

JOHAN
You did that on purpose!

MARIKA *(Not condescending to dissemble)*
Oh dear. The famous Malachi won't come, I hope.

JOHAN
Of course he'll come. There goes my job, right out the window!

MARIKA
You've done nothing wrong.

JOHAN
Tell him that!

MARIKA
I will. He can't be such an ogre as you say he is.

JOHAN
He's such an ogre as you can't imagine.

MARIKA
I can't imagine how I'd paint this room. I can't imagine how Ossian lived here. All right, then, now I'll meet a man I can't imagine.

MALACHI *(Bursts through the door)*
What's going on in here?
(He is a bristling old man in his 70s, twisted with malice, without a drop of moisture in his scaly skin from head to foot. He wears black trousers and shoes and a cutaway coat; their formality combined with their filthy condition is a calculated insult to his customers.)

JOHAN
It's just me, Malachi.

MALACHI *(Eyeballing Marika)*
It's just you, is it? What's this, then? Your left foot, perhaps? Or your left testicle?

JOHAN
She's no one you should talk that way in front of.

MALACHI
Should I talk that way on top of her?

JOHAN
You shouldn't talk that way at all.

MALACHI
Why shouldn't I?

JOHAN
This lady is — a lady.

MALACHI
Oh, a lady.

MARIKA
Yes, a lady. What's more, she isn't deaf, so you can speak to her directly.

MALACHI
May I really take that liberty?

MARIKA
You may, till I revoke it.

MALACHI
Well, then. May I see your papers?

JOHAN
Oh no, Malachi—

MARIKA
Be quiet, Johan. *(To Malachi)* I don't know what papers you can mean.

MALACHI
I'm sure you're registered.

MARIKA
Registered where?

MALACHI
It is the law, you know.

MARIKA
The law, that I be registered? I've never heard of such a thing.

MALACHI
It really works to your advantage. You get free treatment when you need it. In the course of your profession you must need it fairly often.

JOHAN
You don't know who you're talking to!

MALACHI
I don't care who I'm talking to. What is she doing in the Back Room?

JOHAN
This is Mrs. Ossian Borg! *(To Marika)* Tell him!

MARIKA
That's right. Ossian Borg is my husband.

MALACHI *(Despite himself is taken aback)*
You're Ossian's wife?

MARIKA
Since he's my husband, that's right, I'm his wife. The two things go together.

MALACHI
Well well well! That's not an answer to my question. What I asked was what you're doing here. But still... Ossian's wife. That's really very interesting. I can have you arrested, though.

MARIKA
Can you? I'm not arguing the point, I'm only curious. On what charge?

MALACHI
Even if you weren't back here, if you'd just come into the tavern with no escort—

JOHAN
I'm her escort.

MALACHI
You're not anybody's escort. You're my waiter.

JOHAN
I conducted Mrs. Borg here.

MALACHI
Well, I can't deny that's interesting as well. If I pressed charges, would you say that in a court of law? Would the lady want you to? Excuse me for thinking out loud. I'm just considering the options that you've handed me. I always like to think what I could do if I decided to. It gives me many happy hours.

MARIKA
I'm sure it does. Consider all the things that you could do. For example, you could die. I'm sure you're old enough.

MALACHI
I'm too old. If I'd ever planned on dying, I'd have done so long ago.

MARIKA
I'm perfectly willing to fight with you. It would help me to know why we're fighting, however. It can't be because I've stirred up the vermin in your storeroom.

MALACHI
Why have you come here?

MARIKA
I'm not sure I know myself.

MALACHI

Let's have no evasive answers.

MARIKA

I don't give evasive answers. If I don't want to answer a question, I don't answer it. I'll say more, though, if you wish to hear it.

MALACHI

Be so kind.

MARIKA

I know I've come here looking for my husband. I'm beginning to suspect I'm also looking for myself, or for a self I've put aside. Is that direct enough?

MALACHI

I can tell you about Ossian. There is a price.

MARIKA

I don't take charity. What is it?

MALACHI

That you stoop to taste a sample of my stocks. Perhaps some wine, or something stronger.

JOHAN *(Eagerly, to Malachi)*

Can I get the lady something?

MARIKA

Your employer has stopped using the third person in my presence. I'd prefer it if you'd stop as well.

MALACHI *(To Johan, as he checks his watch)*

 You' re not on duty for ten minutes. And besides—
(To Marika) Third person, please excuse me—
(To Johan) Mrs. Borg might not be comfortable alone with me.

MARIKA

I'm comfortable with either of you, thank you very much.

MALACHI

I insist on serving you myself. What can I offer you?

MARIKA

Why not an "Ossian Borg"?

MALACHI *(With a glance toward Johan)*

You've heard about our tourist trade? It's pretty well played out now, I'm afraid. You understand our so-called absinthe –

MARIKA

Isn't absinthe, yes, I know. That's quite all right.

MALACHI

And, Johan, what for you?

JOHAN

For me...?

MALACHI

Don't inhale your tongue. I can't have you strangling before you start your shift.

JOHAN

Well – I'll have an "Ossian Borg" myself.

MALACHI

Two "Ossian Borgs" coming up.

(To Johan) Clear Mrs. Borg a place, you noodle! Do you mean to keep her standing up all evening? *(Tossing him a white cloth from his belt)*

Dust down the table and give her a chair! She's our particular guest!

(He exits)

MARIKA

There, you see? You didn't lose your job. In fact, he's pleased with you for bringing me. Have you discussed me with him?

JOHAN

I've told him that we went to school together, and I've said how well you paint –

MARIKA

How well I used to paint.

JOHAN

I've only just found out you'd stopped.

MARIKA

Shouldn't you clear off the table before he comes back?

JOHAN *(Going into action)*

Oh yes, I'd better, thanks.

(He tramples on a piece of the vase and stoops to pick it up)

MARIKA

I broke the vase. I'll clean it up.

JOHAN

No, that's all right.

MARIKA

I'll do it. Clear the table.

JOHAN *(Lifting broken chairs, stools, and small tables off the big table)*

Malachi should put all this out back for the dustman to carry away. Instead he dumps it here.

MARIKA

He's right to dump it here. It suits the room.

(Examining a shard of the smashed vase) Violet is Ossian's favorite color. I'm sure this vase was his. I'm going to keep a piece. What shall I do with the rest?

JOHAN *(Indicating a pile of refuse L)*
Throw it there. All right now, hold your breath. I'm going to dust the table.
(Marika takes out a handkerchief and covers her mouth and nose. Johan pelts the table with the white cloth, raising suffocating clouds of ancient dust. Coughing, he completes his task, wiping the surface as clean as he can.)

JOHAN
The front room is almost as filthy as this one. Most tavern keepers put out salted biscuits so their customers stay thirsty. Malachi leaves layers of dust for his.
(Malachi has come in and heard the last of this. An uncomfortable moment for Johan. Malachi is carrying a small tray with two drinks on it: liqueur glasses filled with a crystal-clear liquor.)

MALACHI
Here we are, then. Have you made our guest comfortable, Johan? Seat her where her husband used to sit
(Johan places a chair for Marika as indicated, dusts it off and holds it as Marika sits. Malachi serves her the drink, which she will scarcely touch.)

MALACHI *(To Johan, setting down his drink)*
You can sit opposite. *(To Marika)* If I may sit with you, I'll set a chair right here.
(He does so, as Johan seats himself. Malachi has a second cloth with which he dusts down his own chair before sitting.)

MALACHI
Ossian always locked the door whenever he was in here. I had a key, however, and the privilege of entering at will. I didn't even have to knock. There were no secrets between Ossian and me. You don't mind if I call him Ossian, incidentally?

MARIKA
If he allowed you to, it's not for me to quarrel.

MALACHI
No, it's not

MARIKA
You think you knew my husband.

MALACHI
I knew Ossian. I know him still.

MARIKA
Tell me how he first came here.

MALACHI

He came alone, one midnight. He told me he'd been drinking for ten hours and I said he was a liar. Men with blue skin on their necks can't hold more liquor than a squirrel I told him, "If you've come here to get drunk, show me your money and we'll get to work". He'd been drinking wine. I guessed that brandy ought to be his drink. Not right, but near enough for starters. Before too long, he'd shown me why he wanted to be drunk, or to believe that he was drunk. He had some things to say no sober man could listen to, not even from himself.

MARIKA

You listened, though.

MALACHI

Of course I listened. I'm a barkeep.

MARIKA

What did Ossian say?

MALACHI

He talked about his father — or the man he swore was not his father. You know what he said. It's in his first book.

JOHAN

She's never read his first book.

MARIKA

Tell me how he talked.

MALACHI

In every slanderous sentence he uttered, you could taste how he depended on the old professor, both financially and otherwise. Does he need you very badly? If he does, take care. That puts him in a very weak position. He'll exact revenge.

MARIKA

Is that a friendly warning or a threat?

MALACHI

There's no reason I should threaten you, but I'm not friendly either, so I'd say it's neither one.

MARIKA

Get back to Ossian.

MALACHI

In my young years, when I was working at the Grand Hotel, I served men who, just with words, could change how people saw the world. Ossian had that power, or the spark of it. I saw that right away. That first night it was very faint, though. By the time he'd drunk enough to free his feelings, his tongue had turned to muck. I'd gotten the prescription wrong. The next night, when he came back, I'd figured out his drink.

JOHAN

Absinthe.

MALACHI

Not this sugar-water, though. The real poison.

JOHAN *(Of his anisette)*

I'm enjoying this.

MALACHI

I wouldn't serve it to a woman. *(Graciously, to Marika)* Except, of course, at her request.

MARIKA

What did the wormwood do for Ossian?

MALACHI

It helped him see the good professor's kindness as the folly of a doting cuckold. Ossian's mother had died — as Ossian saw it — just to spite them both. From that time on, the widower forwent his every comfort to cram Ossian with learning. Half the languages of Europe were dunned into him. Old Borg set back his own career to take a puny post in Germany, then one in France, to help the boy master those languages. However cramped and insect-ridden Ossian's room was, the professor's was always filthier and smaller. Now they'd come back to Sweden. At the age of twenty-three, Ossian was about to reap the harvest of the old man's years of sacrifice: a triple doctorate from the University of Stockholm. In all that time, the man had asked for nothing. But Ossian knew what he owed, and he knew he didn't have it.

MARIKA

That was...?

MALACHI

Gratitude. No man feels a debt like a man who can never repay it. Every night, out in the front room, Ossian labored at his libels, going over them and over them — revising them, I came to see, like chapters in a novel. At last his picture of the old man grew so rank that Ossian couldn't live with him. I offered Ossian the Back Room. I'd give him food. I'd give him absinthe. When his mind was racing faster than his hand could write, I'd take dictation for him. My one condition was that what he spoke here, what he wrote here, was my property, lock stock and barrel. I could profit by it any way I saw the chance.

MARIKA

Did he know you meant to have it published?

MALACHI

Of course he knew. How else would he take revenge on everyone — most cruelly on himself? I only stole what Ossian threw away. I'm as honest a man as you'll find in this world.

MARIKA

You got rich off his writings, while old Mr. Borg has been shamed into exile. He's back teaching at that miserable school in Bonn.

MALACHI

Ossian's second book was just as hard on me.

MARIKA

You get the royalties, however, and the tourist trade.

MALACHI

They don't amount to much, now that the flurry's died down. But I somehow feel, this evening, that things could pick up very quickly. In the meantime, I'm not destitute. If you'll empty your glass I can fill it again.

MARIKA

I find that I don't care for anisette.

JOHAN (*Rising*)

I can fetch you something else.

MARIKA

What time is it?

JOHAN

Twenty five minutes to six.

MARIKA

Ossian's nearly due home from the office. I like to be there when he comes.

MALACHI

Johan! You call yourself an escort. Ask your friend to stay awhile longer.

JOHAN

I'd love it if she stayed, but if she has to go —

MARIKA

Third person again. That's a truly irksome habit that you both should break.

MALACHI

I shouldn't scold you, Johan, when I've been remiss myself. Mrs. Borg has asked for something and I've brought her a poor substitute.

MARIKA

You brought me what I asked for.

MALACHI

You asked for an "Ossian Borg," and you deserve the real thing. We were ordered to destroy our stocks, but I held onto mine.

JOHAN
You've kept real absinthe here?

MALACHI *(Takes a key from his pocket and tosses it to Johan)*
I thought it might prove useful. Open that box there. The one with iron bands around it.

JOHAN *(Finding a small, sturdy wooden crate among the rubble to L)*
This one?

MALACHI
That one.
(Johan puts the key into the crate's large padlock. It snaps open with a sound like the report of a pistol. He opens the lid and removes an ancient-looking bottle.)
Hand it here. *(Johan gives him the bottle)* The key too. *(Johan returns the key, which Malachi pockets)*

MARIKA
So that's absinthe, then.

MALACHI *(Looking proudly at his precious contraband)*
The medicine of choice for Ossian Borg. It transformed what in another man would be suspicion, envy, jaundice, into vision. It made the shames that he experienced as resonant as holy revelations. It forced him to give voice to what he knew. It showed him he was set about with enemies and had to fight them off by naming and exposing them.

MARIKA
The wormwood gave him phantom foes to grapple with?

MALACHI
Not phantoms. His dead mother, the professor — who's to say they weren't his enemies? All of us are threatened by the people we depend on. They have us at their mercy, and they know it very well. The sentimentalists among us hope their loved ones won't abuse their power. Ossian knew better. With the help of the wormwood, he wrote what he knew.

MARIKA
Does he know less now that he doesn't drink wormwood?

MALACHI
What he knows, he knows — he can't know less. But he can know the same things less disruptively. He can know but not let knowing determine the course of his life. Ossian's stopped writing. He has got married. That's the life he's chosen. For the present. Have you made a choice? Are you equipped to make a choice? Do you know your alternatives? *(He has extended the bottle an inch or so towards her)*

MARIKA
Your wormwood wouldn't give me new alternatives.

MALACHI

No, but it would bring the old ones out. It would show you who your husband is. Isn't that the knowledge that you've come to seek?

MARIKA

I have enemies. I know I have. I don't need to drug myself to feel their hatred. You're my enemy.

MALACHI

I take that as a compliment.

MARIKA

You may. It is a compliment. Johan, for example, is my friend.

JOHAN

I hope so, Marika.

MARIKA

You are. But your employer knows that friends are paltry things compared to enemies.

MALACHI

Is Ossian your friend?

MARIKA

I'd hardly call my husband paltry.

MALACHI

It's for such as you that absinthe was distilled. Think of it seeping through the charcoal, clear as crystal, and then turning faintly greenish as the oil of wormwood started bleeding in.

MARIKA

Ossian is due home. He lives according to the clock, and that makes sense to me, and more sense now I've seen the way he used to live.

MALAGHI

Johan, get her to stay.

JOHAN

How can I if she wants to leave?

MALAGHI

You'd best persuade her. It's your job if you don't.

MARIKA

I'm going, but don't worry, Johan. If I hear you've lost your job because of me — or for any other reason — I'll report your boss for keeping back contraband liquor.

JOHAN (*To Marika*)

You don't have to —

MARIKA
I say this for Malachi's own good. You're an excellent waiter, I'm sure. I wouldn't want to think he'd lost you on account of me. After all, aren't he and I the best of enemies?
(She goes unhurriedly out the door, leaving it open behind her.)
MALAGHI *(With sudden violence slams his hand on the table)*
Damnation!

JOHAN
What's the matter?

MALACHI
What's the matter? You idiot, I wanted her to stay here!

JOHAN
Why? Before you found us, I was scared you'd fire me for bringing her.

MALACHI
I ought to. She says I can't fire you All right, I'll put you back to running errands. You've got Axel's job.

JOHAN
Axel's job? What about Axel?

MALAGHI
Axel's through. I'm getting rid of him.

JOHAN
What for?

MALACHI *(Putting the bottle of absinthe back in the crate and snapping shut the padlock)*
Because he didn't deliver my note in time. He dawdled on the way. I told him Ossian would leave his office punctually.

JOHAN
You sent Axel with a note for Mr. Borg?

MALACHI
That's what I just said.

JOHAN
What was in this note?

MALACHI
I told Ossian his wife was in the Back Room with a young man.

JOHAN
You suggested....?

MALACHI
I suggested nothing. I told him the state of affairs.

JOHAN
All right, he didn't come, though, did he? He must not have believed you.

MALACHI

He didn't get the message. He'd believe me. Ossian knows that I don't lie.

JOHAN

How would he know such a thing as that?

MALACHI

I don't lie. You probably haven't noticed. You assume malicious people must be liars. But I've found the truth is much more damaging than any falsehood, so I always speak with perfect honesty. Ossian knows that.

JOHAN

But he hasn't come.

MALACHI

Axel must have stopped to have a pastry. I'll have his hide. You'll have his job.

JOHAN

I don't want his job.

MALACHI

I don't want his hide, but he does, so I'll have it. I did stretch one point in the note. I said the young man was a painter. That's more than an exaggeration. Yes, I must admit, that just may be an outright lie.

JOHAN

It just may be.

MALACHI

But it should have brought Ossian running. It would have. Axel dawdled.

JOHAN

Axel wouldn't dawdle. Axel's too afraid of you to dawdle.

MALACHI

Ossian would have come. I can't be wrong. I'm not wrong. I know Ossian. Why isn't he here?

(A man's voice, incisive and arresting, is heard through the open doorway. We can't see the speaker.)

VOICE

I am here, Malachi. You're not wrong.

(Ossian Borg appears in the doorway. He is 29, and dressed in frigidly correct dark clothes: a suit with vest and ribbon tie. Only his thick mane of hair, refusing to be tamed, betrays the mildness in the man.)

OSSIAN

You do know me, to my everlasting shame.

MALACHI

Hello, Ossian.

OSSIAN

Don't call me Ossian. Call me Mr. Borg.

MALACHI

You've just missed Mrs. Borg.

OSSIAN

When your message came I went straight home. She's always there to greet me.

MALACHI

Not tonight.

OSSIAN

No, not tonight.

JOHAN

You must have passed her on the way here, Mr. Borg. She was heading for your house to meet you.

OSSIAN *(To Malachi)*

Who is this? *(To Johan)* You're not by any chance a painter?

JOHAN

If you stretch a point

OSSIAN

I haven't stretched a point in years. I made a practice of it once, when I was writing. I've reformed. Writing didn't only rob me of all self-respect — it put me in the company of painters.

(Without taking his eyes off Johan) Malachi, get out of here.

MALACHI

Delighted, Mr. Borg. You have a right to turn me out of course. This room is yours. So is the larder. I assume you've missed your supper. Would you like a chop?

OSSIAN

I'd like to see your back.

MALACHI

Will you have a drink, then?

OSSIAN

I'll have your last remaining twitch of life if you don't quit my sight!

MALACHI *(Clearing his tray and Johan's glass)*

I'm always glad to offer all support.

OSSIAN *(To Malachi)*

What's your painter's name?

JOHAN

My name is Johan Ekdahl, Mr. Borg. I'm a waiter here.

MALACHI

You'll want privacy. I'll close the door behind me. *(He exits, doing so)*

JOHAN

Mr. Borg, I met your wife by accident this afternoon. A former fellow student had a show — we'd been all three at the Institute together. When I told your wife I worked here, she asked if I could show her the Back Room, which she was curious to see —

because of you, of course — well, why else? She was curious to see it... Mr. Borg.

OSSIAN

You knew my wife before I met her.

JOHAN

At the Institute, that's right, sir. We were classmates.

OSSIAN

Back before I'd ever seen her, and before she'd ever seen me.

JOHAN

I think she'd graduated, sir, before she'd met you. I believe that's right.

OSSIAN

Are you a sapper and a miner, Johan?

JOHAN

Sir?

OSSIAN

Do you dig holes and plant explosives?

JOHAN

No.

OSSIAN

You've run a tunnel underneath my marriage, though, isn't that so?

JOHAN

No, sir, that isn't so. I haven't.

OSSIAN

You knew my wife before I knew her. Nobody should have known my wife before I did. Nobody should have known me before she did. Don't you think that's the best basis for a marriage?

JOHAN

Ideally I suppose it is. But it hardly ever happens, does it? It couldn't happen. There's the parents, in the first place.

OSSIAN

Yes, her father. He's got the jump on me, and don't you think he doesn't know it.

JOHAN

I didn't really know your wife that well.

OSSIAN

You knew her. More importantly, she knew you.

JOHAN

She never really paid me any mind, to speak of.

OSSIAN

You say so, but you could be lying, couldn't you? Or you could be mistaken. It's a subject for conjecture. Happily, I don't conjecture anymore. I translate business letters — Swedish into French and German, French and German into Swedish. I improve on the originals in both directions. That's all the writing I do now.

JOHAN

There's nothing to conjecture about Mrs. Borg and me.

OSSIAN

There's always something to conjecture. You're a painter. Is there ever not something to look at?

JOHAN

No, but looking's not conjecturing.

OSSIAN

Painting is.

JOHAN

No, Mr. Borg. You just paint what you see.

OSSIAN

You look past what you see to what you know to be behind it and you paint that. Else why paint at all?

JOHAN

Your wife's stopped painting.

OSSIAN

That's right. In the name of simple decency.

JOHAN

I paint. Is that indecent of me?

OSSIAN

Not if you're completely without talent, as I'd guess you are.

JOHAN

What's talent got to do with it?

OSSIAN

A painter, or a writer, uses the people around him. The more talented he is, the more cruelly he exposes them. He strips the skin off his nearest and dearest, then offers the skin up for sale. He vivisects people like rabbits.

He cuts the tail off his dog, eats the flesh, and gives the dog the bone to chew. What could be more loathsome?

JOHAN

He exposes himself too, doesn't he?

OSSIAN

He exposes himself most shamefully of all. That's hardly compensation to the people he humiliates. I wrote two novels in this room.

JOHAN

I know.

OSSIAN

Of course you know. Everybody knows, to my disgrace. The first one showed a father and his son — his wife's son — in a wretched symbiosis. It revealed the old man's martyrdom as the cramped manipulations of a crippled weasel. At the same time, it revealed the child's ingratitude as no less vicious. No quarter. No prisoners. Art in full deadly career, scything all before it into severed limbs and torsos.

JOHAN

I'm happy I'm not talented, if that's what happens.

OSSIAN

So you should be.

JOHAN

Your wife is very talented.

OSSIAN

Of course she is. If she'd been a dabbler like you, she could have gone on painting till the earth ran out of pigment.

JOHAN

You stopped her, though.

OSSIAN

She stopped herself. Her motives were the same as mine had been. Of course, there'd been some damage done already. My books were in print and some people had ogled her self-portraits.

JOHAN

They were staggering.

OSSIAN

No one but I should have seen them, and not even I. Not even Marika herself should have seen them. You surely shouldn't have. Better I should find you back here drinking with her.

JOHAN

Your wife and I drank absinthe in your honor.

OSSIAN

Absinthe?

JOHAN

Anisette. Real absinthe has been outlawed.

OSSIAN

Yes, I know. Quite rightly, too. Did you sit in my place, or was this glass Marika's?

JOHAN

That glass was hers.

OSSIAN

She hardly touched it.

JOHAN

She took a taste.

OSSIAN

It looks as thin as water. Absinthe used to swell with winding layers of greenish oil ready to suck at your tongue like a harlot.

JOHAN

There's some absinthe in that crate.

OSSIAN

Not real absinthe?

JOHAN

Yes.

OSSIAN

With wormwood?

JOHAN

Yes, sir. Malachi's illegal stock.

OSSIAN

I should have known he'd keep some back. One of the notes he sent me hinted that he had. It had been a grace to think there wasn't any wormwood left in Sweden — like dreaming that this room had caught on fire and burned to cinders. Do you have the key?

JOHAN

No. Malachi.

OSSIAN

The Provider. If I drank a glass of wormwood, I might find out how you met my wife.

JOHAN

I've told you.

OSSIAN

You've told me too much and nothing at all.

JOHAN
I've told you all there is to tell.

OSSIAN
You've said you met at school, without my introducing you.

JOHAN
We met before you knew each other!

OSSIAN
Don't you see that only makes it worse? You were able to impress yourself on Marika before I'd even come into the picture. One person's consciousness has only so much space for unalloyed impressions. That space is filled early in life, before the gestures of the face have carved their creases. My image in Marika's mind lies over images of people she knew earlier. A former image might one day bleed through, and where will I be then?

JOHAN
I've told you Marika paid no attention to me.

OSSIAN
No attention to you?

JOHAN
None.

OSSIAN
What teachers did you both hate?

JOHAN (*Automatically*)
Mr. Elstad...How did you know? Does she still talk about him?

OSSIAN
There always is one teacher all the students hate. He's usually the best.

JOHAN
Mr. Elstad was a rotten teacher. He taught History of Art when he explained a painting, I could hardly see the colors on the canvas for Elstad's description of them.

OSSIAN
Did you and Marika make fun of Mr. Elstad?

JOHAN
He had a stupid moustache. It stuck straight out sideways like the bristles on a pig. Marika said it would have made a fine pair of brushes.

OSSIAN
Did she?

JOHAN
Oh, she hated Mr. Elstad.

OSSIAN
Where were you when she joked about his moustache?

JOHAN
Where? I don't remember that,

OSSIAN
Of course you do. Think back. Were you at school?

JOHAN
Well, most likely we probably were.

OSSIAN
Only probably? Then you might have both been someplace else.

JOHAN
We might have.

OSSIAN
Where?

JOHAN
I don't know. What does it matter?

OSSIAN
It's grist for the mill.

JOHAN
What grist for what mill?

OSSIAN
You're hiding something, Johan.

JOHAN
No I'm not. I don't have anything to hide.

OSSIAN
Then tell me. Where did Marika make this moustache joke to you about poor Mr. Elstad?

JOHAN (*Concentrates a moment*)
I don't think she made it just to me. I think she might have made it to a group of us.

OSSIAN
A group of students?

JOHAN (*"Yes."*)
All of us clustered around her when she talked down the teachers. She'd get really very nasty.

OSSIAN
Where did all you students cluster? If not at the Institute?

JOHAN
Well, sometimes we'd go visit the museums together. Sometimes we'd go to the shore.

OSSIAN
The shore?

JOHAN
The beach, yes. During lunch, or in the evening.

OSSIAN
In the evening?

JOHAN
When the sun stayed out, in summer.

OSSIAN
On Midsummer Evening?

JOHAN
Maybe so. I don't remember.

OSSIAN
That's when the sun stays out the longest.

JOHAN
Yes, I think we all went to the shore together one year on Midsummer Evening. When our last class was dismissed we all trooped over.

OSSIAN
Did you stay all night?

JOHAN
I stayed all night. There were bonfires and dancing on the sand.

OSSIAN
Some of the others stayed all night too?

JOHAN
I think most of them.

OSSIAN
Did Marika stay?

JOHAN
I don't remember if she stayed till morning. She stayed pretty late. *(Explanatorily)* Midsummer Evening.

OSSIAN
It won't offend you if I drink from my wife's glass?

JOHAN
Of course not

OSSIAN
If you drank from it, that would offend me very deeply. *(He sniffs the glass of anisette)*
Your pseudo-absinthe smells invisible, just as it looks. *(He drinks. Disapprovingly)* It tastes like licorice.

JOHAN
I like having the taste come from something that's clear. It s almost magical.

OSSIAN
If I think the wormwood into it — the taste like blackened sulfur from a burnt match — maybe we can manage our Midsummer Night. Now.... we have a group of students, all clustered around Marika.

JOHAN
That wasn't on Midsummer Night, though. At least, I don't remember that it was.

OSSIAN (*Ignoring Johan's cavil, sips his drink, as he will continue to do at intervals*)
Gradually the group got smaller, didn't it? The students fell away in couples. There were Marika and you, and there were others, fewer and fewer as time went by. They fell away in couples.

JOHAN (*Assents, as he comes under the influence of the picture Ossian is developing*)
It was Midsummer Night.

OSSIAN
You didn't fall away, though, did you?

JOHAN
I fell away.

OSSIAN
You fell away with Marika — and left the last few stragglers standing, young men and women making an odd number, a sad little number.

JOHAN
I didn't leave with Marika. I left alone, to walk along the water.

OSSIAN
And left Marika alone.

JOHAN
She was alone quite often. Yes, I think I see her standing up the bank a little way, alone.

OSSIAN
You'd been alone together, then, before you left.

JOHAN
She was comfortable with me. I wasn't jealous of her talent like the others.

OSSIAN
She stayed all alone while you went down to walk along the shore.

JOHAN
She liked to stand among the trees. She did a painting of them once — several paintings.

OSSIAN
She liked it there among the shadows.

JOHAN
Yes.

OSSIAN
What else?

JOHAN
What else?

OSSIAN
There's more.

JOHAN
There's more what?

OSSIAN
There's more to the picture.

JOHAN
That's all I can remember. It's more than I remember.

OSSIAN *(Begins filling the vacuum)*
There's the Midsummer sun. You must remember that the sun rode sideways until, right around eleven, it eased into the ocean at an angle almost flat with the horizon. The radiance it left behind bled softly through the sky above the skerries and across the beach and up the wooded incline where she stood. She was alone. And then he came back.

JOHAN
Who came back?

OSSIAN
The young man.

JOHAN
Wait a minute. What young man?

OSSIAN
The painter. She was standing on the hillside by the shore and he came back.

JOHAN
Who was this painter? Was he me?

OSSIAN
Her fellow student

JOHAN
And her fellow student's name was what?

OSSIAN
His name was Johan.

JOHAN
Mr. Borg, this story isn't true. You know that, don't you?

OSSIAN
What?

JOHAN
This story isn't true.

OSSIAN
Why not?

JOHAN
Why not? It isn't, that's all. It just isn't.

OSSIAN
Because it didn't happen?

JOHAN
Right, because it didn't happen.

OSSIAN
Aristotle knew two thousand years ago that history is inferior to poetry. History, he said, is just what happened. Poetry is what happens.

JOHAN
I didn't go to Marika on any hillside by the water.

OSSIAN
Why didn't you?

JOHAN
I didn't.

OSSIAN
But you might have.

JOHAN
No!

OSSIAN
Why mightn't you?

JOHAN
No reason, but—

OSSIAN
Why mightn't you have been a man of talent, even genius, a man whose will was just as strong as Marika's? You weren't, but that was purely accidental, just a random fact It says nothing about anything. It doesn't help us fathom what the world is like.

JOHAN
I'm not a man of genius and I never was.

OSSIAN

You're like a cork that slips down in the bottle when I try to pop it out. Go get Malachi.

JOHAN

All right, I will, but —

OSSIAN

I don't want to hear you anymore. You've given me all that I needed.

JOHAN

Mr. Borg, I'm not the Johan in this fantasy.

OSSIAN

You're not, no. You're not worthy of yourself. You lack your own dimensions. I can't correct that with you standing here in front of me. Fetch Malachi and don't come back.

JOHAN *(Starting out)*

I'll go. Just so you know –

OSSIAN

I won't know what I don't believe. Don't bother me with facts. They lie like algae on a lake. I want the close green depths to swim in — or to drown in, as the case may be. Vanish. Send in Malachi.

JOHAN *(At the door)*

I'm gone, but –

OSSIAN

You are gone. You're not there. Don't say another word. You're on the shore. Midsummer Evening.

(He empties his glass at a gulp and pays no further attention to the literal Johan) You're walking up the hillside from the beach with slow firm steps. You come to Marika, whose face, though it's addressed to you, seems not to see you. It's as if she heard you with her eyes. The color of her eyes has darkened, getting deeper in their fear of getting deeper which then makes them deeper still and still more fearful, then still deeper.... *(Johan makes to speak)*

You won't make another sound. You'll disappear and send in Malachi.

(Johan has only the strength of will to hesitate before silently obeying. He goes out and softly shuts the door behind him. Ossian moves to the crate of absinthe and grasps it with both hands as if tasting the wormwood through contact with the crate. His nails scrape the wood. Malachi comes in. Without moving not even looking at Malachi.)

OSSIAN

Did you bring pen and paper?

MALACHI

They're where we've always kept them.

(He opens a drawer in the table and takes out some paper, a pen and a bottle of ink.)

OSSIAN

Is our contract there too?

MALACHI

We never drew one up. Not in writing. The commitment that we made was verbal.

OSSIAN

I'd have sworn there was a document, with my signature in blood.

MALACHI

Blood flakes and falls away. Paper turns to powder. Our agreement lives.

OSSIAN

Open one bottle. I want to see the color, if it still looks like a patina of tarnish on old silver.

(Malachi opens the lock, which makes the same violent snap as before, opens the box and lifts out a bottle. Ossian listens but he doesn't watch. Malachi breaks the seal and opens the bottle.)

OSSIAN

The glass is still damp from the substitute. Pour half an inch to rinse out the nothingness. *(Malachi puts a small amount of absinthe in Ossian's glass. Ossian holds it to the light.)*

The real green. A half-inch, deep as all the oceans. *(He swirls the liquor around in the glass, then flicks it broadcast over the table)*

Will that lay the dust? The room remembers. The ceiling's lowering to concentrate the fumes. The walls are closing in a little — just three inches, three or maybe four, or maybe only two. There were nights when it pressed in the size of a coffin.

(He breathes in the bouquet of the empty glass)

MALACHI

Shall I fill your glass?

OSSIAN *(Makes a sign that he shouldn't. Malachi sets down the bottle.)*

I've always heard that the muses descended, but it isn't so. I've descended. You've stayed where you were.

MALACHI

So you could find me.

(Still without looking at Malachi, Ossian starts to speak. Malachi sits and takes down what Ossian dictates.)

OSSIAN

The air among the trees was full of hovering pockets of warmth. One seemed to burst— the gentlest of explosions — against her ankle. It sent a shudder up along her leg. Midsummer Night, when the sun, even during the few hours it was set, left a softly swelling crest of light as hostage for its swift return. She and Johan walked together down the incline toward the water. Day in night. The sky carried the sun's pledge — the grains of light the sun had left behind it, like pollen in the air above a bursting field. The coastline wound away on both sides as the lovers reached the sand. There were bonfires blaring in the distance. All around them women danced in pairs. The women spun each other, leaning back. Their hair, like torch flames, swept soft circles, and their mouths were gaped in silent laughter. With Johan leading her at one unbroken pace, they waded to, then past, the water's edge. Now they had moved into another element, more mysterious than air or earth or fire. The water, like the air, was warm. She scarcely felt a change. Before she was aware of it, the ocean swirled around her softly as a swaddling cloth and sweetly as a shroud and she was floating, lost and floating...

(The door opens. Marika is standing there.)

MARIKA

Johan came and told me you were here. I should have guessed that Malachi had sent for you, and that this time you'd come.

MALACHI

Johan left his station without asking me? I'll have his guts for garters.

MARIKA

No you won't. He saw me to the front door, then he went his way.

MALACHI

You mean he's left for good, right in the middle of a shift?

MARIKA

That's right.

MALACHI

Just like the young scarperer, to quit before I had the chance to fire him.

MARIKA

Ossian, it's odd, you know. He took this job because you'd been here. Now you're back, he runs away.

OSSIAN

There's nothing odd about it. Some people recreate battles with chessmen on maps.

But when a real war breaks out you don't expect them to enlist.

MARIKA

From what he's told me, I assume you're back to stay.

OSSIAN

You haven't left me any choice.

MARIKA

If you don't have a choice, then it's because you never wanted one. You wanted to come back here.

OSSIAN

Did I?

MARIKA

Yes, you did. You wanted me to force you to come back here.

OSSIAN

I suppose, then, I arranged your assignation with your lover?

MARIKA

There was no assignation. For my "lover," I must say Johan Ekdahl is a rather far fetched candidate. He told me that you're glorifying him to make him fill the bill, but that will take some doing, won't it?

OSSIAN

It wasn't I who chose him. It was you. I think he'll fill the bill quite nicely.

MARIKA

He's told you I came here in search of you.

OSSIAN

Yes, what a shame you missed me. I was at the office. I thought you knew.

MARIKA

You were here in spirit. You've been here for months in spirit. Your body has been at the office or at home or on the streets between, hewing strictly to its schedule. Your spirit has been here. Do you think I haven't noticed?

OSSIAN

It isn't true, so how can you have noticed?

MARIKA

From your growing distaste for our life together. "Distaste" is much too weak a word.

"Disgust" is better. "Nausea" is better still.

OSSIAN

I can't even guess what you mean.

MARIKA

All right I'll tell you if you'll listen.

OSSIAN

I'll listen, but I warn you. What you say is your responsibility. What I hear is mine.

MARIKA

Why don't you hear what I tell you?

OSSIAN

I will. But once I've heard it, it belongs to me. Fair warning.

MARIKA

Fair warning. Will your landlord kindly leave us?

OSSIAN

Why?

MARIKA

I'd rather speak with you in private.

OSSIAN

I don't keep any secrets from Malachi. Whatever I discover at the basis of my life, I reveal to him exhaustively. Before long, all the world knows.

MARIKA *(Looking at Malachi's papers)*

You've begun another book.

OSSIAN

I've finished it.

MARIKA

You've finished it? How can you have finished it?

OSSIAN

Women misconceive artistic creation the same way they misconceive sexual union. A woman thinks the act of love should be like a massage, but in its purest form it ought to be a flash of lightning. My third novel is written. It's a vile thing, a tumor, a putrescence. I regret having brought it into being. But I had no choice. You'd killed me.

I had to wash my body for the coffin.

MARIKA

When did you write this book? It isn't true. You've been losing me and I've been losing you — we've both been losing this third thing, our marriage. But you hadn't started writing.

OSSIAN

Malachi and I have only just set pen to paper, but the book is written. All the rest is just mechanics.

MARIKA *(Waving a hand at Malachi)*

And now this creature's going to reap whatever profit's in this new thing you've created.

OSSIAN

I've recorded it, and truly that's degenerate enough. But you've created it. You're the book's first mover and its subject.

MARIKA

Make Malachi get out of here. *(To Malachi)* Ossian will repeat to you, in due course, everything I say that compromises either me or him. You'll make your money, but for now get out.

OSSIAN

I don't know who you think should profit from the book. Should I? I should be flayed until the shirt falls off my back in strips, and then my skin. You have some claim to some part of the profits. Do you want them?

MARIKA

Come away with me where we can talk, or make him leave.

OSSIAN

Go on, Malachi.

MALACHI *(To Marika, fawning but with genuine respect)*

May I bring you a glass? I'll just leave it and withdraw again. Your husband's using yours.

MARIKA *(To Ossian)*

Are you drinking wormwood?

OSSIAN

Not yet.

MALACHI

Let me bring you a glass.

MARIKA

Get out and stay out

MALACHI *(As he backs out of the room)*

You remind me of the days when, half a century ago, I was a waiter at the Grand Hotel. It was a pleasure taking orders from people who knew how to give them. At your will, then...

(He goes softly through the door and closes it behind him.)

MARIKA

Ossian, I don't know if you remember, but you said some very silly things when you proposed to me. I was touched that such a brilliant man should talk so foolishly. It showed me that your heart was full. You said that in the little house we'd have, the coffee grinder wouldn't rasp and growl. All coffee grinders rasp and growl, but ours would play sweet music. For these last months, though, you couldn't bear to hear me grind the coffee. The only way that you could stand the noise was to grind it yourself.

OSSIAN

You ground it at me.

MARIKA

No I didn't. Why would I do that?

OSSIAN

I don't know yet. I'll find out the reason when I've written it.

MARIKA

In our first year and our second year, you came into my room sometimes to sit with me — not share my bed but just to sit while I combed out my hair or sewed garments that I couldn't take outside into the parlor. You stopped coming in.

OSSIAN

I showed more modesty on your behalf than you yourself. You ought to thank me.

MARIKA

You've made me learn to walk on eggshells. I used to live quite comfortably inside my body.

OSSIAN

Yes. Your comfort was cacophonous.

MARIKA

The quieter I got the sharper you pricked up your ears. Should I thank you for that?

OSSIAN

Should I have slit my eardrums?

MARIKA

During our engagement you wrote me that you longed to kiss my milk teeth. In the past few months you've seen they weren't my baby teeth. They're the teeth that I'll have till they drop from my head. I use these teeth to chew with. That revolts you.

You can hardly bear to eat with me.

OSSIAN

I've never liked eating in company. Eating is a functional necessity, and not a pretty one.

MARIKA

You used to like to share your meals with me.

OSSIAN

I did at first. Then, later on, I didn't. I couldn't help my changing feelings — or returning feelings — little as I welcomed them. Still, I take responsibility for how I feel. You can't help it, any more than I can, that you have to eat, but nonetheless you have to be responsible. The world demeans us by giving us animal needs, but we demean ourselves still further if we fight shy of our guilt for them. To do so is undignified.

MARIKA

It's human.

OSSIAN (*As if she'd made his point*)

It's human. That's the perfect word.

MARIKA

My "humanness" is in your novel, I suppose. No doubt quite prominently.

OSSIAN

You know it has to be. It is there, if I'm foul enough to leave it in. It belongs there.

MARIKA

If you feel it belongs there, then you'll dose yourself with wormwood till you think I crunched my radishes and slurped my soup just to offend your sensibilities.

OSSIAN

You chewed at me. You swallowed at me.

MARIKA

No I didn't, Ossian.

OSSIAN

Maybe not. It's possible that someone might, though, isn't it? It wouldn't be against the laws of nature?

MARIKA

Someone might. I didn't.

OSSIAN

Then perhaps you didn't. Perhaps it wasn't you. I only know that it was Marika.

MARIKA

I am Marika. Marika is my name and I claim it.

OSSIAN

It's been used by other people. I can use it too.

MARIKA

You can use the name. I can't prevent you. You can use me too. You will. I only want to know that you know there's a difference between Marika and "Marika."

(She has used herself to illustrate the first, Malachi's papers to illustrate the second)

OSSIAN

The distinction doesn't interest me. It confuses me the way a pair of ears confuses hearing, the way a pair of eyes confuses sight. Think how a noise confuses smell. Surely the world's fragrances are better served by recreation in the mind than being snuffed up through a fungus on the face.

MARIKA

What's the Marika you're writing like?

OSSIAN

She's someone to be reckoned with. She's helpless. She's a liar.

MARIKA

I'm not a liar, Ossian.

OSSIAN

Marika's a walking lie.

MARIKA

She's your lie. She's your fiction.

OSSIAN

She's my fiction, yes, but not my lie. She's the world's lie, and my only truth. The deepest truth I'm learning.

MARIKA

I married you because I knew it wouldn't last. I loved you, but I knew it wouldn't last. I didn't want it to. That's why we haven't had children. You kept on saying we should wait until we'd saved more money, but that wasn't your real reason. You were terrified of art's destructive power, and you made a grand spasmodic gesture toward escaping from it. Look at who you married, though. An artist. One as gifted as yourself, whose addiction was as fatal. You knew we'd both go back.

OSSIAN

You went back. You came here with a painter. Before that you'd been to a gallery. That was your true infidelity. You were going back to painting.

MARIKA

I always knew, for years before I met you, that I'd have to marry someone. I didn't have the courage to throw off all the things that I'd been raised to want. I couldn't leave my father's house and forge into the world to paint. I couldn't have my inmost feelings scrutinized in public.

OSSIAN

Yes, the public. Their praise is as degrading as their mockery. They have the right to criticize, of course — the clay we mould in is their flesh. But, still, they stare and we can't turn away our faces.

MARIKA

I loved you and respected you, but underneath I knew you'd force me out into the open on my own, the former wife of the notorious Ossian Borg. You'd leave me nothing to protect from the ravages of my own talent. I'd be a painter by default. No one could blame me for a choice I hadn't made. I would have had no choice. And now it's come to pass. Half Europe's going to read your book. I'll be an outcast only fit to stand outside the world, at my easel. You've forced me into freedom. Deep down I always knew that's what would happen. Ossian, you knew too. I want you to admit it. Then I'll leave you here with Malachi and "Marika."

OSSIAN

If you'd been someone else than who you are, we would have stayed together.

MARIKA

You knew who I was the day you saw my paintings.

OSSIAN

You promised to reform.

MARIKA

I couldn't, any more than you could, and you knew it. Can't you see that?

OSSIAN

In the Back Room I invent what I see. I don't choose what to invent, though. I invent according to the world's laws. The world being what it is, what I invent is what no one would choose.

MARIKA

I'm beginning to see how I should paint this room. Perhaps I've painted it already. Yes, the painting's finished. I haven't dabbed the oils on the canvas yet, but that's just mechanics. Next I'm going to paint you.

OSSIAN

No. I paint myself. I'm matter for my pen, not for your brushes.

MARIKA

You're matter for my brushes if I'm matter for your pen. I'll be painting you for years to come — perhaps as often as I paint myself. We'll paint each other searchingly.

OSSIAN

And shamelessly. And pitilessly.

MARIKA

Yes.

OSSIAN

It isn't any worse than we deserve.

MARIKA

We're invulnerable, aren't we, in a certain way. For ordinary people, people like Johan, any suffering they undergo is suffering and nothing else. They have no alchemy to turn it to advantage.

OSSIAN *(Fills her liqueur glass with wormwood and slides it toward her)*

You'll want to try this if you're going to paint me.

MARIKA

I don't need to drink delusion.

OSSIAN

It will let you see more clearly. Paranoia's no distortion when it only shows the truth. I am your enemy, as you are mine. When we pledged ourselves one to the other, we struck a truce. We laid our weapons at each other's feet. Maybe we disarmed ourselves to save ourselves from suicide. In any case, we made peace. One makes peace with one's enemies, not with one's friends.

MARIKA

To you, then, Ossian.
(She drinks half the absinthe and hands him the glass.)

OSSIAN

To you.
(He finishes the glass and sets it down. Marika picks up her hat from the table.)
May I take a feather from your hat?
(She hands him her hat. He pulls out a large feather and returns the hat. Marika goes out through the door, leaving it open. Ossian takes a penknife from his pocket, makes a quill pen of the feather and substitutes it for Malachi's pen, which he puts back into the drawer.

Malachi comes in. Ossian moves to his place at the table. He sits facing Downstage. Malachi, with soft, deliberate movements — calculated not to interfere with Ossian's train of thought — fills the glass with wormwood, recaps the bottle, and sits himself down with his writing materials. He dips the new pen in the ink and sits patiently waiting as Ossian continues to look outward.
Slow fade to black.)

Close of play

Ionescapes

A tribute to Eugene Ionesco

Scenes from
• The Lesson • The Bald Soprano • Rhinoceros • Amedee • The Leader

The play script published in this volume includes narratives developed at Bangalore Little Theatre as part of the workshop production.

FOR
PRITHAM KUMAR

CHARACTERS IN THE PLAY

First performed By Bangalore Little Theatre in association with Alliance de Francaise in October 2002

The ensemble of artists in the SPOT 2001 group played multiple parts from a selection of scenes of plays by Eugene Ionesco.
ANKURA RANADE, APARNA RAO, ASHWIN R, BIDDAPA KC CHARULATA KASHINATH, INDU MURALI, JACOB CHERIAN, MANSI SONI, NANDAN SINGH, NILANJAN PAUL CHOUDHURY, NISHA KUMAR, PAYAL SHAH, PRANAV KUMAR, RONALD PHILIP, SABREEN BAKER, SAZANA JAYADEVA, SUDARSHAN RAJAGOPAL, TANISHA PEREIRA, VENKATARAGHAVAN, VISHAL SACHDEV, VRINDA SAMARTHA, YESHWANTHI

Trainer-Facilitators
PRITHAM KUMAR
MADHU SMRITI SHUKLA

The play designed and directed by
VIJAY PADAKI

LANGUAGE NOTES

Angrez hain kya?:
  Are they English?

Dekhne mey toh desi lagte hain.
  They look native.

Dekhne mey toh pataa nahin lagta ki yeh
  From their looks we cannot make out if

yahaan ke desi hain ki vilayati desi.
  they are local natives or foreign natives.

Angrezi mey zara koshish Karen?Shall we try English?
  Zaroor.Sure

PART 1
INTRODUCTION AND THE LESSON

The play opens with a bare stage. In the round. A floor stage, with seating on four sides, perhaps raised. Above the acting area is suspended an elaborate mobile that remains as the "updrop" throughout the play.

Enter four Chorus members from two directions, meeting at the perimeter, circling it in two groups, in two opposite directions. They begin to speak – in French. They are shown as C below.

C1

It is customary to begin by greeting the audience.

C2

Greetings, ladies and gentlemen!

C3

And a very good evening to you.

C4

And welcome to this evening's programme on the life and work of Eugene Ionesco.

ALL 4

The life and work of Eugene Ionesco.

(By now the mobiles have been lit. The acting area is clear. Two members of the chorus continue with the introduction, in French, while the others look at the audience intently.)

C1

(In French) Eugene Ionesco. 1912-1994. On the day of his death in Paris, his first two plays, The Bald Soprano and The Lesson were given their 11,944th consecutive performance in the city.

C2

In 1948 Ionesco started taking lessons in English. He was to say later...

C3

(In English, tugging at his sleeve) Professor, Professor...

C2

(In French) Now leave me alone! Let me be! What is the meaning of this?

C4

(Joining C3) No, Professor, no!

C2

(In French) You are going too far!

C3

(Getting C2 to look at the audience) It's not Paris!

C4

Not Pondicherry either.

C1

It looks like they have a point.

C2

Anglais?

C4

Whatever that means.

C1

English, maybe.

C2

(In Hindi) Angrez hain kya?

C3

Dekhne mey toh desi lagte hain.

C4

Dekhne mey toh pataa nahin lagta ki yeh yahaan ke desi hain ki vilayati desi.

C1

Angrezi mey zara koshish Karen?

C2

You mean, shall we try English?

C1

Zaroor. Maney, of course.

C2

In 1948 Ionesco started taking lessons in English. He was to say later...

C3

(Tugging at his sleeve) Professor, Professor...

C1

(Looking at the audience) It's working!

C4

They are Angrez in desi clothing after all.

C1

Or the other way about.

C4

You are sounding absurd.

C1

Thank you. We can continue, then. *(Signals to C2)*

C2

You are introduced to an author from Gujarat. Meet Sureshbhai Shah. Imaginary name, of course. He wrote the first absurd play in Gujarati. Hmmm.

C1

You are introduced to an author from Karnataka. Meet Seshagiri Rao. Nom de plume again. He wrote the first absurd play in Kannada *(Pause)*.

C3

How absurd! Many of us delight in writing in a style that we would fondly like to believe is the absurd form. Is that all there is to the "theatre of the absurd"?

C4

The great pioneers of the form that we call the absurd did not apply the label on themselves. It came from the keen observations of critics, art historians and social analysts. There was something common to all their observations, strong agreements on patterns seen, and the term Theatre of the Absurd seemed both apt and timely. The label stuck.

C2

Just how powerful an influence the absurdist movement was is reflected in the hundreds of Sureshbhai Shahs and Seshagiri Raos in countries all around the world who believe that their portfolios are incomplete without at least one piece of writing in the so-called absurd form.

C1

And drama companies all over the world who must include in their repertoires an absurd play as early as possible in the company's life.

C2

It must be recognized that under the surface of form there must always be substance – even if that substance is a profound non-substance, a pointlessness, a conspicuous monotony, a surrealistic disjointedness in images.

C1

There might be more elegant descriptions of absurdist writing.

C4

And there is no dearth of scholarship on the subject. What is too easily overlooked is that this form of writing – indeed the movement itself – was largely a European phenomenon. Two great wars within the space of one generation must be a traumatic experience for any society.

C3

For this to happen to a society that had great pride in its civilization and all that the great civilization offered to its membership – art and culture, education and learning, science and technology, as well as the products of science and technology in instruments of war – could only result in depression, disillusionment and disenchantment without parallel.

C4

And a pessimism about solutions from the social institutions revered thus far.

(By now the cast of the first play are ready. The actor playing the Professor steps in.)

PROFESSOR

The Europeans, and especially the French, with their finely developed artistic sensibility, chose to sublimate their feelings according to their own genius. A touch of the bizarre, a dash of the ridiculous, yes, but never for themselves. For no form can be sustained by such pat recipes. The novelty wears off. Above all else, plays in the absurd form were explorations in abstraction to go way beyond the familiar allegorical abstractions so cleverly constructed in countless plots throughout the history of drama...

(Another woman is tugging at his sleeve. She is to become the Maid in the play.)

MAID

Professor, Professor...

PROFESSOR

Now, leave me alone! Let me be! What's the meaning of this? *(Continues with his speech)*...Yet, it must be clear that every idea, every form, is a product of its time. The elements of linguistics and of comparative philology...

MAID

No, Professor, no! You mustn't do that!

PROFESSOR

Marie, you're going too far!

MAID

Professor, especially not philology. Philology leads to calamity...
(A third woman, reacts to this. She is the Pupil in the same play.)

PUPIL

Calamity? That's hard to believe.

PROFESSOR

That's enough now. Get out of here.

MAID

All right, Professor, all right. But you can't say that I didn't warn you. Philology leads to calamity!

PROFESSOR

I'm an adult, Marie!

MAID

As you wish *(Withdraws)*

PROFESSOR

Let's continue, miss

PUPIL

Yes, Professor.

PROFESSOR

I want you to listen now with the greatest possible attention to a lecture I have prepared...

PUPIL

Yes, Professor!

(A pause. The three actors return to their narrator roles.)

PROFESSOR

(To audience) Sorry, we slipped into that a trifle prematurely. It needed just a wee bit more of an introduction. We get carried away. Ionesco has done that to so many of us. That was from...? *(Seeks response from the audience.)* That's right. The Lesson. An almost automatic inclusion in any contemporary drama course, it has been estimated that the script has had the largest number of translations and productions of all post-war European short plays.

C1

The Lesson shares with at least six other Ionesco plays the interplay of three themes that seemed to be the playwright's fascination at that time.

C2

The critique of language; the haunting presence of death; and the transformation of personalities as if by a force unseen, even unknown to them, mocking smug notions of human will.

C3

The critique of formal language appears in one form or the other in the writing of all authors in the absurd tradition. Martin Esslin sums this up most neatly in his introductory essay on Absurd Drama. Quote:

C4

In the aftermath of the great war...The spread of spiritual emptiness in the outwardly prosperous and affluent societies of Western Europe and the United States. There can be no doubt: for many intelligent and sensitive human beings the world of the mid twentieth century has lost its meaning and has simply ceased to make sense.

C2

Previously held certainties have dissolved, the firmest foundations for hope and optimism have collapsed. Suddenly man sees himself faced with a universe that is both frightening and illogical – in a word, absurd.

MAID

In 1948 Ionesco started taking lessons in English. He was to say later...

PROFESSOR

"I learned not English but some astonishing truths – that, for example, there are seven days in a week, something I already knew; that the floor is down, the ceiling up, things I knew as well, perhaps, but that I had never seriously thought about or had forgotten, and that seemed to me, suddenly, as stupefying as they were indisputably true..."

PUPIL

(Moving towards him) I have a great thirst for knowledge, Professor. My parents want me to get an education.

PROFESSOR

Then, if you'll permit me, pardon me, please, I do think that we ought to get to work. We have scarcely any time to lose.

PUPIL

Oh, but certainly, Professor, I want to. I beg you to.

PROFESSOR

I am only your humble servant.

PUPIL

Oh, Professor...
(They slip into the scene: EXCERPT 1)

PUPIL

Oh, really, Sir...

PROFESSOR

Well, then, if you... er... we... er... we, that is to say, I... I'll begin by giving you a brief examination on the knowledge you have acquired so far, and that will give me an idea about the lines we must work on in the future...Good.

How do you feel about your perception of plurality?

PUPIL

A little vague... and confused.

PROFESSOR

Fine. We'll have a look at it.
(He rubs his hands. The MAID comes in, and this seems to upset the PROFESSOR She makes for the dresser, looks for something inside, and lingers.)

Well now, Mademoiselle, what do you say to doing a little arithmetic... that is, if you don't mind...

PUPIL

But of course, Sir. Willingly. I couldn't ask for anything better.

PROFESSOR

It's a fairly new science, a modern science: strictly speaking I suppose one should call it a method rather than a science... It is also a therapy. *(To the Maid)* Marie, have you finished?

MAID

Yes, Sir. I've found the plate I was looking for. I'm just going...

PROFESSOR

Hurry up, please, and go back to the kitchen.

MAID

Yes, Sir, I'm going. *(Offers to go on, then)* I beg pardon, Sir, but please be careful. Not too much excitement.

PROFESSOR

Don't be so ridiculous, Marie. Nothing whatever to worry about.

MAID

But that's what you always say.

PROFESSOR

Your insinuations are entirely without foundation. I am perfectly capable of behaving myself. After all, I'm old enough.

MAID

That's just it, Sir. You'd much better not start Mademoiselle off with arithmetic. That arithmetic never did anyone any good. It makes you tired and upsets you.

PROFESSOR

I'm too old for that now. And what business is it of yours, anyway? It's my concern and I know what I'm doing. You've no right to be here, anyway.

MAID

Very well, Sir. But don't you go telling me I didn't warn you.

PROFESSOR

I'm not interested in your warnings, Marie.

MAID

Monsieur must do as he thinks best.
(She goes out.)

PROFESSOR

I'm sorry about this stupid interruption, Mademoiselle... You must understand that this poor woman is always afraid I shall tire myself. She's worried about my health.

PUPIL

Oh, it really doesn't matter, Sir. It shows she's devoted to you. She must be very fond of you. Good servants are hard to find.

PROFESSOR

She really goes too far. It's stupid to be so nervous. Let us get back to our arithmetical sheep.

PUPIL

I follow you, Sir.

PROFESSOR *(wittily)*
But without leaving your seat, I see!

PUPIL *(appreciating the joke)*
Just like you, Sir!

PROFESSOR
Good! Then shall we arithmetize a little?

PUPIL
I'll be pleased to, Sir.

PROFESSOR
Then perhaps you wouldn't mind telling me...

PUPIL
Not in the slightest, Sir. Please go ahead.

PROFESSOR
What do one and one make?

PUPIL
One and one make two.

PROFESSOR *(astounded by his pupil's erudition)*
But that's very good indeed! You're extremely advanced in your studies. You'll have very little difficulty in passing all your Doctorate examinations.

PUPIL
I'm very pleased to hear it, Sir. Especially from you.

PROFESSOR
Let us proceed a little further. What do two and one make?

PUPIL
Three.

PROFESSOR
Three and one?

PUPIL
Four.

PROFESSOR
Four and one?

PUPIL
Five.

PROFESSOR
Five and one?

PUPIL
Six.

PROFESSOR
Six and one?

PUPIL
Seven.

PROFESSOR
Seven and one?

PUPIL
Eight.

PROFESSOR
Seven and one?

PUPIL
Still eight.

PROFESSOR
Very good answer. Seven and one?

PUPIL
Eight again.

PROFESSOR
Excellent. Perfect. Seven and one?

PUPIL
Eight for the fourth time. And sometimes nine.

PROFESSOR
Magnificent! You're magnificent! Sublime! My warmest congratulations, Mademoiselle. There's no point in going on. You're quite first- rate at addition. Let's try subtraction. Just tell me, that is if you're not too tired, what is left when you take three from four?

PUPIL
Three from four... three from four?

PROFESSOR
Yes, that's it. I mean to say, what is four minus three?

PUPIL
That makes... seven?

PROFESSOR
I'm extremely sorry to have to contradict you, but three from four doesn't make seven. You're muddling it up. Three plus four makes seven, take three away from four and that makes...? It's not a question of adding up, now you have to subtract.

PUPIL (*struggling to understand*)
Yes... I see...

PROFESSOR
Three from four, that makes... How many... how many?

PUPIL
Four?

PROFESSOR

No, Mademoiselle. That's not the answer.

PUPIL

Three then?

PROFESSOR

That's not right either, Mademoiselle...I really do beg your pardon... It doesn't make three... I'm terribly sorry...

PUPIL

Four minus three... three away from four...four minus three? I suppose it woudn't make ten?

PROFESSOR

Oh, dear me, no, Mademoiselle. But you mustn't rely on guesswork, you must reason it out. Shall we try and solve it together? Would you be so good as to count?

PUPIL

Yes, Sir. One... two... three...

PROFESSOR

You know how to count all right? You can count up to what number?

PUPIL

I can count up to... infinity.

PROFESSOR

That's impossible.

PUPIL

Up to sixteen, then.

PROFESSOR

That's quite far enough. We must all recognize our limitations. Go on counting then, if you please.

PUPIL

One... two... and then after two comes three... four...

PROFESSOR

Stop there, Mademoiselle. Which number is the greater? Three or four?

PUPIL

Er... three or four? Which is the greater? The greater number out of three and four? In what way greater?

PROFESSOR

Some numbers are smaller than others. In the greater numbers there are more units than there are in the smaller ones.

PUPIL

Than in the smaller numbers... ?

PROFESSOR
Unless, of course, the small numbers are made up of smaller units. If all the units are very small, there may be more units in the small numbers than in the big ones... that is, if they are not the same units...

PUPIL
In that case small numbers can be bigger than big numbers?
(Pause. The actors turn Narrators.)

PROFESSOR
Ionesco's instructions to the actors in The Lesson are in great detail. The pupil is described as a well brought up girl...

MAID
She seems to be a well-brought-up girl, polite, but lively, gay, dynamic; a fresh smile is on her lips. During the course of the play she progressively loses the lively rhythm of her movement and her carriage, and becomes withdrawn. From gay and smiling she becomes progressively sad and morose; from very lively at the beginning, she becomes more and more fatigued and somnolent. Towards the end of the play her face must clearly express a nervous depression; her way of speaking shows the effects of this, her tongue becomes thick, words come to her memory with difficulty. Firm and determined at the beginning, so much so as to appear to be almost aggressive, she becomes more and more passive, until she is almost a mute and inert object, seemingly inanimate in the Professor's hands.

PUPIL
And the Professor... Excessively polite, very timid...

MAID
Excessively polite, very timid, his voice deadened by his timidity, very proper, very much the teacher. During the course of the play his timidity will disappear progressively, imperceptibly; and the lewd gleams in his eyes will become a steady devouring flame in the end. From the manner that is inoffensive at the start, the Professor becomes more and more sure of himself, more and more nervous, aggressive, dominating, until he is able to do as he pleases with the Pupil, who has become, in his hands, a pitiful creature. Of course, the voice of the Professor must change too, from thin and reedy, to stronger and stronger, until at the end it is extremely powerful, ringing, sonorous...

PROFESSOR *(Changing)*
I realize that this is not easy, it is very, very abstract...
(They slip into the scene: EXCERPT 2)

PROFESSOR
It's obvious that it's very very abstract... but if you've not mastered these elementary propositions, how can you ever hope to make mental calculations such as – and this would be as easy as winking to an average

engineer — such as this, for example: how much is three billion, seven hundred and fifty- five million, nine hundred and ninety-eight thousand, two hundred and fifty-one, multiplied by five billion, one hundred and sixty-two million, three hundred and three thousand, five hundred and eight?

PUPIL *(very rapidly)*

That makes nineteen quintillion, three hundred and ninety quadrillion, two trillion, eight hundred and forty-four billion, two hundred and nineteen million, a hundred and sixty-four thousand, five hundred and eight...

PROFESSOR *(astonished)*

No, I don't think so. That must make nineteen quintillion, three hundred and ninety quadrillion, two trillion, eight hundred and forty-four billion, two hundred and nineteen million, a hundred and sixty-four thousand, five hundred and nine!

PUPIL

No... five hundred and eight.

PROFESSOR *(growing more and more astonished and calculating in his head)*

Yes... you're right, by Jove... yours is the correct product... *(Muttering unintelligibly)*... quintillion, quadrillion, trillion, billion, million... *(Distinctly)*... a hundred and sixty four thousand, five hundred and eight... *(Stupefied)*

But how did you arrive at that, if you don't understand the principle of arithmetical calculation?

PUPIL

Oh! It's quite easy, really! As I can't depend on reasoning it out, I learned off by heart all the possible combinations in multiplication.

PROFESSOR

But the combinations are infinite!

PUPIL

I managed to do it, anyway!

PROFESSOR

It's quite astounding!... Nevertheless, you will allow me to point out to you that I am by no means satisfied, Mademoiselle, and you must do without my congratulations. In mathematics, and particularly in arithmetic, what counts — and you can't get away from counting in arithmetic — what counts above all else is the ability to understand what you are doing. You ought to have found the answer by a dual process of inductive and deductive mathematical reasoning, and that is the way you should arrive at all your answers.

Memory is a deadly enemy to mathematics, and though it has certain advantages, arithmetically speaking, memory is a bad thing! And so I'm not at all happy about you... that just won't do at all...

PUPIL *(crushed)*

No, Sir.

PROFESSOR

We'll forget about it for the moment. Let us pass on to another kind of exercise.

PUPIL

Yes, Sir.

MAID *(as she comes in)*

Hmm... Hmm... Monsieur!

PROFESSOR *(not hearing her)*

It's a great pity, Mademoiselle, that you're not more advanced in special mathematical studies...

MAID *(pulling at his sleeve)*

Monsieur! Monsieur!

PROFESSOR

I am afraid you can hardly think of going in for the total Doctorates...

PUPIL

Oh, what a shame, Sir!

PROFESSOR

At least, if you... *(To the Maid)* Leave me alone, Marie, what on earth do you think you're up to? Back to the kitchen and your washing up! Go on! Go on!

(To the Pupil) Still, we'll try to prepare you at least for the partial Doctorate...

MAID *(pulling at his sleeve)*

Monsieur... Monsieur!

PROFESSOR *(to the Maid)*

For goodness' sake, let me go! Leave me alone! What the devil do you mean by this?

(To the Pupil) I think perhaps I should teach you then, if you're really anxious to go in for the partial Doctorate...

PUPIL

Oh yes, please, Sir!

PROFESSOR

The essentials of linguistics and comparative philology.

MAID

No, Monsieur, no! I shouldn't do that if I were you!

PROFESSOR

Marie! Now you're really going too far!

MAID

Of all things, not philology, Monsieur. Philology is the worst of all...

PUPIL *(surprised)*

The worst of all? *(Smiling a little stupidly)* What a funny thing to say!

PROFESSOR *(to the Maid)*

That's too much! Leave the room!

MAID

Very well, Monsieur, very well. But you won't say I didn't warn you! Philology is the worst of all!

PROFESSOR

I am over twenty one, Marie!

PUPIL

Yes, Sir.

MAID

Monsieur must do as he thinks best!
(She goes out.)

PROFESSOR

Shall we go on, Mademoiselle?

PUPIL

Please, Sir.

PROFESSOR

Thanks to which you may, in fifteen minutes, acquire the fundamental principles of the comparative and linguistic philology of the neo-Spanish languages.

PUPIL *(Clapping her hands)*

Oh, Sir! How marvellous!

PROFESSOR *(with authority)*

Silence! What's all this for?

PUPIL

I'm sorry, Sir! (Slowly, she lays her hands on the table again.)

PROFESSOR

Silence!

(He gets up and paces the room, his hands behind his back; now and again he stops, in the centre of the room or close to the Pupil, and reinforces his words with a gesture of the hand; he declaims his lecture, but without overdoing it; the PUPIL follows him with her eyes, sometimes with difficulty, for she is always having to twist her head round; once or twice, but no more, she makes a complete turn.)

PROFESSOR
Spanish, then, Mademoiselle, is actually the mother language that gave birth to all the neo-Spanish languages, among which we include Spanish, Latin, Italian, our own French, Portuguese, Rumanian, Sardinian or Sardanapalus, Spanish and neo-Spanish, and in certain respects we may add Turkish, itself however rather closer to Greek, which is after all perfectly logical, Turkey being Greece's neighbour and Greece lying closer to Turkey than either you or I. This is but one more illustration of a very important linguistic law, according to which geography and philology are twins...You may take notes, Mademoiselle.

PUPIL *(in a strangled voice)*
Yes, Sir!

MAID *(As Narrator)*
He underlines his words with gestures of his hand. He orates. His tone changes. His voice hardens. The pupil appears progressively unwell, in pain, slipping into a stupor.

EXCERPT 3

PROFESSOR *(Continuing))*
At last! In order to learn to distinguish all these different languages, I've already said that there's nothing like practice... Let us proceed in an orderly fashion. I'll try to teach you all the possible translations of the word 'Knife'.

PUPIL
All right, if you want to... After all...

PROFESSOR *(calling the Maid)*
Marie! Marie! She can't hear me. Marie... Marie! Oh really! Marie!
(He opens the door on the right.) Marie!
(He goes out. The PUPIL is left alone for a few moments, gazing blankly into space, quite besotted. The Professor's voice is heard offstage in a shrill voice.)

PROFESSOR *(Offstage)*
Marie! What's the meaning of this? Why don't you come when I want you? You know you must come at once when I call!
(He returns, followed by the MAID.)
I'm the one who gives the orders here, you understand? *(Pointing to the Pupil)* This girl doesn't understand anything. Not a thing!

MAID
Don't take on so, Monsieur. Think what it may lead to! It'll take you further than you want to go, you'll go too far, you know.

PROFESSOR

I shall be able to stop in time.

MAID

I've heard that before. I'd like to see it happen.

PUPIL

I've got the toothache.

MAID

What did I tell you! It's beginning! That's the sign!

PROFESSOR

What sign! What do you mean? What are you talking about?

PUPIL (*in a flabby voice*)

Yes, what are you talking about? I've got the toothache.

MAID

It's the final symptom! The worst symptom!

PROFESSOR

Nonsense! Nonsense! Nonsense!

(*The MAID makes to leave.*)

Don't go away like that! I called you to go and look for the knives: the Spanish, neo-Spanish, Portuguese, French, Oriental, Rumanian, Sardanapolitan, Latin, and Spanish ones.

MAID (*severely*)

You needn't think you can count on me.

(*She goes out. The PROFESSOR makes a movement of protest, then controls himself, rather at a loss. Suddenly he remembers.*)

PROFESSOR

Ah!

(*He goes quickly to the drawer and finds a big imaginary knife; he takes hold of it and brandishes it exultantly.*)

Here's one, Mademoiselle, here's a knife! It's a pity this is the only one; but we'll try to make it serve for all the languages! All you need to do is to pronounce the word Knife in each language, while you stare closely at the object and imagine it belongs to the language you're using.

PUPIL

I've got the toothache.

PROFESSOR (*almost chanting, melodiously*)

Come along then: Say Kni, like Kni, Fff, like Fff... and watch it carefully, don't take your eyes off it...

PUPIL

What is it, this one? French, Italian, or Spanish?

PROFESSOR
It doesn't matter... It doesn't matter to you. Say: Kni.

PUPIL
Kni.

PROFESSOR
Fff... Watch it. *(He moves the knife in the Pupil's face.)*

PUPIL
Fff...

PROFESSOR
Again... Watch it.

PUPIL
No! No! No more! That's enough! I've had enough! Besides, my teeth ache and my feet ache and my head aches...

PROFESSOR
Knife... Watch it... Knife... Watch it... Knife... Watch it...

PUPIL
You make my ears ache, too. What a voice you've got! How piercing it is!

PROFESSOR
Say Knife... Kni... Fff...

PUPIL
No, no! My ears are aching. I'm aching all over...

PROFESSOR
I'll soon have those little ears of yours off, my poppet, and then they won't hurt you any more...

PUPIL
Ow! You're hurting me, it's you that's hurting me...

PROFESSOR
Look, come along now, quick, say it after me: Kni...

PUPIL
Oh, if I must... Kni... Knife... *(A moment of lucidity, of irony)*
It must be neo-Spanish...

PROFESSOR
If you like. Yes, it is neo-Spanish, but hurry up now... we haven't got much time...
And what are you insinuating! You're getting too big for your shoes!
(The PUPIL is growing more and more tired and desperate, more and more tearful, at once distraught and exalted.)

PUPIL
Ah!

PROFESSOR

Say it again, watch it. *(Like a child)* Knifey... Knifey... Knifey... Knifey...

PUPIL

Oh, my head!... My head aches...
(She passes her hand over each part of her body as she names it, like a caress.)
My eyes...

PROFESSOR *(Like a child)*

Knifey... Knifey... Knifey...

MAID *(As Narrator)*

As described by the playwright, they are both standing: she, against the table, he, still brandishing his invisible knife, almost beside himself, and turning about her as though executing a sort of scalp dance. Nothing is exaggerated and the Professor's steps are barely indicated.

(The next lines are along with action from the Professor and the pupil.)

In due course the knife descends in a spectacular blow. The Professor remains standing in front of the collapsed body. There is a second slash of the knife, bottom to top. After that a noticeable convulsion shakes his whole body.

EXCERPT 4 – TO END

PROFESSOR

Come along, Mademoiselle, the lesson is over now... You can go home...
You can pay me another time... Oh! She's dead... dead... And with my knife... She's dead... It's terrible.
(The Maid enters the scene.)
I don't know you, Marie.

MAID

Then you are satisfied with your pupil? She has profited by your lesson?

PROFESSOR *(hiding his knife behind his back)*

Yes, the lesson is over now... but... she's still here... she won't go away...

MAID *(not sympathetically)*

Well, well!

PROFESSOR *(quivering)*

It wasn't me... I didn't do it, Marie... No... I promise you... it wasn't me, Marie... dear Marie...

MAID

Who was it, then? Who else was it? Me?

PROFESSOR

I don't know... perhaps...

MAID

Or was it the cat?

PROFESSOR

Perhaps it was... I don't know...

MAID

And it's the fortieth time today! And every day it's the same story! Every day! Aren't you ashamed of yourself? At your age too! But you'll go and make yourself ill! There soon won't be any more pupils left. And a good thing, too.

PROFESSOR *(vexed)*

It's not my fault! She wouldn't learn anything! She was disobedient! She was a bad pupil! She didn't want to learn!

MAID

Liar!

PROFESSOR *(approaching the Maid slyly, his knife behind his back)*

It's none of your business!

(He tries to strike her a terrific blow, but she seizes his wrist and twists it; the PROFESSOR drops his knife.)

Forgive me!

(The MAID strikes the PROFESSOR twice, forcibly and noisily, so that he falls to the ground on his behind, snivelling.)

MAID

You little murderer! Revolting little swine! Wanted to do that to me, did you?!

I'm not one of your blessed pupils!

(She hauls him up by the back of his collar, picks up his skull-cap, and puts it back on his head. He is afraid of being hit again and protects himself with his elbow, like a child.)

Put the knife back where you found it! Come along now!

(The PROFESSOR puts it back in the drawer of the dresser and comes back to her.)

And I gave you proper warning, too, only a little while ago! Arithmetic leads to Philology, and Philology leads to Crime...

PROFESSOR

You said Philology was the worst of all!

MAID

It all comes to the same in the end.

PROFESSOR

I didn't quite understand. I thought when you said Philology was the worst of all, you just meant it was the hardest to learn...

MAID

Liar! Old fox, you! A clever man like you doesn't go making mistakes about what words mean. You can't fool me!

PROFESSOR *(sobbing)*

I didn't kill her on purpose!

MAID

At least you're sorry you did it?

PROFESSOR

Oh yes, Marie, I swear I am.

MAID

I can't help feeling for you. Come now! You're not a bad boy after all! We'll try and do what we can to put things right. But don't you go doing it again... Why, it could give you heart trouble...

PROFESSOR

Yes, Marie!... What are we going to do then?

MAID

We're going to bury her... at the same time as the other thirty-nine... forty coffins that'll be. We're going to call in the undertakers and my boyfriend Auguste, the priest... we're going to order the wreaths...

PROFESSOR

Yes. Thank you, Marie, very much.

MAID

Come to think of it, it's hardly worth asking Auguste, not when you're a bit of a priest yourself, when you want to be, if you can believe what people say.

PROFESSOR

Not too dear, though, the wreaths. She hasn't paid for her lesson.

MAID

Don't worry... better just cover her with her apron, anyway; she's not decent. And then we'll carry her away.

PROFESSOR

Yes, Marie, yes. *(He covers her.)* Could get sent to jail for this, you know... forty coffins... Just think of it... People would be surprised... What if anyone asks us what's inside?

MAID

Don't go making trouble for yourself. We'll say they're empty. Besides, no one will ask any questions. They're used to it.

PROFESSOR

All the same...

MAID *(bringing out an armband bearing a device, the Swastika perhaps)*

Here you are! Put this on, if you're frightened, then you won't have anything to be afraid of.

(She puts it round his arm.)...It's political.

PROFESSOR

Thank you, thank you, kind Marie. I feel much safer like that... You're a good girl, Marie.

You're a good girl, Marie... very faithful...

MAID

That's all right. Well, Monsieur? Are you ready?

PROFESSOR

Yes, Marie. I'm ready.

(The MAID and the PROFESSOR take the young girl's body, one by the shoulders, the other by the legs, and go towards the door on the right.)

Take care, now, not to hurt her.

(They go out. The stage is empty a few moments. A ring at the bell at the door on the left.)

VOICE OF THE MAID

I'm coming! Just a minute!

(She appears as at the beginning of the play and goes towards the door. The bell rings a second time.)

MAID *(to herself)*

She's in a good old hurry, this one!

(Aloud) Coming!

(She goes to the door and opens it.)

Good Morning, Mademoiselle. Are you the new pupil? You've come for your lesson? The professor's expecting you. I'll go and tell him you've arrived. He'll be down in a minute! Come in, won't you, Mademoiselle!

Close of play

PART 2
THE BALD SOPRANO

The Chorus resets the scene. Actors for Part 2 stand by, the chorus seating them.

C1

Oh, how do you do? *(To the others)* It's the Fire Chief!

FIRE CHIEF

Good evening, ladies and gentlemen... Good evening, Mrs. Smith. You appear to be angry.

MRS. SMITH

Oh!

MR. SMITH

Oh, my dear, this is not so serious. The Fire Chief is an old friend of the family. His mother courted me, and I knew his father. He asked me to give him my daughter in marriage if ever I had one. And he died waiting.

C2

Ionesco had a perfect ear for nonsense. At the drop of a banality he would weave an enchanting series of non sequiturs. Beneath the blitz of hilarious language, though, there were the unmistakable themes...

C3

For instance, the opening scene of The Bald Soprano.

C4

A middle class English interior, with English armchairs. An English evening. Mr. Smith, an Englishman, seated in his English armchair and wearing English slippers, is smoking his English pipe and reading an English newspaper, near an English fire.

C3

He is wearing English spectacles, and a small gray English moustache. Beside him, in another English armchair, Mrs. Smith, an Englishwoman, is darning some English socks.

C2

A long moment of English silence. The English clock strikes 17 English strokes.

(The actors slip into the scene.)

MRS. SMITH

There, it's nine o'clock. We've drunk the soup, and eaten the fish and chips, and the English salad. The children have drunk English water. We've eaten well this evening. That's because we live in the suburbs of London, and because our name is Smith.

(Mr. Smith, continuing to read, clicks his tongue)

MRS. SMITH

Potatoes are very good fried in fat. The salad oil was rancid. The oil from the grocer at the corner is better quality oil than the oil from the grocer across the street. It is even better than the oil from the grocer at the bottom of the street. However, I prefer not to tell them that their oil is bad.

(Mr. Smith, continuing to read, clicks his tongue)

MRS. SMITH

However, the oil from the grocer at the corner is still the best.

(Mr. Smith, continuing to read, clicks his tongue)

MRS. SMITH

Mary did the potatoes very well this evening. The last time she did not do them well. I do not like them when they are well done.

FIRE CHIEF *(As narrator)*

She continues with her weather report. He continues to read his newspaper, clicking his tongue in response.

MRS. SMITH

Yogurt is excellent for the stomach, the kidneys, the appendicitis, and apotheosis. It was Dr. Mackenzie-King who told me that. He's the one who takes care of the children of our neighbours, the Johns. He's a good doctor. One can trust him. He never prescribes any medicine that he has not tried out on himself first. Before operating on Parker, he had his own liver operated on first, although he was not the least bit ill.

MR. SMITH

But how does it happen that the doctor pulled through while Parker died?

MRS. SMITH

Because the operation was successful in the doctor's case, and it was not in Parker's.

MR. SMITH

Then Mackenzie is not a good doctor. The operation should have succeeded with both of them, or else both should have died.

MRS. SMITH

Why?

MR. SMITH

A conscientious doctor must die with his patient if they can't get well together. The captain of a ship goes down with the ship into the briny deep. He does not survive alone.

FIRE CHIEF *(As narrator)*

A moment of silence. The clock strikes seven times. Silence. The clock strikes three times. Silence. The clock doesn't strike.

MR. SMITH

Tch tch, it says here that Bobby Watson died.

MRS. SMITH

My god, the poor man! When did he die?

MR. SMITH

Why do you pretend to be astonished? You know very well that he's been dead these past two years. Surely you remember that we attended his funeral a year and a half ago.

MRS. SMITH

Oh yes, of course I do remember. I remembered it right away. But I don't understand why you were yourself so surprised to see it in the paper.

MR. SMITH

It wasn't in the paper. It's been three years since his death was announced. I remembered it through an association of ideas.

MRS. SMITH

What a pity! He was so well preserved.

MR. SMITH

He was the handsomest corpse in Great Britain. He didn't look his age. Poor Bobby, he's been dead for four years, and he was still warm. A veritable living corpse. And how cheerful he was!

MRS. SMITH

Poor Bobby.

MR. SMITH

Which poor Bobby do you mean?

MRS. SMITH

It is his wife that I mean. She is called Bobby too, Bobby Watson. Since they both had the same name, you could never tell one from the other when you saw them together. It was only after his death that you could really tell which was which. And there are still people today who confuse her with the deceased, and offer their condolences to him. Do you know her?

MR. SMITH

I met her only once, by chance, at Bobby's burial.

MR. SMITH

She's still young. She might very well remarry. She looks so well in mourning.

MRS. SMITH

But who would take care of the children? You know very well that they have a boy and a girl. What are their names?

MR. SMITH

Bobby and Bobby, like their parents. Bobby Watson's uncle, old Bobby Watson, is a rich man and very fond of the boy. He might very well pay for Bobby's education.

MRS. SMITH

That would be proper. And Bobby Watson's aunt, old Bobby Watson, might very well, in her turn, pay for the education of Bobby Watson, Bobby Watson's daughter. That way Bobby, Bobby Watson's mother, could remarry. Has she anyone in mind?

MR. SMITH

Yes, a cousin of Bobby Watson's.

MRS. SMITH

Who? Bobby Watson?

MR. SMITH

Yes, of course. Bobby Watson.

MRS. SMITH

Why, Bobby Watson, the son of old Bobby Watson, the late Bobby Watson's other uncle.

MR. SMITH

No, it's not that one, it's someone else. It's Bobby Watson, the son of old Bobby Watson, the late Bobby Watson's aunt.

FIRE CHIEF *(As narrator)*

The clock strikes five times. A long silence. Mary, the maid, enters briskly.

MARY *(entering)*

I'm the maid. I have spent a very pleasant afternoon. I've been to the cinema...

(The next excerpt is enacted, including the arrival of the Martins, the Maid's exit and the travel dialogue of the Martins.)

MARY *(entering)*

I'm the maid. I have spent a very pleasant afternoon. I've been to the cinema with a man and I've seen a film with some women. After the cinema, we went to drink some brandy and milk and then read the newspaper.

MRS. SMITH

I hope that you've spent a pleasant afternoon, that you went to the cinema with a man and that you drank some brandy and milk.

MR. SMITH

And read the newspaper.

MARY

Mr. and Mrs. Martin, your guests, are at the door. They were waiting for me. They didn't dare come in by themselves. They were supposed to have dinner with you this evening.

MRS. SMITH

Oh, yes. We were expecting them. And we were hungry. Since they didn't put in an appearance, we were going to start dinner without them. We've had nothing to eat all day. You should not have gone out!

MARY

But it was you who gave me permission.

MR. SMITH

We didn't do it on purpose.

(Mary bursts into laughter, then she bursts into tears. Then she smiles.)

MARY

I bought me a chamber pot.

MRS. SMITH

My dear Mary, please open the door and ask Mr. and Mrs. Martin to step in. We will change quickly.

(Mr. and Mrs. Smith exit right. Mary opens the door at the left by which Mr. and Mrs. Martin enter.)

MARY

Why have you come so late! You are not very polite. People should be punctual. Do you understand? But it down there, anyway, and wait, now that you're here.

(She exits. Mr. and Mrs. Martin sit facing each other, without speaking. They smile timidly at each other. The dialogue which follows must be spoken in voices that are drawling, monotonous, a little singsong, without nuances.)

MR. MARTIN

Excuse me, madam, but it seems to me, unless I'm mistaken, that I've met you somewhere before.

MRS. MARTIN

I, too, sir. It seems to me that I've met you somewhere before.

MR. MARTIN

Was it, by any chance, at Manchester that I caught a glimpse of you, madam?

MRS. MARTIN

That is very possible. I am originally from the city of Manchester. But I do not have a good memory, sir. I cannot say whether it was there that I caught a glimpse of you or not!

MR. MARTIN

Good God, that's curious! I, too, am originally from the city of Manchester, madam!

MRS. MARTIN

That is curious!

MR. MARTIN

Isn't that curious! Only I, madam, I left the city of Manchester about five weeks ago.

MRS. MARTIN

That is curious! What a bizarre coincidence! I,too, sir,I left the city of Manchester about five weeks ago.

MR. MARTIN

Madam, I took the 8: 30 morning train which arrives in London at 4:45.

MRS. MARTIN

That is curious! How very bizarre! And what a coincidence! I took the same train, sir, I too.

MR. MARTIN

Good Lord, how curious!

FIRE CHIEF (*As narrator*)

After much exchange of data and deep reflection on their meaning, the two look at each other in silence. The clock strikes 29 times. Mr. Martin moves towards Mrs. Martin, who also rises quietly.

MR. MARTIN

Then, dear lady, I believe there can be no doubt about it, we have seen each other before, and you are... my own wife. Elizabeth, I have found you again!

FIRE CHIEF (*As narrator*)

The clock strikes once, very loud, loud enough to make the audience jump. The Martins do not hear it.

MRS. MARTIN

Donald, it's you, darling!

FIRE CHIEF (*As narrator*)

They sit together, their arms around each other, and fall asleep. The clock strikes several more times.

(Mary, on tiptoe, a finger to her lips, enters quietly and addresses the audience, providing the link to the next excerpt.)

MARY

Elizabeth and Donald are now too happy to be able to hear me. I can therefore let you in on a secret. Elizabeth is not Elizabeth, Donald is not Donald. And here is the proof: the child that Donald spoke of is not Elizabeth's daughter, they are not the same person. Donald's daughter has one white eye and one red eye like Elizabeth's daughter. Whereas Donald's child has a white right eye and a red left eye, Elizabeth's child has a red right eye and a white left eye! Thus all of Donald's system of deduction collapses when it comes up against this last obstacle which destroys his whole theory. In spite of the extraordinary coincidences which seem to be definitive proofs, Donald and Elizabeth, not being the parents of the same child, are not Donald and Elizabeth. It is in vain that he thinks he is Donald, it is in vain that she thinks she is Elizabeth. He believes in vain that she is Elizabeth. She believes in vain that he is Donald. They are sadly deceived. But who is the true Donald? Who is the true Elizabeth? Who has any interest in prolonging this confusion? I don't know. Let's not try to know. Let's leave things as they are.

(She takes several steps toward the door, then returns and says to the audience)
My real name is Sherlock Holmes. *(She exits.)*
(Mr. and Mrs. Smith enter)

MRS. SMITH

Good evening, dear friends! Please forgive us for having made you wait so long. We thought that we should extend you the courtesy to which you are entitled and as soon as we learned that you had been kind enough to give us the pleasure of coming to see us without prior notice we hurried to dress for the occasion.

MR. SMITH *(Annoyed)*

We've had nothing to eat all day. And we've been waiting four whole hours for you. Why have you come so late?
(They sit. Mr. Smith lets the fire chief in)
Oh, how do you do? *(To the others)* It's the Fire Chief.

FIRE CHIEF

Good evening, ladies and gentlemen... Good evening, Mrs. Smith. You appear to be angry.

MRS. SMITH

Oh!

MR. SMITH

Oh, my dear, this is not so serious. The Fire Chief is an old friend of the family. His mother courted me, and I knew his father. He asked me to give him my daughter in marriage if ever I had one. And he died waiting.

MR. MARTIN

That's neither his fault, nor yours.

FIRE CHIEF

Well, what's it all about?

MRS. SMITH

My husband was claiming...

MR. SMITH

No, it was you who was claiming.

MR. MARTIN

Yes, it was she.

MRS. MARTIN

No, it was he.

FIRE CHIEF

(To the audience) I have stories to tell. I must get to them fast.

(To the others) Excuse me, but I can't stay long. I should like to remove my helmet, but I haven't time to sit down.

(He sits down, without removing his helmet.) I must admit that I have come to see you for another reason. I am on official business.

MRS. SMITH

And what can we do for you, Mr. Fire Chief?

FIRE CHIEF

I must beg you to excuse my indiscretion... *(terribly embarrassed)* Uhm... *(He points a finger at the Martins)* you don't mind...in front of them...

MRS. MARTIN

Say whatever you like.

MR. MARTIN

We're old friends. They tell us everything.

MR. SMITH

Speak.

FIRE CHIEF

Eh, well... is there a fire here?

MRS. SMITH

Why do you ask us that?

FIRE CHIEF

It's because... pardon me... I have orders to extinguish all the fires in the city.

MRS. MARTIN

All?

FIRE CHIEF

Yes, all .

MRS. SMITH *(confused)*

I don't know...I don't think so. Do you want me to go and look?

MR. SMITH *(sniffing)*

There can't be one here. There's no smell of anything burning.

FIRE CHIEF *(aggrieved)*

None at all? You don't have a little fire in the chimney, something burning in the attic or in the cellar? A little fire just starting, at least?

MRS. SMITH

I am sorry to disappoint you but I do not believe there's anything here at the moment. I promise that I will notify you when we do have something.

FIRE CHIEF
Please don't forget. it would be a great help.

MRS. SMITH
That's a promise.

FIRE CHIEF *(to the Martins)*
And there's nothing burning at your house either?

MRS. MARTIN
No, unfortunately.

MR. MARTIN *(to the Fire Chief)*
Things aren't going so well just now.

FIRE CHIEF
Very poorly. There's been almost nothing, a few trifles - a chimney, a barn. Nothing important. It doesn't bring in much. And since there are no returns, the profits on output are very meager.

MR. SMITH
Times are bad. That's true all over. It's the same this year with business and agriculture as it is with fires, nothing is prospering.

MR. MARTIN
No wheat, no fires.

FIRE CHIEF
No floods either.

MRS. SMITH
But there is some sugar.

MR. SMITH
That's because it is imported.

MRS. MARTIN
It's harder in the case of fires. The tariffs are too high!

FIRE CHIEF
All the same, there's an occasional suffocation by gas, but that's unusual too. For instance, a young woman asphyxiated herself last week. She had left the gas on.

MR. SMITH
These confusions are always dangerous!

MRS. SMITH
Did you go to see the match dealer?

FIRE CHIEF
There's nothing doing there. He is insured against fires.

MR. MARTIN
Why don't you go see the Vicar of Wakefield, and use my name?
(They go on to the next excerpt.)

MRS. SMITH

Mr. Fire Chief, since you are not too pressed, stay a little while longer. You would be doing us a favor.

FIRE CHIEF

Shall I tell you some stories?

MRS. SMITH

Oh, by all means, how charming of you. *(She kisses him.)*

MR. SMITH, MRS. MARTIN, MR. MARTIN *(together)*

Yes, yes, some stories. Hurrah!
(They applaud)

MR. SMITH

And what is even more interesting is the fact that firemen's stories are all true, and they're based on experience.

FIRE CHIEF

I speak from my own experience. Truth, nothing but the truth. No fiction.

MR. MARTIN

That's right. Truth is never found in books, only in life.

MRS. SMITH

Begin!

MR. MARTIN

Begin!

MRS. MARTIN

Be quiet, he is beginning.

FIRE CHIEF *(coughs slightly several times)*

Excuse me, don't look at me that way. You embarrass me. You know that I am shy.

MRS. SMITH

Isn't he charming! *(She kisses him)*

FIRE CHIEF

I'm going to try to begin anyhow. But promise me that you won't listen.

MRS. MARTIN

But if we don't listen to you we won't hear you.

FIRE CHIEF

I didn't think of that!

MRS. SMITH

I told you, he's just a boy.

MR. MARTIN AND MR. SMITH

Oh, the sweet child! *(They kiss him)*

MRS. MARTIN
Chin up!

FIRE CHIEF
Well, then! *(He coughs again in a voice shaken by emotion)*
"The Dog and the Cow," an experimental fable. Once upon a time another cow asked another dog: "Why have you not swallowed your trunk?"
"Pardon me," replied the dog, "it is because I thought that I was an elephant."

MRS. MARTIN
What is the moral?

FIRE CHIEF
That's for you to find out.

MR. SMITH
He's right.

MRS. SMITH
Tell us another.

FIRE CHIEF
(To audience) Another. Then another. The others try their hand at storytelling too, but nobody can tell a story like the Fire Chief.

MRS. MARTIN
Tell us another.

FIRE CHIEF
Oh, no, it's too late.

MR. MARTIN
Tell us one, anyway.

FIRE CHIEF
I'm too tired.

MR. SMITH
Please do us a favor.

MR. MARTIN
I beg you.

FIRE CHIEF
No.

MRS. MARTIN
You have a heart of ice. We're sitting on hot coals.

MRS. SMITH
I implore you!

FIRE CHIEF
Right-ho.

MR. SMITH *(in Mrs. Martin's ear)*
He agrees! He's going to bore us again.

MRS. MARTIN
Shhh.

MRS. SMITH
No luck. I was too polite.

FIRE CHIEF
"The Headcold." My brother-in law had, on the paternal side, a first cousin whose maternal uncle had a father-in-law whose paternal grandfather had married as his second wife a young native whose brother he had met on one of his travels, a girl of whom he was enamored and by whom he had a son who married an intrepid lady pharmacist who was none other than the niece of an unknown fourth-class Petty Officer of the Royal Navy and whose adopted father had an aunt who spoke Spanish fluently and who was, perhaps, one of the granddaughters of an engineer who died young, himself the grandson of the owner of a vineyard which produced mediocre wine, but who had a second cousin, a stay-at-home, a sergeant-major, whose son had married a very pretty young woman, a divorcee, whose first husband was the son of a loyal patriot who, in the hope of making his fortune, had managed to bring up one of his daughters so that she could marry a footman who had known Rothschild, and whose brother, after having changed his trade several times, married and had a daughter whose stunted great-grandfather wore spectacles which had been given him by a cousin of his, the brother-in-law of a man from Portugal, natural son of a miller, not too badly off, whose foster-brother had married the daughter of a former country doctor, who was himself a foster-brother of the son of a forrester, himself the natural son of another country doctor, married three times in a row, whose third wife...

MR. MARTIN
I knew that third wife, if I'm not mistaken. She ate chicken sitting on a hornet's nest.

FIRE CHIEF
It's not the same one.

MRS. SMITH
Shhh!

FIRE CHIEF
As I was saying...whose third wife was the daughter of the best midwife in the region and who, early left a widow...

MR. SMITH
Like my wife.

FIRE CHIEF

...Had married a glazier who was full of life and who had, by the daughter of a station master, a child who had burned his bridges...

MRS. SMITH

His britches?

MR. MARTIN

No his bridge game.

FIRE CHIEF

And had married an oyster woman, whose father had a brother, mayor of a small town, who had taken as his wife a blonde schoolteacher, whose cousin, a fly fisherman...

MR. MARTIN

A fly by night?

FIRE CHIEF

...Had married another blonde schoolteacher, named Marie, too, whose brother was married to another Marie, also a blonde schoolteacher...

MR. SMITH

Since she's blonde, she must be Marie.

FIRE CHIEF

...And whose father had been reared in Canada by an old woman who was the niece of a priest whose grandmother, occasionally in the winter, like everyone else, caught a cold.

MRS. SMITH

A curious story. Almost unbelievable.

MR. MARTIN

If you catch a cold, you should get yourself a colt.

MR. SMITH

It's a useless precaution, but absolutely necessary.

MRS. MARTIN

Excuse me, Mr. Fire Chief, but I did not follow your story very well. At the end, when we got to the grandmother of the priest, I got mixed up.

MR. SMITH

One always gets mixed up in the hands of a priest.

MRS. SMITH

Oh yes, Mr. Fire Chief, begin again. Everyone wants to hear.

FIRE CHIEF

Ah, I don't know whether I'll be able to. I'm on official business. It depends on what time it is.

MRS. SMITH

We don't have the time, here.

FIRE CHIEF

But the clock?

MR. SMITH

It runs badly. It is contradictory, and always indicates the opposite of what the hour really is.

(Enter Mary)

MARY

Madam...sir...

MRS. SMITH

What do you want?

MR. SMITH

What have you come in here for?

MARY

I hope, madam and sir will excuse me...and these ladies and gentlemen too...I would like...I would like to tell you a story, myself.

MRS. MARTIN

What is she saying?

MR. MARTIN

I believe that our friends' maid is going crazy...she wants to tell us a story, too.

MARY

I'm going to recite a poem, then, is that agreed? It is a poem titled "The Fire" in honor of the Fire Chief:

The Fire
   The polypoids were burning in the wood.
   A stone caught fire
   The castle caught fire
   The forest caught fire
   The men caught fire
   The women caught fire
   The birds caught fire
   The fish caught fire
   The water caught fire
   The sky caught fire
   The ashes caught fire
   The smoke caught fire
   The fire caught fire
   Everything caught fire
   Caught fire, caught fire.
(She recites the poem while the Smiths are pushing her offstage.)

MRS. MARTIN
That sent chills up my spine...

MR. MARTIN
And yet there's a certain warmth in those lines...

FIRE CHIEF
I thought it was marvellous.

MRS. SMITH
All the same...

MR. SMITH
You're exaggerating...

FIRE CHIEF
Just a minute...I admit...all this is very subjective...but this is my conception of the world. My world. My dream. My ideal... And now this reminds me that I must leave. Since you don't have the time here, I must tell you that in exactly three-quarters of an hour and sixteen minutes, I'm having a fire at the other end of the city. Consequently, I must hurry. Even though it will be quite unimportant.

MRS. SMITH
What will it be? A little chimney fire?

FIRE CHIEF
Oh, not even that. A straw fire and a little heart- burn.

MR. SMITH
Well, we're sorry to see you go.

MRS. SMITH
You have been very entertaining.

MRS. MARTIN
Thanks to you, we have passed a truly Cartesian quarter of an hour.

FIRE CHIEF (*moving towards the door, then stopping*)
Speaking of that – the bald soprano?
(*General silence, embarrassment.*)

MRS. SMITH
She always wears her hair in the same style.

FIRE CHIEF
Ah! Then goodbye, ladies and gentlemen.

MR. MARTIN
Good luck, and a good fire!
(*The Maid links the next excerpt.*)

MAID
(*To audience*) And the evening rolls on. The conversation rolls on. They speak to each other, at each other, above each other and beneath each other.

Presently, there is a certain nervous irritation. The strokes of the clock are nervous too. The four speak in the manner of bougainvillea creepers racing up an old tree. It races to the end of the play.

(In the Bangalore production the Maid moved Down-Centre. With her back to the audience she "conducted" the following cacophony of the four other actors.)

MR. SMITH

I'm going to live in my cabana among my cacao trees.

MRS. MARTIN

Cacao trees on cacao farms don't bear coconuts, they yield cocoa! Cacao trees on cacao farms don't bear coconuts, they yield cocoa! Cacao trees on cacao farms don't bear coconuts, they yield cocoa.

MRS. SMITH

Mice have lice, lice haven't mice.

MR. SMITH

Groom the goose, don't goose the groom.

MRS. MARTIN

The goose grooms.

MRS. SMITH

Groom your tooth.

MR. MARTIN

Groom the bridegroom, groom the bridegroom.

MR. SMITH

Seducer seduced!

MRS. MARTIN

Scaramouche!

MR. SMITH

I've been goosed.

MR. MARTIN

Robert!

MR. SMITH

Browning!

MRS. MARTIN AND MR. SMITH

Rudyard.

MRS. SMITH AND MR. MARTIN

Kipling.

MRS. MARTIN AND MR. SMITH

Robert Kipling!

MRS. SMITH AND MR. MARTIN

Rudyard Browning!

MRS. MARTIN
Silly gobblegobblers, silly gobblegobblers.

MR. MARTIN
Marietta, spot the pot!

MRS. SMITH
Krishnamurti, Krishnamurti, Krishnamurti!

MR. SMITH
The pope elopes! The pope's got no horoscope. The horoscope's bespoke.

MRS. MARTIN
Bazaar, Balzac, bazooka!

MR. MARTIN
Bizarre, beaux-arts, brassieres!

MR. SMITH
A, e, i, o, u, a, e, i, o, u, a, e, i, o, u, i!

MRS. MARTIN
B, c, d, f, g, l, m, n, p, r, s, t, v, w, x, z!

MR. MARTIN
From sage to stooge, from stage to serge!

MRS. SMITH *(imitating a train)*
Choo, choo, choo, choo, choo, choo, choo, choo, choo, choo, choo!

MR. SMITH
It is!

MRS. MARTIN
Not!

MR. MARTIN
That!

MRS. SMITH
Way!

MR. SMITH
It is!

MRS. MARTIN
O!

MR. MARTIN
Ver!

MRS. SMITH
Here!
(The lights go off. In the darkness we hear them speak all together, completely infuriated, in an increasingly rapid rhythm. They are screaming in each others' ears.)

ALL TOGETHER

It's not that way, it's over here, it's not that way, it's over here, it's not that way, it's over here, it's not that way, it's over here!

(The words cease abruptly. The lights come on again. Mr. and Mrs. Smith and the Maid have left the stage. Mr. and Mrs. Martin are seated like the Smiths at the beginning of the play. The play begins again with the Martins, who say exactly the same lines as the Smiths in the first scene, while the curtain softly falls.

Or there is a slow fade out.)

MRS. MARTIN

There, it's nine o'clock. We've drunk the soup, and eaten the fish and chips, and the English salad. The children have drunk English water. We've eaten well this evening. That's because we live in the suburbs of London, and because our name is Smith.

(Mr. Martin, continuing to read, clicks his tongue)

MRS. MARTIN

Potatoes are very good fried in fat. The salad oil was rancid. The oil from the grocer at the corner is better quality oil than the oil from the grocer across the street. It is even better than the oil from the grocer at the bottom of the street. However, I prefer not to tell them that their oil is bad.

(Mr. Martin, continuing to read, clicks his tongue)

MRS.MARTIN

However, the oil from the grocer at the corner is still the best.

(Mr. Martin, continuing to read, clicks his tongue)

MRS.MARTIN

Mary did the potatoes very well this evening. The last time she did not do them well. I do not like them when they are well done.

Close of play

PART 3
RHINOCEROS

The Chorus resets the scene.

There are (at least) eighteen characters in the original play. The ensemble cast touches on some of the characters. They stand in a semi-circle at the periphery and step in to play the selected scenes.

C1

The real test of validity for an art form is the test of time. Fads come and go, here today, gone tomorrow. A form sustains when it is part of a movement.

C2

And a movement is characterized by parallel developments in other art forms – in fine arts, in poetry, in sculpture and music and dance, as well as in film and in the graphic arts.

C3

Within the theatre, too, the explorations in script are incomplete without the parallel explorations in the use of stage space, the use of body and voice, and innovations in all the technical departments of stagecraft to produce wholly new sensory experiences.

C4

Making a beginning in the early fifties the theatre of the absurd appears to have succeeded in meeting all the criteria of a movement. It certainly seems to have stood the test of time.

C2

By all the traditional standards of critical appreciation of drama, these plays are not only abominably bad, they do not even deserve the name of drama.

HOUSEWIFE

If the critical touchstones of traditional drama did not apply to these plays, this must surely have been due to a difference in objective, the use of different artistic means, to the fact, in short, that these plays were both creating and applying a different contract of drama.

LOGICIAN

Samuel Beckett, Jean Genet, Arthur Adamov and Eugene Ionesco are often regarded as the vanguard of the movement in the early fifties. All of their first performances took place in Paris – the crucible for new art forms in post-war Europe. Interestingly, three of the four were exiles in Paris from other parts of Europe.

GROCER (OR WIFE)

Of the four, Ionesco was undoubtedly the most fertile and original and, in spite of a streak of clowning and fun in his work, one of the most profound.

PROPRIETOR

Ionesco never failed to denounce forces that destroy the individuality of man, the oppressive social systems that force man "to become a rhinoceros".

WAITRESS

The 1960 script The Rhinoceros has become a modern classic, developed on the premise that people will go to any length to keep up with the Joneses.

JEAN (AS NARRATOR)

At first it is simply a baffling sight in the town square.
(Slipping into the role of Jean in the play)
Well, of all things!
The actors spring into action. An excerpt of the play is enacted.

JEAN *(also averting his head a little, but very much awake)*
Well, of all things! *(He sneezes.)*

HOUSEWIFE *(Her provisions scattered on the ground round her)*
Well of all things! *(She sneezes.)*
(The OLD GENTLEMAN, GROCER'S WIFE and GROCER are up-stage, re-opening the door of the Grocer's shop that the Old Gentleman has closed behind him.)

ALL THREE

Well, of all things !

JEAN

Well, of all things! *(To Berenger)* Did you see that?
(The noise of the rhinoceros and its trumpeting is now far away; the people are still staring after the animal, all except for Berenger who is still apathetically seated.)

ALL *(except Berenger)*
Well, of all things !

BERENGER *(to Jean)*
It certainly looked as if it was a rhinoceros. It made plenty of dust.
(He takes out a handkerchief and blows his nose.)

HOUSEWIFE

Well, of all things! Gave me such a scare.

GROCER *(to the Housewife)*
Your basket...and all your things...
(The Old Gentleman approaches the lady, bending to pick up her things scattered about the stage. He greets her gallantly, raising his hat.)

PROPRIETOR

Really, these days, you never know...

WAITRESS
Fancy that !

OLD GENTLEMAN *(to the Housewife)*
May I help you pick up your things?

HOUSEWIFE *(to the Old Gentleman)*
Thank you, how very kind! Do put on your hat. Oh, it gave me such a scare!

LOGICIAN
Fear is an irrational thing. It must yield to reason.

WAITRESS
It's already out of sight.
(Continuing as Narrator) But, then, there must be a logical explanation for all things. The logician in the group is going to explain what a syllogism is...
(The next excerpt of the play is enacted)

LOGICIAN *(to the Old Gentleman)*
I'm going to explain to you what a syllogism is.

OLD GENTLEMAN
Ah yes, a syllogism.

JEAN *(to Berenger)*
I can't get over it! It's unthinkable! *(Berenger yawns)*

LOGICIAN
A syllogism consists of a main proposition, a secondary one, and a conclusion.

OLD GENTLEMAN
What conclusion?
(The Logician and the Old Gentleman go out)

JEAN
I just can't get over it.

BERENGER
Yes, I can see you can't. Well, it was a rhinoceros. All right, so it was a rhinoceros! It's miles away by now... miles away...

JEAN
But you must see it's fantastic! A rhinoceros loose in this town, and you don't bat an eyelid! It shouldn't be allowed! *(Berenger yawns)*
Put your hand in front of your mouth!

BERENGER
Yais...yais...It shouldn't be allowed. It's dangerous. I hadn't realized. But don't worry about it, it won't get us here.

JEAN
We ought to protest to the Town Council! What's the Council there for?

BERENGER (*yawning, then quickly putting his hand to his mouth*)
Oh, excuse me...perhaps the rhinoceros escaped from the zoo.

JEAN
You're day-dreaming.

BERENGER
But I'm wide awake.

JEAN
Awake or asleep, it's the same thing.

BERENGER
But there is some difference.

JEAN
That's not the point.

BERENGER
But you just said being awake and being asleep were the same thing...

JEAN
You didn't understand. There's no difference between dreaming awake and dreaming asleep.

BERENGER
I do dream. Life is a dream.

JEAN
You're certainly dreaming when you say the rhinoceros escaped from the zoo!

BERENGER
I only said perhaps.

JEAN
Because there's been no zoo in our town since the animals were destroyed in the plague...ages ago.

BERENGER (*with the same indifference*)
Then perhaps it came from a circus.

JEAN
What circus are you talking about?

BERENGER
I don't know...some travelling circus.

JEAN
You know perfectly well that the Council banned all travelling performers from the district. There haven't been any since we were children.

BERENGER (*trying unsuccessfully to stop yawning*)
In that case, maybe it's been hiding ever since in the surrounding swamps?

JEAN

The surrounding swamps! The surrounding swamps! My poor friend, you live in a thick haze of alcohol.

BERENGER *(naively)*

That's very true...it seems to mount from my stomach...

JEAN

It's clouding your brain! Where do you know of any surrounding swamps? Our district is known as 'Little Castille' because the land is so arid.

BERENGER *(surfeited and pretty weary)*

How do I know, then? Perhaps it's been hiding under a stone? Or maybe it's been nesting on some withered branch?

JEAN

If you think you're being witty, you're very much mistaken! You're just being a bore with... with your stupid paradoxes. You're incapable of talking seriously!

PROPRIETOR *(as Narrator)*

Meanwhile, another of the beasts has thundered by. There is much consternation. Was it an Asiatic rhinoceros or an African one? Did it have one horn or two of them?

WAITRESS

Well, let's say there were two. Does the single horned one come from Asia?

OLD GENT

No, it's the one from Africa with two I think.
(The next excerpt is enacted)

OLD GENTLEMAN

No. It's the one from Africa with two, I think.

PROPRIETOR

Which is two-horned?

GROCER

It's not the one from Africa.

GROCER'S WIFE

It's not easy to agree on this.

OLD GENTLEMAN

But the problem must be cleared up.

LOGICIAN *(emerging from his isolation)*

Excuse me gentlemen for interrupting. But that is not the question. Allow me to introduce myself...

HOUSEWIFE *(coming out of the cafe in tears)*

He's a logician.

PROPRIETOR
Oh! A logician, is he?

OLD GENTLEMAN *(introducing the Logician to Berenger)*
My friend, the Logician.

BERENGER
Very happy to meet you.

LOGICIAN *(continuing)*
Professional Logician. My card. *(He shows his card)*

BERENGER
It's a great honour.

GROCER
A great honour for all of us.

PROPRIETOR
Would you mind telling us then, sir, if the African rhinoceros is single-homed.

OLD GENTLEMAN
Or bicorned...

GROCER'S WIFE
And is the Asiatic rhinoceros bicorned...

GROCER
Or unicorned.

LOGICIAN
Exactly, but that is not the question. Let me make myself clear.

GROCER
But it is still what we want to find out.

LOGICIAN
Kindly allow me to speak, gentlemen.

OLD GENTLEMAN
Let him speak!

GROCER'S WIFE *(to the Grocer, from window)*
Give him a chance to speak.

PROPRIETOR
We're listening, sir.

LOGICIAN *(to Berenger)*
I'm addressing you in particular. But all the others present as well.

GROCER
Us as well...

LOGICIAN

You see, you have got away from the problem which instigated the debate. In the first place you were deliberating whether or not the rhinoceros which passed by just now was the same one that passed by earlier, or whether it was another. That is the question to decide.

GROCER

Yes, but how?

LOGICIAN

Thus: you may have seen on two occasions a single rhinoceros bearing a single horn...

GROCER *(repeating the words, as if to understand better)*

On two occasions a single rhinoceros...

PROPRIETOR *(doing the same)*

Bearing a single horn...

LOGICIAN

Or you may have seen on two occasions a single rhinoceros with two horns.

OLD GENTLEMAN *(repeating the words)*

A single rhinoceros with two horns on two occasions...

LOGICIAN

Exactly. Or again, you may have seen one rhinoceros with one horn, and then another also with a single horn.

GROCER'S WIFE *(from window)*

Ha, ha...

LOGICIAN

Or again, an initial rhinoceros with two horns, followed by a second with two horns...

PROPRIETOR

That's true.

LOGICIAN

Now, if you had seen...

GROCER

If we'd seen...

OLD GENTLEMAN

Yes, if we'd seen...

LOGICIAN

If on the first occasion you had seen a rhinoceros with two horns...

PROPRIETOR

With two horns...

LOGICIAN
And on the second occasion, a rhinoceros with one horn...

GROCER
With one horn...

LOGICIAN
That would not be conclusive either.

OLD GENTLEMAN
Even that wouldn't be conclusive.

PROPRIETOR
Why not?

GROCER'S WIFE
 Oh, I don't get it at all!

GROCER
Shoo! Shoo!
(The Grocer's Wife shrugs her shoulders and withdraws from her window.)

LOGICIAN
For it is possible that since its first appearance, the rhinoceros may have lost one of its horns, and that the first and second transit were still made by a single beast.

BERENGER
I see, but...

OLD GENTLEMAN *(interrupting Berenger)*
Don't interrupt !

LOGICIAN
It may also be that two rhinoceroses both with two horns may each have lost a horn.

OLD GENTLEMAN
That is possible.

PROPRIETOR
Yes, that's possible.

BERENGER
Why not? But in any case...

OLD GENTLEMAN *(to Berenger)*
Don't interrupt.

LOGICIAN
If you could prove that on the first occasion you saw a rhinoceros with one horn, either Asiatic or African...

OLD GENTLEMAN
Asiatic or African...

LOGICIAN
And on the second occasion a rhinoceros with two horns...

GROCER
One with two...

LOGICIAN
No matter whether African or Asiatic...

OLD GENTLEMAN
African or Asiatic...

LOGICIAN
We could then conclude that we were dealing with two different rhinoceroses, for it is hardly likely that a second horn could grow sufficiently in a space of a few minutes to be visible on the nose of a rhinoceros.

OLD GENTLEMAN
It's hardly likely.

LOGICIAN (*enchanted with his discourse*)
That would imply one rhinoceros either Asiatic or African...

OLD GENTLEMAN
Asiatic or African...

LOGICIAN
...and one rhinoceros either African or Asiatic.

PROPRIETOR
African or Asiatic.

BERENGER
Er...yais.

LOGICIAN
For good logic cannot entertain the possibility that the same creature be born in two places at the same time...

OLD GENTLEMAN
Or even successively.

LOGICIAN (*to Old Gentleman*)
Which was to be proved.

BERENGER (*to LOGICIAN*)
That seems clear enough. But it doesn't answer the question. (*The Chorus steps in to take the narration forward.*)

C2
While the debate goes on, it is becoming clear that it is the people of the town turning into rhinoceroses.

C1
More and more of them, at a faster and faster rate. Those still retaining the human form are afraid to step out.

WAITRESS

Meanwhile, Berenger is shaken out of his complacence when he finds that his friend Jean is one of those turned into a rhinoceros.

JEAN

He decides to do something about it. He goes to a government office to register a formal report.

WAITRESS

The people in the office are not easily convinced he has a case. They think he should go out for a breath of fresh air.

BERENGER

Go out? I suppose I'll have to...
(The next excerpt is enacted.)

BERENGER

Go out? I suppose I'll have to. I'm dreading the moment. I'll be bound to meet some of them...

DUDARD

What if you do? You only have to keep out of their way. And there aren't as many as all that.

BERENGER

I see them all over the place. You'll probably say that's being morbid, too.

DUDARD

They don't attack you. If you leave them alone, they just ignore you. You can't say they're spiteful. They've even got a certain natural innocence, a sort of frankness. Besides I walked right along the avenue to get to you today. I got here safe and sound, didn't I? No trouble at all.

BERENGER

Just the sight of them upsets me. It's a nervous thing. I don't get angry, no, it doesn't pay to get angry, you never know where it'll lead to, I watch out for that. But it does something to me, here! *(He points to his heart.)*

I get a tight feeling inside.

DUDARD

I think you're right to a certain extent to have some reaction. But you go too far. You've no sense of humour. That's your trouble, none at all. You must learn to be more detached, and try and see the funny side of things.

BERENGER

I feel responsible for everything that happens. I feel involved, I just can't be indifferent.

DUDARD

Judge not, lest ye be judged. If you start worrying about everything that happens you'd never be able to go on living.

BERENGER

If only it had happened somewhere else, in some other country, and we'd just read about it in the papers. One could discuss it quietly, examine the question from all points of view and come to an objective conclusion. We could organize debates with professors and writers and lawyers, and bluestockings and artists and people. And the ordinary man in the street, as well. It would be very interesting and instructive. But when you're involved yourself, when you suddenly find yourself up against the brutal facts you can't help feeling directly concerned. The shock is too violent for you to stay cool and detached. I'm frankly surprised, I'm very very surprised. I can't get over it.

DUDARD

Well I'm surprised, too. Or rather I was. Now I'm starting to get used to it.

BERENGER

Well, I don't want to accept the situation.

DUDARD

What else can you do? What are your plans?

BERENGER

I don't know for the moment. I must think it over. I shall write to the papers. I'll draw up manifestos. I shall apply for an audience with the mayor – or his deputy, if the mayor's too busy.

DUDARD

You leave the authorities to act as they think best! I'm not sure if morally you have the right to butt in. In any case, I still think it's not all that serious. I think it's silly to get worked up because a few people decide to change their skins. They just didn't feel happy in the ones they had. They're free to do as they like.

BERENGER

We must attack the evil at the roots.

DUDARD

The evil! That's just a phrase! Who knows what is evil and what is good? It's just a question of personal preferences. You're worried about your own skin, that's the truth of the matter. But you'll never become a rhinoceros, really you won't...you haven't got the vocation!

DUDARD *(as Narrator)*

The big question is: can the galloping phenomenon be halted? Can the shrinking minority hold on?

BERENGER *(as Narrator)*

They conclude that the rhinoceroses are anarchic because they are not the majority.

(Daisy enters with a lunch hamper.)

DUDARD *(as Narrator)*
Meanwhile, Daisy, a girl who works in the office is getting friendly with Berenger.
(The next excerpt is enacted)
BERENGER
It's the rhinoceroses which are anarchic, because they're in the minority.
DUDARD
They are, it's true – for the moment.
DAISY
They are a pretty big minority, and getting bigger all the time. My cousin is a rhinoceros now, and his wife. Not to mention leading personalities like the Cardinal de Retz...
DUDARD
A prelate!
DAISY
Mazarin.
DUDARD
This is going to spread to other countries, you'll see.
BERENGER
And to think it all started with us!
DAISY
And some of the aristocracy. The Duke of St. Simon.
BERENGER *(with uplifted arms)*
All our great names!
DAISY
And others too. Lots of others. Maybe a quarter of the whole town.
BERENGER
We're still in the majority. We must take advantage of that. We must do something before we're inundated.
DUDARD
They're very potent, very.
DAISY
Well for the moment, let's eat. I've brought some food.
BERINGER
You're very kind, Miss Daisy.
DAISY *(unpacking her basket)*
You know, I had a lot of trouble finding food. The shops have been plundered, they just devour everything. And a lot of the shops are closed. It's written up outside: 'Closed on account of transformation.'

BERENGER

They should be all rounded up in a big enclosure, and kept under strict supervision.

DUDARD

That's easier said than done. The Animal Protection League would be the first to object.

DAISY

And besides everyone has a close relative or a friend among them, and that would make it even more difficult.

BERENGER

So everybody's mixed up in it!

DUDARD

Everybody's in the same boat!

BERENGER

But how can people be rhinoceroses? It doesn't bear thinking about!

DAISY *(to Berenger)*

You get used to it, you know. Nobody seems surprised any more to see herds of rhinoceroses galloping through the streets. They just stand aside, and then carry on as if nothing had happened.

DUDARD

It's the wisest course to take.

BERENGER

Well I can't get used to it.

DUDARD *(reflectively)*

I wonder if one oughtn't to give it a try.

DAISY

Well, right now, let's have lunch.

BERENGER

I don't see how a legal man like yourself can...

(A great noise of rhinoceroses travelling very fast is heard outside. Trumpets and drums are also heard.)

What's going on?

(They rush to the down-stage window.)

What is it?

(The sound of a wall crumbling is heard. Dust covers part of the stage, enveloping , if possible, the characters. They are heard speaking through it.)

BERENGER

You can't see a thing! What's happening?

DUDARD

You can't see, but you can hear all right.

BERENGER
That's no good!

DAISY
The plates will be all covered in dust.

BERENGER
How unhygienic!

DAISY
Let's hurry up and eat. We won't pay any attention to them.
(The dust disperses.)

BERENGER *(pointing into the auditorium)*
They've demolished the walls of the Fire Station.

DUDARD
That's true, they've demolished them!
(Daisy, after moving from the window to near the table holding the plate which she is endeavouring to clean, rushes to join the other two.)

DAISY
They're coming out.

BERENGER
All the firemen... They are a whole regiment of rhinoceroses, led by drums.

DAISY
They're pouring up the streets!

BERENGER
It's gone too far, much too far !

DAISY
More rhinoceroses are streaming out of the courtyard.

BERENGER
And out of the houses...

DUDARD
And the windows as well!

DAISY
They're joining up with the others.
(A man comes out of the landing door left and dashes downstairs at top speed; then another with a large horn on his nose; then a woman wearing an entire rhinoceros head.)

DUDARD
There aren't enough of us left any more.

BERENGER
How many with one horn, and how many with two?
(The Chorus steps in to take the narration forward.)

C2

One by one they are all gone... All transformed, converted. Berenger and Daisy are the only ones left.

C3

Ionesco's instructions to the actors performing this play...

C1

Noises from everywhere at once. Rhinoceros heads fill the entire upstage wall.

C4

From left and right the noises of rushing feet and the panting breath of the animals.

C1

But all these disquieting sounds are nevertheless somewhat rhythmical, making a kind of music.

C3

The loudest noises come from above, a noise of stampeding

C4

Plaster falls from the ceiling. The house shakes violently.
(The next excerpt is enacted.)

BERENGER

Listen, Daisy, there is something we can do. We'll have children, and our children will have children. It'll take time, but together we can regenerate the human race.

DAIS

Regenerate the human race?

BERENGER

It happened once before.

DAISY

Ages ago. Adam and Eve...They had a lot of courage.

BERENGER

And we, too, can have courage. We don't need all that much. It happens automatically with time and patience.

DAISY

What's the use?

BERENGER

Of course we can, with a little bit of courage.

DAISY

I don't want to have children – it's a bore.

BERENGER

How can we save the world, if you don't?

DAISY

Why bother to save it?

BERENGER

What a thing to say! Do it for me, Daisy. Let's save the world.

DAISY

After all, perhaps it's we who need saving. Perhaps we're the abnormal ones.

BERENGER

You're not yourself, Daisy, you've got a touch of fever.

DAISY

There aren't any more of our kind about anywhere, are there?

BERENGER

Daisy, you're not to talk like that!
(They look all around. There are rhinoceros heads on the walls, on the landing door, and now starting to appear along the footlights.)

DAISY

Those are the real people. They look happy. They're content to be what they are. They don't look insane. They look very natural. They were right to do what they did.

C1

It is inevitable.
(Daisy leaves BERENGER)

C4

There is a long, agonizing monologue by Berenger, ending with the voice of optimism for mankind. Let us listen to just the closing words.

BERENGER

I should have gone with them while there was still time. Now it's too late! Now I'm a monster, just a monster. Now I'll never become a rhinoceros, never, never! I've gone past changing. I want to, I really do, but I can't, I just can't. I can't stand the sight of me. I'm ashamed!
(He turns his back on the mirror)
I'm so ugly! People who hang on to their individuality always come to a bad end!
(He suddenly snaps out of it)
Oh well, too bad! I'll take on the whole of them! I'll put up a fight against the lot of them, the whole lot of them! I'm the last man left, and I'm staying that way until the end. I'm not capitulating!

Close of play

PART 4
AMEDEE

The Chorus resets the scene.

C1

Ionesco's influence spread rapidly and spread wide.

C2

In Britain, N.F. Simpson, James Saunders, David Campton and Harold Pinter, among others, have acknowledged their intellectual debt to him. Gunter Grass was once recognized as an exponent of the absurd form in Germany.

C1

Across the Atlantic, Edward Albee and Woody Allen, contrasting in style but common in purpose, introduced lashings of the absurd in their work.

C3

Prof. K. Madavane on the Faculty of Jawaharlal Nehru University says that although Ionesco wrote on many themes, dealt with many situations, death remained by far the most important undercurrent in his work.

C4

Amedee. Or How To Get Rid Of It. Ionesco's first full length play was performed in public in April 1954, that is, how many years ago?

C2

A middle aged husband and wife are shown in a situation which is clearly not from real life. They have not left their flat for years.

C3

The wife earns her living by operating some sort of telephone switchboard. The husband is writing... a play.

C4

But has never gone beyond the first few lines.

C1

In the bedroom is a corpse. It has been there for many years.

C2

Whose corpse? This is by no means certain.

C4

The oddest thing about it is that it keeps growing larger and larger.

C3

It is suffering from "geometric progression – the incurable disease of the dead".

(By now the actors playing Madeleine and Amedee are onstage and guided to their positions by the chorus.)

MADELEINE

All this is wildly fantastic, yet not altogether unfamiliar. For it is not unlike our experiences at one time or another in dreams and nightmares.

AMEDEE

Ionesco has in fact put a dream situation on stage.
(The actors slip into the opening scene.)

EXCERPT 1

AMÉDÉE *(finally closes the door and then comes towards Madeleine)*
I was only looking to see if he'd grown!...You'd almost think he had, a little.

MADELEINE *(sharply)*
Not since yesterday...or at least not that you'd notice!

AMÉDÉE
It may be all over, you know. Perhaps he's stopped.

MADELEINE
Oh, you and your silly 'look on the bright side'. We know all about your forecasts. I'd rather you wrote that play of yours. *(She looks at the table while dusting.)* You don't seem to have made much progress. You're still on the first scene. You'll never finish it!

AMÉDÉE
I shall...I've added another speech, anyway.
(He opens the notebook. Madeleine stops working, broom or duster in hand, and listens while he reads.)

AMEDEE
The old man says to the old woman: 'It won't do by itself!'

MADELEINE
Is that all?

AMÉDÉE *(laying the notebook down)*
I've no inspiration. With all I have on my conscience...the life we're leading... it's not exactly the right atmosphere.

MADELEINE
You've never been short of excuses.

AMÉDÉE
I feel so tired, so tired... worn out, heavy. I've got indigestion and my tummy's all blown out. I feel sleepy all the time.

MADELEINE
Well, you sleep all day!

AMÉDÉE

That's because I'm sleepy.

MADELEINE

I'm tired, too, dog-tired. And I go on working, working, working.

AMÉDÉE

I can't stick it. Perhaps it's my liver. I feel I've aged. Of course, I'm not exactly young any more. Still, to feel like this...

MADELEINE

Then rest. What's to stop you resting? Sleep at night and give up dozing during the day. Stop overeating. It's all the result of self-indulgence. You drink too much.

AMÉDÉE

You've never seen me drunk.

MADELEINE

More than once!

AMÉDÉE

That's not true.

MADELEINE

You don't need to be drunk all the time to become an alcoholic! It's that little drink before dinner. That's what gradually poisons your whole system!

AMÉDÉE

You know I never touch anything but tomato juice.

MADELEINE

Well, then, if you've always been such a sober-sides, if you've nothing seriously wrong with you, if all your faculties are still intact, wake yourself up a bit, get to work, write your masterpiece.

AMÉDÉE

I tell you I've no inspiration.

MADELEINE

Always the same old story! How do other people manage, I wonder? It's fifteen years since you had any inspiration!

AMÉDÉE

Fifteen years. You're right! *(He points to the left-hand door.)* I've not written more than two speeches since he...*(He picks up the notebook and reads)* The old woman says to the old man, 'Do you think it will do?' and the one I managed to write today, the one I've just read you: The old man replies, 'It won't do by itself.' *(He sits down at his table.)* I simply must get down to it. Write, in the state I'm in! A man should be in a state of elation to do creative work. You'd need to be a hero, a superman, to write in my situation, in such wretched poverty.

MADELEINE

Have you ever seen a superman living in poverty? You must be the first!

AMÉDÉE

I must, I must get down to it. It's hard, terribly hard, but I simply must get down to it!

(*He has collapsed at his table, leaning on his elbows, his head in his hands, staring vacantly, drawn and haggard; then slowly his arm falls along the table with his forehead resting on it. Dumb show. Meanwhile MADELEINE has finished her cleaning; when she sees her husband's attitude, she shrugs her shoulders and mutters between her teeth.*)

· ·

AMEDEE (*as Narrator*)

They try to return to their respective routines, but it is not easy to ignore the strange

(*Goings-on in the house, the changing atmosphere.*)

MADELEINE (*as Narrator*)

It's nine o'clock. Time for Madeleine to get to work.

AMEDEE

I don't suppose you often see mushrooms growing in flats?

MADELEINE

It's all because of him.

EXCERPT 2

AMÉDÉE (*trying to explain*)

They are very tiny. It may have nothing to do with him after all. Perhaps it's only the damp...It often happens, you know, in flats. And you never know, they may be good for something. Perhaps they keep spiders away...

MADELEINE

I suppose you've often seen mushrooms growing in flats?

AMÉDÉE

It does happen, I assure you. In small provincial towns, especially. Sometimes in the big one – Lyons, for example.

MADELEINE

I have no idea whether mushrooms sprout in flats in Lyons, but they certainly don't in Paris.

AMÉDÉE

We never go out. We never visit anyone. We've been living shut up here for fifteen years. Perhaps it's different now, in Paris too. Or even in the flats of neighbours. Paris mushrooms! How can you really be sure!

MADELEINE

Don't talk such nonsense! I'm not a child. It's all because of him. *(With a look and a gesture towards the left-hand door)* Only because of him.

AMÉDÉE *(resigning himself to the truth, his arms hanging loosely, overcome)*

Yes. Of course, you're right. There can't be any other reason.

MADELEINE *(raising her head to look at the clock)*

Nine o'clock! It's time. I must go to work, whatever happens, or I shall be late!

AMÉDÉ

Hurry up, then.

MADELEINE *(as she puts on her hat)*

I shall get into a row. They'll be starting any moment now.

(A buzz from the switchboard) They've started already...I'm coming!

(More gently to Amedee) Try and do a little work, too, write something...

AMÉDÉE

I'll try, I promise...

(Madeleine goes quickly to the switchboard, sits down, picks up her headphones and passes on the call, while Amedee too goes and sits down at his table with his notebook before him. The clock advances a quarter of an hour. It is 9.15.)

MADELEINE

Hallo? Can I help you? The President of the Republic? The President in person or his secretary? Ah, the President...

AMÉDÉE *(at his table, re-reading what he has written)*

The old woman to the old man: 'Do you think it will do?'

MADELEINE *(at the switchboard)*

The President of the Republic is on tour, Sir, try again in half an hour!

AMÉDÉE *(at the table)*

The old man to the old woman...

MADELEINE *(at the switchboard as it buzzes again)*

Hallo, hallo...

AMÉDÉE *(at the table, as before)*

The old man to the old woman...

MADELEINE *(as before)*

Mr Charles Chaplin, the grocer? I'll put you through. (Another buzz) Hallo, hallo...

AMÉDÉE *(as before)*

'It won't do by itself!'

MADELEINE *(as before)*

No, sir, no. The President can't take a call for another half hour, I've just told you.

AMÉDÉE *(as before)*

The old woman to the old man: 'Do you think it will do?'

MADELEINE *(as before)*

A call from the King of the Lebanon…
(Another call; she listens in on another line.) Hold on, please! *(She plugs in)* Hallo, the Elysée Palace? The Elysée?!

AMÉDÉE *(as before)*

The old man to the old woman…

MADELEINE *(as before)*

Yes, of course there's a King of the Lebanon…but I tell you he's on the line! Is that the President? There's a call for you, Sir. *(Another line)* Go ahead, please, it's the President of the Republic.

AMÉDÉE *(as before)*

'No, it won't do by itself.'

MADELEINE *(as before, taking another call. The clock shows 9.30)*

Hallo, I'm putting you through. *(Another call, another line)*

No, Sir, there are no gas chambers left, not since the last war. You'd better wait for the next one.

AMÉDÉE *(still at the table, to Madeleine)*

Madeleine, I can't think of the next line…

MADELEINE *(to him)*

Can't you see I'm busy?…*(Buzz)* Hallo…I'm sorry, the firemen are away on Thursdays, it's their day off, they take the children out for a walk…But I didn't say today was Thursday. *(Another buzz)* Yes…Hallo…I'm putting you through…

AMÉDÉE *(standing up, his hands still on the table)*

Oh, how tiring it is to write…I feel worn out!

MADELEINE *(as before, answering another call)*

Yes…you wish to speak to his wife? You don't mind if she takes it from the bathroom?

(Amedee sits down again heavily. Madeleine goes on as before, answering another call, then another, and so on, while the clock hands move round to 9.45, and then 10 o'clock.)

MADELEINE

I'm putting you through…I'm putting you through…

AMÉDÉE *(with a vacant stare)*

The old woman with a vacant stare…

MADELEINE *(as before)*
Hold on, please, I'm putting you through...

AMÉDÉE *(with a sudden glint in his eyes; he's found it)*
'Oh, yes; it will do all right!'...

MADELEINE *(as before)*
You're through...

AMÉDÉE
Madeleine! Would you like me to read you what I've just written? You can tell me if it's any good!

MADELEINE *(lifting her headphones slightly to hear what Amedee is saying)*
I haven't time just now! In a minute! *(Another call)*
Hallo...hold on please... *(The calls follow in quick succession)*
I'm putting him through...I'm putting her through...I'm putting them through...Hallo, hallo...

....

MADELEINE *(as Narrator)*
Amedee, taking advantage of his wife being fully occupied at the board, gets up quietly, goes towards the door, and... wants so badly to look at the corpse in the next room.

AMEDEE *(as Narrator)*
Madeleine is quick to scold him.

EXCERPT 3

AMÉDÉE *(Explaining)*
Suddenly I began to hope...I wondered if...I thought he might have disappeared...

MADELEINE
Just like that, all by himself! You're out of your mind!

AMÉDÉE
The days of miracles are past...unfortunately...

MADELEINE
Come along now, come along!
(Madeleine drags Amedee away from the door.)

AMÉDÉE
I feel quite sick! Every time I look at him.

MADELEINE
Don't look, then! What did you go to his room for?

AMÉDÉE

I feel quite sick...

MADELEINE

Any excuse to stop writing!

AMÉDÉE

He's grown again. Soon, the divan won't be big enough for him. His feet are over the end already. I seem to remember fifteen years ago he was rather short. And so young. Now he's got a great white beard. He's quite imposing with that white beard. Twenty and fifteen, that only makes him thirty-five, after all... He's not really old.

MADELEINE

The dead grow old faster than the living. Everyone knows that...

(Amédée, quite overcome, goes and collapses into the armchair; Madeleine is in the centre of the stage.)

AMÉDÉE

Oh! What big nails he's got!

MADELEINE

I can't cut them every day. I've got other things to do! Last week I threw a whole handful into the dustbin. It's not easy to do either. I'm just a servant, I am, just a drudge, waiting on everyone.

AMÉDÉE

His toenails have grown right through his shoes.

MADELEINE

Then buy him another pair, if you've got money to burn! What do you expect me to do? I'm not giving you any! We're very poor! You don't seem to realize!

AMÉDÉE

Well, I can't very well give him mine, can I? They're my only pair. Besides, they'd never fit him – now his feet have got so large!

(A buzz. Madeleine goes quickly to the switchboard.)

MADELEINE

Hallo, yes? Can I help you?

(Meanwhile Amédée gets up from his armchair, goes once more towards the half-open door on the left and stares out petrified.)

No, Sir, he's not there...At least, I shouldn't think so.

AMÉDÉE *(without moving)*

The shutters are fastened tight. Yet it's not dark in his room.

(Madeleine moves up to AMÉDÉE; each time she leaves her office, she takes off her hat; she puts it on again whenever she goes back.)

MADELEINE

The light comes from his eyes. You've forgotten to close the lids again.

AMÉDÉE

His eyes haven't aged. They're still as beautiful. Great green eyes. Shining like beacons. I'd better go and close them for him.

MADELEINE

And you think they're beautiful! You're talking like a book. You've plenty of inspiration in real life. Funny idea of beauty, though.

AMÉDÉE

I didn't say it was funny.

MADELEINE

We could get along without his kind of beauty, it takes up too much space. *(Slight cracking noises can be heard coming from the adjoining room.)* Did you hear that?

AMÉDÉE

He's growing, it's quite natural. He's branching out.

MADELEINE

What do you take him for? A tree? He's just making himself at home! Why, he'll soon monopolize the whole place! Where am I going to put him? You don't care. You don't have to do the housework!

....

AMEDEE *(as Narrator)*

They try again. She returns to her board, he to his script. Soon enough he is drawn to the mushrooms.

MADELEINE *(as Narrator)*

Madeleine has to take charge of the situation again.

EXCERPT 4

AMÉDÉE *(looking about everywhere on the floor for the mushroom)*
I could have sworn I saw one just now!

MADELEINE *(pointing to the room)*
With him here!

AMÉDÉE *(on his knees, getting up again, a mushroom in his hand)*
Here it is! I've found it!

MADELEINE

The second one in the dining-room! Don't put it on the table, silly, it's not sanitary. And you know they're poisonous. *(A short silence)*
Listen, today I'll let you break your rule. Have a glass of wine, go on, you look so miserable! *(A tremendous crack is suddenly heard from the adjoining room.)*

Oh! I'm frightened!

AMÉDÉE

It's only him, Madeleine, don't be afraid!

(A loud crash of breaking glass from the same direction; AMÉDÉE rushes to the door, followed by MADELEINE.)

MADELEINE

Don't stand there like that! Go and see!

AMÉDÉE

What can have happened now!

(They both disappear through the door, which they leave wide open; coming from the wings, left)

He's smashed the window! His head's gone right through!

MADELEINE *(in the wings)*

He's growing both ends at once! What's he up to now! Do something, Amédée. The neighbours will see him! Pull his head in!

AMÉDÉE *(in the wings)*

That's what I am doing!

MADELEINE *(her back framed in the door)*

Hurry up! *(A dull thud)* Don't drag his head on the floor! You are a clumsy devil!

AMÉDÉE *(in the wings)*

It's not so easy!

MADELEINE

Lift him up. Lay his head on the cushion. Don't forget to close his eyes!

AMÉDÉE *(in the wings)*

I can't. There's not enough room.

MADELEINE *(still framed in the doorway)*

Well, fold him in two then, fold him in two, it's easy enough!
(Amédée can be heard breathing heavily with the effort) No, not like that!
(Madeleine goes back into the room and can be heard saying:) Let me do it!
(Amédée's back now appears, framed in the doorway.)
That's it. Like this. I have to show you everything!

AMÉDÉE *(still in the doorway)*

I was doing my best...you're never satisfied. Are the neighbours looking out of their windows?

MADELEINE *(from the wings)*

No...Come and help me. You always leave me to do the hardest part by myself.
(Amédée disappears once more into the room. He leaves the door wide open.)

AMEDEE *(off-stage)*
But I thought you wanted...

MADELEINE *(louder, but still off stage)*
Now pull, pull harder! *(Their efforts are clearly audible; a dull thud.)*
Look out! Be careful! *(More noise)* Close the shutters properly! It'll be cold in here now, without the glass!

AMÉDÉE
It's not nearly winter yet.
(Amédée and Madeleine reappear.)

MADELEINE
That's that!

AMÉDÉE
You see, it's all right in the end.

MADELEINE *(changes her mind as she is about to shut the door)*
Go and close his eyes! You've forgotten again!
(Amédée starts walking towards the room)
The neighbours must have heard.

AMÉDÉE *(stopping)*
They may not have done. *(Short silence)* There's not a sound from them! Besides, at this time of day...

MADELEINE
They must have heard something. They're not all deaf.

AMÉDÉE
Not all of them, they couldn't be. But as I say, at this time of day...

MADELEINE
What could we tell them?

AMÉDÉE
We could say it was the postman!

MADELEINE *(turning her back to the audience and looking towards the rear window)*
It was the postman who did it! It was the p-o-o-stman! *(To Amédée)* Will they believe us? The postman must have gone by now.

AMÉDÉE
All the better. *(Loudly shouting to the rear of the stage)* It was the p-o-o-stman!

....

MADELEINE *(as Narrator)*
Act Two opens with a visible change in the stage – altered to accommodate the huge legs and feet of the dead man. They have now intruded into the room.

AMEDEE *(as Narrator)*

Also, on one side, there are giant mushrooms growing at the foot of the walls.

MADELEINE

Every now and then the dead man's feet jerk forward, occupying more stage space.

(Every time this happens Amedee measures the fresh ground covered.)

AMEDEE

He's growing faster than ever...

EXCERPT 5

Amédée and Madeleine are on the left of the stage. They are barely visible, concealed by the lumber. Neither of them speaks for a moment, then the dead man's feet suddenly slide forward to the right. At once Madeleine's head appears, only to disappear again a moment later among the furniture. Amédée steps into the open stage.

MADELEINE

You can actually see him growing.

(Amédée makes a chalk mark on the floor by the stool on which the dead man's feet are resting, and then carefully measures the distance between the old mark and the new one; when he has done this, he speaks.)

AMEDEE

Six inches in twenty minutes. He's growing faster than ever! Oh dear, oh dear!

(For a moment he gazes at the part of the body that is on the stage, then at the enormous mushrooms.) They're still getting bigger too! *(A silence)*

If they weren't the poisonous variety, we could eat them, or sell them! Oh! I'm really no good at anything – whatever I try! I can never make a go of it.

MADELEINE *(emerging, straighteninging her hair in front of the mirror)*

I've been telling you that for ages...

(Silence. With his hands behind his back, rather round-shouldered, Amedee strolls meditatively round the left-hand part of the stage; then he stops.)

AMÉDÉE

If only my morale was a little higher. It's being so tired. Yet I don't do anything special...*(He starts making for the bed on the right and brushes against the dead man's legs.)* Oh, I'm so sorry...

(He gently rearranges the legs and glances at Madeleine to see if she has noticed or not; as he sees she is still busy with her hair, he looks a little more relieved. Then, after a few more paces, he suddenly stops. He has an idea. He glances again at Madeleine, then towards the open door to the left, then again

at Madeleine; once more towards the door. He has made up his mind. He tiptoes quietly towards the next room. He has just reached the doorway when Madeleine sees him.)

MADELEINE *(coming forward)*

Amédée, where are you going? *(He stands stock still)* Can't you hear me, Amédée? I want to know where you're going?

AMÉDÉE

Nowhere, nowhere at all...where could I be going?

MADELEINE

I'm coming with you.

AMÉDÉE

I can't move an inch without you following me! I'm a free man, aren't I?

MADELEINE *(annoyed)*

Do as you please, my dear, go ahead, go ahead if you like...If you always want to be by yourself! If only getting your own way got you somewhere!

AMÉDÉE *(retracing his steps)*

Very well. I'll never go in again, so there! Now are you satisfied?
(She makes for the left-hand room.)

AMÉDÉE

Where are you going?

MADELEINE

I can't leave him as he is! Someone's got to clean him up, and I can't see you doing it!

AMÉDÉE

Why bother! What's the good!
(Madeleine does not in fact go; the dead man's feet advance again.)

MADELEINE

He's growing! Growing again! *(AMÉDÉE moves towards the bed.)* What are you doing? You still haven't closed his eyes! You've got a memory like a sieve!

AMÉDÉE

I feel so tired!
(He goes and collapses on the bed.)

MADELEINE

As usual, when it's time for you to do something! Are you going to get rid of him? If you're really so tired, take some medicine, take a tonic... take something.

AMÉDÉE

They have no effect on me any more. They just make me more tired.

....

MADELEINE *(as Narrator)*
A fatigue is setting into the scene, in their lives. A resignation.
AMEDEE *(as Narrator)*
Madeleine reminds Amedee... his is a fine time for him to be giving in.
MADELEINE
Amédée complains he has no strength left, no will-power.
MADELEINE
At the critical moment his energy always desertshim, and his will power
dwindles away. He'll never change!

EXCERPT 6

MADELEINE *(taking it up again)*
You've let fifteen years go by. Fifteen years! Now we'll never make anyone
believe that nothing's happening here, that nothing's ever happened...And
it's all because you've no initiative.
*(The dead man makes another sudden jerk forward. Amédée rises painfully
to his feet, like a robot, and goes to measure the latest progress, makes a new
chalk mark, returns to his armchair and falls heavily into it, while Madeleine,
with hardly a pause, goes on with her tirade.)*
MADELEINE
It might be better to tell the police after all, if you won't do anything else.
AMÉDÉE
There'd be such a fuss...
MADELEINE
Anyway, if we could prove he'd been dead for fifteen years...they can't
prosecute when a man's been dead for fifteen years.
AMÉDÉE
Thirteen...
MADELEINE
You see, even thirteen's enough, and in our case it's fifteen. If you'd
reported his death at the time, we'd be all right now. We'd be feeling much
safer...Not so afraid of the neighbours. This place would be more cheerful
and we shouldn't be living like prisoners, like criminals. *(She indicates the
dead man.)* Because of him, everything goes wrong...
AMÉDÉE
I'll never succeed, Madeleine, in teaching you logic. If we'd gone to the
authorities the day he died, we'd have been in prison long ago or probably
been executed. The fifteen years would never have had time to elapse.

MADELEINE

Obviously I must be wrong. According to you I'm always wrong. But I still think...Yes, you could still have gone to the police station the next day, after the murder, and told them you'd killed him in a ft of anger, out of jealousy. After all, it would have been perfectly true. You always said you thought he was my lover...And I never denied it.

AMÉDÉE

Oh? Is that why I killed him? I'd forgotten...

MADELEINE

Scatterbrain! As though anyone could forget a thing like that! *(Continuing)* And as it was a crime of passion, you wouldn't have had any trouble; they'd have given you some little statement to sign and then let you go free. The statement would have been stuffed into a file, it would all be over and done with...the whole affair would have been forgotten ages ago.

AMÉDÉE

But as it is, we're still talking about it!

MADELEINE *(still sweeping on)*

Whenever I asked you, while there was still time, to go and register his death, you answered as you did just now: 'tomorrow', 'tomorrow', 'tomorrow', 'tomorrow'...

AMEDEE

I say, what if I went tomorrow?

MADELEINE *(forcefully)*

No! Today, today, today, today!

AMÉDÉE

Perhaps it's easier to go to the police station...

MADELEINE

Anyway, I can't see you going to the police station. Besides, it wouldn't do any good now. Fifteen years after the murder, they'd never believe you did it in anger. If you wait fifteen years, that proves it was premeditated.

AMÉDÉE

I'm wondering what we could say to the police...As he's grown so old. He does look very old, doesn't he? Perhaps I could say it was my father and I killed him yesterday...

MADELEINE

Oh, I don't think that'd be a very bright idea...

AMÉDÉE

No, perhaps not. You're right...

MADELEINE

Officially, there's nothing we can do now. But we can still get round the law. You've got to act on your own...and as quickly as possible.

(Amédée gets up slowly and walks round the walls of the room, avoiding the body.)

AMEDEE
In point of fact, Madeleine, I'm just wondering if I really...

MADELEINE
What's the matter now? You're hesitating, aren't you? You don't want to do anything!

AMÉDÉE
Yes I do. I was going to say something else.

MADELEINE
What then? What's puzzling you?

AMÉDÉE
Did I really kill him?

MADELEINE
You don't think it was a poor weak woman like me?

AMÉDÉE
No, no. Of course not.

MADELEINE
Well?

AMÉDÉE
Of course, of course! *(A second later, his face lit up by a glimmering of hope)* But why shouldn't he have died a natural death anyway? Why do you insist I killed him?

....

MADELEINE *(as Narrator)*
At last Madeleine and Amedee find a plan – and the courage – to get rid of it.

AMEDEE *(as Narrator)*
The first thing to do of course is to get the enormous corpse out of the house.

MADELEINE
It's specially important to be careful now.

AMEDEE
They have a look through the window.

MADELEINE
The street is still empty. Still, they must watch out.

AMEDEE
They can't see any police on their beat.

EXCERPT 7

AMÉDÉE

The streets are empty at this time of night.

MADELEINE

You mustn't throw him in the water where there are any barges; the moon doesn't affect barges. Don't choose a place like that.

AMÉDÉE *(pointing through the window)*

I'll go a hundred yards farther up. It only means a little extra effort. Whatever I do, I can't help crossing little Torco Square, there, at the end of the street.

MADELEINE *(still looking through the window in the same direction)*

Can't you go another way? That's a nuisance, right at the end there are lights in some of the windows. You might be spotted.

AMÉDÉE

That's the bar and brothel kept by the owner of our flat. It's used by American soldiers. You can see them sometimes walking about with their girls. There's not much risk. They don't know a word of the language, most of them!

MADELEINE

Try and avoid them.

AMÉDÉE

That's not very easy. I'll have to chance it. It's a lovely night.

(Madeleine is still looking through the window, her back to the audience. Amédée starts pulling the legs round in the middle of the stage; then goes back to the window.)

MADELEINE

Amédée...I'm frightened...Oh dear...I suppose we must...We must... You'd better get on with it...

(Standing at the window, Amédée pulls the body; it is obviously going much more easily. The clock strikes. The feet are over the window-sill and hang down the other side.)

AMÉDÉE

He's rolling out, now...It's a lot easier...rolling out!

....

(The Chorus steps in now to provide the links.)

C2

Amedee is pulling at his legs, and the long, long body is winding out of the room – interminably.

C3

At each pull he rests it on the window sill, while the long legs go sliding down, presumably to the pavement below.

C4

The trunk has not appeared yet. The legs continue to issue from the other room.

C1

Amedee decides to go down to the pavement and pull from there.

EXCERPT 8

MADELEINE (*egging her husband on from the window*)

Pull... That's it... Again... again... Pull... There's still some more to come. Pull! Pull!

(*Amedee is still off-stage, in the street, pulling. He must have gone some distance, as far as Torco Square. His voice sounds a long way off.*)

AMEDEE

I've got to the Square! Torco-o-o!

MADELEINE (*gazing down at the street*)

No-o-o! Go on pulling! There's more to come! It's not finished yet! Have you met anybody?

AMEDEE

No-o-o-body! Don't be afraid! And you – have you? Can you see anyone?

MADELEINE

No-o-o one! Go on, now, pull... Pull... Pull!

(*She is still at the window, the body is still sliding out. Finally, the shoulders appear, then the head, which is so large that there is hardly room for it to pass through the doorway on the left. It has tremendously long air and an enormous white beard. When the head reaches the window the long hair is still not quite out of the room.*)

MADELEINE

Pull Amedee, pull... Amedee... Pull... Pull... Pull! Watch out for the barges! Hurry up... Don't catch a cold... Go straight there... Don't hang about!

(*The head is near the window, almost hiding Madeleine.*)

Pul-l-l... Pul-l-l-l

....

C1

That's not the end of the play!

C3

The last act has various townspeople involved in the denouement – the owner of a bar-brothel, an American soldier, two policemen and a man and a woman at their windows. In a spectacular display of stagecraft Ionesco has the body turn into a sail and float away, carrying Amedee away with him.

C2

A year later Ionesco wrote an alternative ending in which the technical demands were less formidable but no less intriguing in effect. Amedee floats away to the sky anyway, but with the dead man's hat and beard on himself.

C4

As the policemen scramble to grab him, there are various droppings from the sky – his shoes, the hat and the beard.

(All the actors scramble onto the stage. They follow the flight path of Amedee from 1 o'clock through 6 o'clock to amedee's desk. Madeleine goes to her desk.)

MADELEINE

Amedee, you haven't even finished your play!

ACTOR 1

Perhaps he was a genius!

ACTOR 2

All that talent wasted!

ACTOR 3

It's a bad day for literature!

ACTOR 4

No one is indispensable!

ACTOR 5

He left her the flat, anyway!

MADELEINE

Amedee, you may have gone up in the world, but you are not going up in my estimation!

ACTOR 6

(Blowing a whistle) The show is over!

ACTOR 7

(Blowing a whistle) Move along then, please, ladies and gentlemen. Move along, please. Move along, please...

(To the blowing of the two whistles the actors leave upstage, carrying away the stage props. The chorus appears from two sides onto the empty stage.)

Close of play

Link to The Leader

C1

What was that?

C3

That was Ionesco!

C2

That was a play?

C3

That was Ionesco!

C4

There is an audience for that? OK, OK...

ALL FOUR

That was Ionesco!

C1

Bhaisaheb, it sounds much too foreign for me.

C2

Look who's talking!

C1

No, seriously...

C3

What does all this mean to ordinary people like us?

C4

You mean sadharan vilayati desi like us?

C2

Like... *(Referring to the audience)*

C3

Like all of us.

C1

Maybe the The Leader can tell us.

C2

Maybe

C4

The Leader, maybe.

C3

Let's try The Leader.

C2

So, we try?

ALL FOUR

The Leader!

C2
So, we try?
ALL FOUR
The Leader!

PART 5
THE LEADER

Characters

- The Announcer
- The Young Lover
- The Girlfriend
- The Admirer
- The Girl Admirer
- The Leader

A chant has begun backstage: LEA-DER, LEA-DER... The announcer and the two admirers enter and take positions. The chorus withdraws. The play begins.

Standing with his back to the public, centre-stage, and with his eyes fixed on the up-stage exit, the ANNOUNCER waits for the arrival of the LEADER. To right and left, riveted to the walls, two of the Leader' s ADMIRERS, a man and a girl, also wait for his arrival. After a few moments of suspense the announcer comes to life.

ANNOUNCER

There he is! There he is! At the end of the street!

(Shouts of "Hurrah" etc. are heard.)

There's the leader! He's coming, he's coming nearer!

(Cries of acclaim and applause are heard from off stage.)

It's better if he doesn't see us...

(The two ADMIRERS hug the wall even closer.)

Watch out! *(The ANNOUNCER gives vent to a display of enthusiasm.)*

Hurrah! Hurrah! The leader !The leader! Long live the leader!

(The two ADMIRERS, with their bodies rigid and flattened against the wall, thrust their necks and heads as far forward as they can to get a glimpse of the LEADER.)

The leader! The leader!

TWO ADMIRERS *(in unison)*

Hurrah! Hurrah!

(Other 'Hurrahs!' mingle with 'Hurrah! Bravo!' from the wings and gradually die down.)

Hurrah! Bravo !

(The ANNOUNCER takes a step up-stage, stops, then goes up-stage, followed by the TWO ADMIRERS, exclaiming as he goes.)

ANNOUNCER

Ah! Too bad I He's going away! He's going away! Follow me quickly! After him!

(The ANNOUNCER and the two ADMIRERS leave, crying 'Leader! Lee-ee-eader! Lee-ee-eader! This last 'Lee-ee-eader !' echoes in the wings like a bleating cry.

Silence. The stage is empty for a few moments. The young LOVER enters from right, and his GIRLFRIEND from left; they meet centrestage.)

YOUNG LOVER

Forgive me, Madame, or should I say Mademoiselle?

GIRLFRIEND

I beg your pardon, I'm afraid I don't happen to know you!

YOUNG LOVER

And I'm afraid I don't know you either!

GIRLFRIEND

Then neither of us knows each other.

YOUNG LOVER

Exactly. We have something in common. It means that between us there is a basis of understanding on which we can build the edifice of our future.

GIRLFRIEND

Huh? That leaves me cold. I'm afraid.
(She makes as if to go)

YOUNG LOVER

Oh, my darling, I adore you.

GIRLFRIEND

Darling, so do I!
(They embrace)

YOUNG LOVER

I'm taking you with me, darling. We'll get married straightaway. *(They leave left. The stage is empty for a brief moment.)*

ANNOUNCER *(entering up-stage, followed by the two ADMIRERS)*
But the leader swore that he'd be passing here.

ADMIRER

Are you absolutely sure of that?

ANNOUNCER

Yes, yes, of course.

GIRL ADMLRER

Was it really on his way?

ANNOUNCER

Yes, yes. He should have passed by here, it was marked on the Festival programme.

ADMIRER

Did you actually see it yourself and hear it with your own eyes and ears?

ANNOUNCER

He told someone. Someone else!

ADMIRER

But who? Who was this someone else?

GIRL ADMIRER

Was it a reliable person? A friend of yours?

ANNOUNCER

A friend of mine who I know very well.

(Suddenly in the background one hears renewed cries of 'Hurrah!' and 'Long live the leader!')

ANNOUNCER

That's him now! There he is! Hip! Hip! Hurrah! There he is! Hide yourselves! Hide yourselves!

(The two ADMIRERS flatten themselves as before against the wall, stretching their necks out towards the wings from where the shouts of acclamation come; the ANNOUNCER watches excitedly upstage, his back to the public.)

ANNOUNCER

The leader's coming. He approaches. He's bending. He's unbending.

(At each of the ANNOUNCER'S lines, the ADMIRERS give a start and stretch their necks even farther; they shudder.)

He's jumping. He's crossed the river. They're shaking his hand. He sticks out his thumb. Can you hear? They're laughing.

(The ANNOUNCER and the two ADMIRERS also laugh.)

Ah... they're giving him a box of tools. What's he going to do with them? Ah...he's signing autographs. The leader is stroking a hedgehog, a superb hedgehog! The crowd applauds. He's dancing... with the hedgehog in his hand. He's embracing his dancer. Hurrah! Hurrah!

(Cries are heard in the wings.)

He's being photographed, with his dancer on one hand and the hedgehog on the other... He greets the crowd...

(He spits! A tremendous distance.)

GIRL ADMIRER

Is he coming past here? Is he coming in our direction?

ADMIRER

Are we really on his route?

ANNOUNCER *(turning his head to the two ADMIRERS)*

Quiet! And don't move, you're spoiling everything...

GIRL ADMIRER

But even so...

ANNOUNCER
Keep quiet, I tell you! Didn't I tell you he'd promised, that he had fixed his schedule himself...
(He turns back up-stage and cries out)
Hurrah! Hurrah! Long live the leader! *(Silence)*
Long live, long live, the leader! *(Silence)*
Long live, long live, long live the leead-er !
(The two ADMIRERS, unable to contain themselves, also give a sudden cry.)

ADMIRERS
Hurrah! Long live the leader!

ANNOUNCER *(to the ADMIRERS)*
Quiet, you two! Calm down! You're spoiling everything ! *(Then, once more looking up-stage)*
Long live the leader! *(Wildly enthusiastic)* Hurrah! Hurrah! He's changing his shirt. He disappears behind a red screen. He reappears! *(The applause intensifies.)*
Bravo! Bravo!
(The ADMIRERS also long to cry 'Bravo' and applaud; they put their hands to their mouths to stop themselves.)
He's putting his tie on! He's reading his newspaper and drinking his morning coffee! He's still got his hedgehog... He's leaning on the edge of the parapet. The parapet breaks. He gets up... he gets up unaided!
(Applause, shouts of 'Hurrah!')
Bravo! Well done! He brushes his soiled clothes.

TWO ADMIRERS *(stamping their feet)*
Oh! Ah! Oh! Oh! Ah! Ah !

ANNOUNCER
He's mounting the stool! He's climbing piggyback, they're offering him a thin-ended wedge, he knows it's meant as a joke, and he doesn't mind, he's laughing.
(Applause and enormous acclaim.)

ADMLRER *(to the GIRL ADMIRER)*
You hear that? You hear? Oh! If I were king...

GIRL ADMIRER *(In an exalted tone)*
Ah...! The leader!

ANNOUNCER *(still with his back to the public)*
He's mounting the stool. No. He's getting down. A little girl offers him a bouquet of flowers... What's he going to do ? He takes the flowers. He embraces the little girl... calls her 'my child'...

ADMIRER
He embraces the little girl...calls her 'my child'...

GIRL ADMIRER

He embraces the little girl...calls her 'my child'...

ANNOUNCER

He gives her the hedgehog. The little girl's crying... Long live the leader! Long live the lee-ee-der!

ADMIRER

Is he coming past here?

GIRL ADMIRER

Is he coming past here?

ANNOUNCER *(suddenly dashing out up-stage)*

He's going away! Hurry! Come on!

(He disappears, followed by the two ADMIRERS, all crying 'Hurrah! Hurrah"!
The stage is empty for a few moments. The two LOVERS enter, entwined in an embrace; they halt centre-stage and separate; she carries a basket on her arm.)

GIRLRIEND

Let's go to the market and get some eggs!

YOUNG LOVER

Oh! I love them as much as vou do!

(She takes his arm. From the right the ANNOUNCER enters running, quickly regaining his place, back to the public, followed closely by the two ADMIRERS, arriving , one from the left and the other from the right; the two ADMIRERS knock into the two LOVERS who were about to leave right.)

ADMIRER

Sorry !

YOUNG LOVER

Oh! Sorry!

GIRL ADMIRER

Sorry! Oh! Sorry!

GIRLFRIEND

Oh! Sorry, sorry, sorry, so sorry!

ADMIRER

Sorry, sorry, sorry, oh! Sorry, sorry, so sorry!

YOUNG LOVER

Oh, oh, oh, oh, oh, oh! So sorry, everyone!

GIRLFRIEND *(to her lover)*

Come along, Adolphe! *(To the two ADMIRERS)* No harm done! *(She leaves, leading her LOVER by the hand.)*

ANNOUNCER *(watching up-stage)*

The leader is being pressed forward... and pressed back. Now they're pressing his trousers !

(The two ADMIRERS regain their places.)

The leader is smiling. Whilst they're pressing his trousers, he walks about. He tastes the flowers and the fruits growing in the stream. He's also tasting the roots of the trees. He suffers the little children to come unto him. He has confidence in everybody. He inaugurates the police force. He pays tribute to justice. He salutes the great victors and the great vanquished. Finally he recites a poem. The people are very moved.

TWO ADMIRERS

Bravo! Bravo! *(Then sobbing)* Boo! Hoo! Hoo!

ANNOUNCER

All the people are weeping.

(Loud cries of weeping are heard from the wings; the ANNOUNCER and the ADMIRERS also start to bellow.)

Silence! *(The two ADMIRERS fall silent; there is silence from the wings.)*

They've given the leader his trousers back. The leader puts them on. He looks happy! Hurrah! *('Bravos' and acclaim from the wings. The two ADMIRERS also shout their acclaim, jump about, without being able to see anything of what is presumed to be happening in the wings.)*

The leader's sucking his thumb! *(To the two ADMIRERS)* Back, back to your places, you two! Don't move! Behave yourselves and shout: 'Long live the leader !'

TWO ADMIRERS *(flattened against the wall, shouting)*

Long live, long live the leader !

ANNOUNCER

Be quiet, I tell you! You'll spoil everything! Look out, the leader's coming!

ADMIRER *(in the same position)*

The leader's coming!

GIRL ADMIRER

The leader's coming!

ANNOUNCER

Watch out! And keep quiet! Oh! The leader's going away! Follow him! Follow me!

(The ANNOUNCER goes out up-stage, running; the two ADMIRERS leave right and left, whilst in the wings the acclaim mounts, then jades. The stage is momentarily empty. The YOUNG LOVER, followed by his GIRLFRIEND, appear le.ft, running across the stage to right.)

YOUNG LOVER *(running)*

You won't catch me! You won't catch me! *(Runs out)*

GIRLFRIEND *(running)*

Wait a moment! Wait a moment! *(She runs out. The stage is empty for a moment; then once more the two LOVERS cross the stage at a run, and leave.)*

YOUNG LOVER
You won't catch me!

GIRLFRIEND
Wait a moment!
(They exit. The stage is empty. The ANNOUNCER reappears up-stage, the ADMIRER from the right, the GIRL ADMIRER from the left. They meet centre.)

ADMIRER
We missed him!

GIRL ADMIRER
Rotten luck !

ANNOUNCER
It was your fault!

ADMIRER
That's not true!

GIRL ADMIRER
No, that's not true!

ANNOUNCER
Are you suggesting it was mine?

ADMIRER
No, we didn't mean that!

GIRL ADMIRER
No, we didn't mean that!
(There is noise of acclaim and 'Hurrahs' from the wings.)

ANNOCNCER
Hurrah !

GIRL ADMIRER *(Pointing up-stage)*
It's from over there!

ADMIRER
Yes, it's from over there! *(He points left.)*

ANNOUNCER
Very well. Follow me! Long live the leader!
(He runs out right, followed by the two ADMIRERS, also shouting.)

TWO ADMIRERS
Long live the leader!

They leave. The stage is empty for a moment.
The YOUNG LOVER and his GIRLFRIEND appear left; the YOUNG LOVER exits up-stage; the GIRLFRIEND shouts 'I'll get you!' and runs out right.

The ANNOUNCER and the two ADMIRERS appear from up-stage.

ANNOUNCER *(to the ADMIRERS)*

Long live the leader!

This is repeated by the ADMIRERS. Then, still talking to the ADMIRERS, he says 'Follow me! Follow the leader !' (He leaves up-stage, still running and shouting) 'Follow him!'

The ADMIRER exits right, the GIRL ADMIRER left into the wings. During all of this, the acclaim off stage is heard louder or fainter according to the rhythm of the stage action.

The stage is empty for a moment. Then the LOVERS appear from right and left, crying out)

YOUNG LOVER

I'll get you!

GIRLFRIEND

You won't get me!

They leave at a run, shouting: 'Long live the leader!'

The ANNOUNCER and the two ADMIRERS emerge from up-stage, also shouting: 'Long live the leader' , by the two LOVERS. They all leave right, in single file, crying out as they run: 'The leader! Long live the leader! We'll get him! It's from over here! You won't get me!'

They enter and leave, employing all the exits; finally, entering from left, from right, and from up-stage they all meet centre, whilst the acclaim and the applause from the wings becomes a fearful din. They embrace each other feverishly, crying at the tops .of their voices: ' Long live the leader! Long live the leader!' Long live the leader!'

(Then, abruptly, silence falls.)

ANNOUNCER

The leader is arriving. Here's the leader. To your places! Attention!

The ADMIRER and the GIRLFRIEND flatten themselves against the wall right; the GIRL ADMIRER and the YOUNG LOVER against the wall left; the two couples are in each others' arms, embracing.

ADMIRER AND GIRLFRIEND

My dear, my darling!

GIRL ADMIRER AND YOUNG LOVER

My dear, my darling!

(Meanwhile, the ANNOUNCER has taken up his place, back to the audience, looking fixedly up-stage; a lull in the applause.)

ANNOUNCER

Silence! The leader has eaten his soup. He is coming. He is nigh.

(The acclaim redoubles its intensity; the two ADMIRERS and the two LOVERS shout.)

ALL

Hurrah! Hurrah! Long live the leader!

They throw confetti before he arrives. Then the ANNOUNCER hurls himself suddenly to one side to allow the LEADER to pass; the other four characters freeze with outstretched arms holding confetti; but still say 'Hurrah!'

The LEADER enters from up stage, advances to centre; to the footlights, hesitates, makes a step to left, then takes a decision and leaves with great, energetic strides by right, to the enthusiastic 'Hurrahs!' of the ANNOUNCER and the feeble, somewhat astonished 'Hurrahs!' of the other four; these, in fact, have some reason to be surprised, as the LEADER is headless, though wearing a hat. This is simple to effect: the actor playing the LEADER needing only to wear an overcoat with the collar turned up round his forehead and topped with a hat. The-man-in-an-overcoat-with-a- hat-without-a-head is a somewhat surprising apparition and will doubtless produce a certain sensation.

After the LEADER'S disappearance, the GIRL ADMIRER speaks.

GIRL ADMIRER

But... but... the leader hasn't got a head!

ANNOUNCER

What's the need a head for when he's got genius!

YOUNG LOVER

That's true! *(To the GIRLFRIEND)* What's your name?

The YOUNG LOVER to the GIRL ADMIRER, the GIRL ADMIRER to the ANNOUNCER, the ANNOUNCER to the GIRLFRIEND, the GIRLFRIEND to the YOUNG LOVER, one after the other:
What's yours? What's yours? What's yours?
Then, all together, one to the other:
What's your name?

Close of play

NARRATOR

Scott Sullivan reporting from Paris in an issue of Newsweek said: In 1979 Ionesco stopped writing plays. He made a new and successful career in painting. He campaigned tirelessly for human rights, especially in his native Romania. He was honoured as one of the forty "immortals" of the French Academy.

Moliere Alive!

*A tribute to Jean-Baptiste Poquelain
otherwise known as Moliere.*

Scenes from
- *The Imaginary Invalid • The Physician in Spite of Himself*
- *School for Wives • Tartuffe • Don Juan • The Would-be Gentleman*

*The play script published in this volume includes narratives developed at
Bangalore Little Theatre as part of the workshop production.*

FOR
SRIDHAR RAMANATHAN

DESIGN AND APPROACH

The basic design

An Indian group of storytellers/artists presenting Moliere to an Indian audience.

The set is meant to be minimal. Two benches, three cubes serving as stools and a short step ladder can be arranged in varying configurations for the different scenes played. Each scene is set by the actors during the narrative preceding the scene. All props and costumes are make-shift and improvised, as in most rehearsal spaces in most theatre companies. (For instance, a brass plate and a serving ladle can serve as a gong, a leather-bound ledger served as "the holy book", two bamboo sticks as swords, etc.) The props and costuming are kept at the start in two piles, in and around two steel trunks, stage DR and DL. Seating spaces for the company players are arranged R and L outside the acting area, in full view of the audience. Actors not on in a scene sit there watching the excerpts being played.

The total duration of the performance is approx. an hour and a half. The scenes are played in one continuous run without an intermission.

Costuming

Folk... minstrels...Indian...earthy...compatible with what they do on stage. For instance:

>> Chaniya-cholis, Gujarati style, colourful, minimal costume jewellery
>> Barefeet, anklets

Likewise, the actors will have minimal costuming to suit story contexts, but add on pieces from costumes/prop boxes for each story.

Musical instruments

Only one tambourine or similar percussion. It may be used by different actors in different sequences.

Used in sung portions as well as to punctuate narration.

Body and movement

Energetic, good footwork, interactive – not static
Applies to use of voice as well... wide range in voice usage, full bodied

Ensemble acting

The team of actors plays multiple parts, slipping out of roles and into roles. A Chorus of rour to six actors are the narrators, providing links to the scenes in the play, singing, setting the scenes, etc. Members of the Chorus may also play multiple parts, but remain the same as Chorus. Casting requirement for Chorus: they sing.

The play has also been done by just two actors in a later version.

FIRST PERFORMED

First performed in September 2005 as part of the Summer Project on Theatre (SPOT) at Alliance Francaise de Bangalore with the following ensemble group:

Men Actors .... VENKATESWARAN, ANSHUK, MANIVANNAN, LINGARAJ, RAGHUNATH, MANEESH, MAHESH, KAMAL

Women Actors .... BHAMINI, MAYURI, SUSHMITA, DEEPA, SHRUTI, NEHA, RIDHI, CHINMAYEE

Trainer-facilitators .... VIJAY PADAKI, PRITHAM KUMAR

The play designed and directed by .... VIJAY PADAKI

OVERVIEW OF SCENES

- Chorus: Introduction
- Opener: Imaginary Invalid
- Chorus link: Second
- Physician in Spite of Himself: 2 excerpts
- Chorus link: Third
- School for wives: 4 Excerpts
- Chorus link: Fourth
- Tartuffe: 5 excerpts
- Chorus link: Fifth
- Don Juan Monologue
- Chorus link: Sixth
- Would-be Gentleman: 6 excerpts
- Reprise: Imaginary Invalid
- Closing

OPENER: FIRST SONG, INTRODUCTION

The stage is dimly lit. It is the rehearsal space of a theatre company. Benches, cubes, props and costumes trunks, a short step ladder, etc. are seen on the stage, which is set for Scene 1, the excerpt from The Imaginary Invalid.

The Chorus enters singing. The song may be developed by the performing group, as done in the Bangalore workshop. The tune and lyrics are folksy and have a catchy rhythm. The song ends. The chorus members introduce the programme.

The lines below are distributed among the Chorus.

ALL

Ta daa!

>> Ladies and gentlemen. Presenting

>> The darling of the court of Louis XIV

>> The founder-director of the Illustre Theatre

>> The mercurial, the mesmeric, the magnetic,

>> The masala maker for the French revolution

>> The one and only

>> Jean-Baptiste Poquelain, also known as...

ALL

Moliere! It's Moliere Tonight!!

>> Moliere without a grand set?

>> Without colourful costumes, props?

>> The only stuff we have right now is what's left over from the last play.

>> "Six Authors in Search of Tipu Sultan".

>> And a zero budget for this show.

ALL

Today...we improvise!

>> Let's see what we can do with whatever we have.

>> LET'S SEE IF WE CAN CAPTURE THE ESSENCE OF MOLIERE

>> Without the trappings

>> What do you say? Shall we give it a go?

ALL

Right! Here we go!

>> He was born on Makara Sankranti day in 1622

>> That was January the 15th...we just wanted to get the Indian Connect!

>> And he bid adieu in 1673

>> Probably because of pulmonary TB

>> After playing the part of Argan in The Imaginary Invalid

>> Collapsing backstage...

>> Let us pick up the action from the end.

The actors in Scene 1 position themselves and freeze.

>> Beralde and Argan talk about doctors and quacks
>> In a play where Moliere ridicules doctors.
>> Ladies and Gentlemen, a nugget from Le Malade imaginaire...

ALL

The Imaginary Invalid.
Two members of the chorus tap the actors, who come to life. The Chorus exits.
Scene 1 is played out.

SCENE 1

EXCERPT: Act III. Beralde talks to Argan about doctors and quacks, and the play by Moliere ridiculing doctors.

BERALDE

Will you allow me brother to ask you above all not to excite yourself during our conversation?

ARGAN

Agreed.

BERALDE

And answer the questions I put to you without asperity?

ARGAN

Right.

BERALDE

And treat whatever we have to discuss together in a spirit of entire detachment?

ARGAN

Lord, yes! What a preamble!

BERALDE

All right, brother. We'll leave your life out of it. She's a woman with the best of intentions towards your family, absolutely disinterested, wonderfully attached to you, and shows inconceivable affection and good will towards your children. That's all beyond question. We'll say no more about that and come to your daughter. What's your idea brother, in wanting to marry her to a doctor's son?

ARGAN

The idea is, brother, for me to have the sort of son-in-law I'm in need of.

BERALDE

But that's no concern of your daughter's and moreover, there's someone available who would suit her much better.

ARGAN

Yes, but this happens to suit me better.

BERALDE

But is she to take a husband for her own sake or yours?

ARGAN

For both brother – hers and mine and because we want to have people in the family who will be useful to me.

BERALDE

I suppose on the same principle if the little one were a bit older you'd marry her to an apothecary?

ARGAN

Why not?

BERALDE

How can you possibly continue to be so infatuated with apothecaries and doctors? Are you determined to go on being ill in spite of all that your friends and nature itself can do for you?

ARGAN

What do you mean by that, brother?

BERALDE

What I mean is that I don't know anybody who's less ill than you are. One couldn't wish for a better constitution than yours. One proof that there is nothing wrong with you and that your health is perfectly sound is that you have survived all the medicines they've given you to swallow. In spite of all your efforts you haven't managed to damage your constitution.

ARGAN

But don't you know, brother, that that's just what keeps me going. Dr.Purgeon says that if he left off attending me for three days I shouldn't survive it.

BERALDE

Purge on! He'll be attending you into the next world if you aren't careful.

ARGAN

Let's pursue this question a bit further. You don't believe in medicine at all then?

BERALDE

No,brother, and I don't see that it's necessary to my salvation that I should.

ARGAN

What! You don't accept the truth of what is universally accepted and has been treated with respect and reverence all down the ages.

BERALDE

Far from accepting it as true, I look upon it, between ourselves, as one of the greatest follies of mankind. Looking at it philosophically I don't know any more absurd piece of mummery, anything more ridiculous, than for one man to set up to cure another.

ARGAN

And why don't you admit that one man may cure another?

BERALDE

Because, brother, the nature of the human organism is still a mystery about which we know very little, because nature has drawn too thick a veil before our eyes for us to understand anything of that matter.

ARGAN

So according to you doctors know nothing?

BERALDE

Precisely. Most of them know their classics, talk Latin freely, can give the Greek names of all the diseases, define them, and classify them, but as for curing them – that's a thing they know nothing about.

ARGAN

Yet you must agree that doctors know more about such things than other folk.

BERALDE

They know what I've told you, which doesn't amount to much when it comes to curing people. All that their art consists of is a farrago of high-sounding gibberish, specious babbling which offers words in place of sound reasons and promises instead of results.

ARGAN

All the same, brother, there are other people as wise and as clever as you and we find that everybody has recourse to a doctor when he's ill.

BERALDE

That's evidence of human frailty not proof of a doctor's skill.

ARGAN

But doctors must believe in their art because they have to resort to it themselves.

BERALDE

That's because there are some of them who share the popular errors from which they profit. There are others who don't share them but still take the profit. Your Mr. Purgeon, for example, makes no bones about it. Full of headlong prejudice, unshakeable self-confidence, and no more common sense and reasoning than a brute beast, he goes on his way purging and bleeding at random and hesitates at nothing. It's no good bearing him ill will for the harm he does to you – he'll send you in to the next world with the best of intentions, and in killing you off do no more for you than he would do for his own wife and children or, if need arose, for himself.

ARGAN

You have your knife in him, brother. Let's come down to facts. What is one to do when one's ill?

BERALDE

Nothing, brother.

ARGAN

Nothing?

BERALDE

Nothing. Rest. That's all that is necessary. Nature, if we will but leave her to it, will find her own way out of the disorder into which she has fallen. Our restlessness, our own impatience is the ruin of everything. Most men die of their remedies not of their diseases.

ARGAN

Ay well! You are a great doctor I can see. I only wish some of those gentlemen were here to answer your arguments and cut your cackle.

....

Second song, second narration.

The actors in The Imaginary Invalid freeze. The Chorus enters singing. They unfreeze the actors and lets one of them exit. They escort the other actor to a stool, stage centre and reposition themselves DR.

CHORUS – TOGETHER

It is the year 1673.

>> The celebrated playwright, actor and theatre director, Moliere, is dead.

>> Denied the sacrament of the church and grudgingly given a burial,

>> His was a life full of struggle and obscurity at first.

>> But perseverance. And then fame.

>> And then also ridicule and ostracism.

>> He died in the arms of two Sisters of Mercy.

>> The priests refused the last consolations of the church to the man who had authored the play Tartuffe.

ALL

What do we do now? Where do we go?

(The actor at Centre speaks...as Moliere.)

MOLIERE

You will survive. I will always be with you.

(The Chorus continues)

CHORUS

Jean-Baptiste acquired a taste for drama even while at school. It was to last a long time.

>> Accompanying his father to the King's palace he was able to see court performers of different kinds.

>> He made up his mind that he could never be a lawyer.

>> One day he met a beautiful young woman.

One of the Chorus (a woman) walks across to Moliere.

WOMAN

Her name was Madeline Bejart.

CHORUS

She shared his passion for the theatre.

WOMAN

It will be a great new idea, Jean-Baptiste. Imagine a group of actors together all the time – traveling, working, learning, entertaining people.

CHORUS

Making some money too. We will write our own plays.

>> We will perform them.

>> Oh, what an exciting life that will be!

MOLIERE

I was convinced. I gave up law, took on the name Moliere and created a theatre group.

CHORUS

She was an independent minded redhead,

A woman several years older than himself

MOLIERE

She extracted from Moliere the privilege to choose whichever role she liked – through a legal document!

CHORUS

He wrote funny plays...made people laugh.

>> Why would that get him into trouble?

>> He did not spare anybody. That's why.

>> Husbands and Wives, Doctors, God men, Critics, and the new rich.

WOMAN

The group was often broke and almost always in debt.

CHORUS

After thirteen years Moliere became the director of the company.

>> The Illustre Theatre.

>> He wrote his first play.

>> You had to be careful with him.

>> People he met found their way into his plays.

>> People he loved, people despised, people admired.

>> Including...his second wife, Armande,

>> Merely sixteen when she came into the company.

Another member of the chorus (a girl) joins the Woman and Moliere.

GIRL

I joined the group thinking I was going to be an apprentice. He told me I was very beautiful and that I fascinated him.

WOMAN *(On the other side of Moliere)*
You cannot do this! I have given the best years of my life to you. Am I not your muse?

CHORUS
Have I not stood by you through the worst of times? She is so young.

GIRL
I was seventeen. He was forty. He loved me.

WOMAN
She is...my little sister, for god's sake!

GIRL
He fussed over me. People noticed. He kept his eye on me.

CHORUS
She was just seventeen, and can't a girl have some fun?
>> He was so jealous.
>> They married. Then they separated, then they came together.
>> They separated and came together many times.

MOLIERE
It was a passionate but difficult marriage.
The Woman and the Girl re-join the Chorus.

CHORUS
There were other wives of other husbands in Moliere's plays.
>> They were older and smarter.
>> Often smarter than the husbands.
>> Bolder, more practical, feet on the ground.
>> Who were they modeled after? His first wife, Madeline?
>> Would the stupid, pig headed husband then be himself? Moliere?
>> The woodcutter Sganarelle and his wife appear in several stories showing just that sort of couple.
>> Most famously in one of Moliere's most successful comedies, The Physician in Spite of Himself.

SCENE 2

By now the two actors to play Sganarelle and Martine have entered with a bang and are running about the stage, agitated.

>> It is a routine quarrel between a husband and his wife
>> The woodcutter Sganarelle and his wife Martine.
EXCERPT: Act I, Scene 1.
Sganarelle and Martine (The domestic quarrel)

SGANARELLE

I tell you I'll have nothing to do with it and it's for me to say. I'm the master.

MARTINE

And I am telling you that I'll have you do as I want. I didn't marry you to put up with your nonsensical goings on.

SGANARELLE

Oh! The misery of married life! How right Aristotle was when he said wives were the very devil!

MARTINE

Just listen to the clever fellow – him and his blockhead of an Aristotle!

SGANARELLE

Yes a clever fellow all right! Produce me a woodcutter who can argue and hold forth like a man who has served six years with a famous physician and had his Latin grammar off by heart from infancy.

MARTINE

A plague on the idiot!

SGANARELLE

A plague on you, you worthless hussy!

MARTINE

A curse on the day and hour when I took it into my head to go and say 'I will'!

SGANARELLE

And a curse on the cuckold of a notary who made me sign my name to my own ruin.

MARTINE

A lot of reason you have to complain, I must say! You ought to thank Heaven every minute of your life that you have me for your wife. Do you think you deserved to marry a woman like me?

SGANARELLE

It's true you did me a great honour and I had good cause to be satisfied with my wedding night! But confound it! Don't set me talking about that. I might say things that should not be heard...

MARTINE

Such as?

SGANARELLE

No, let's leave it at that. We know what we know. That's enough. You were pretty lucky to come across me.

MARTINE

Lucky you call it to come across you – a man who has brought me down to the workhouse, a dissolute scoundrel, a dog who eats me out of house and home?

SGANARELLE

That's a lie. I drink as well as eat!

MARTINE

Who has sold every stick in the house.

SGANARELLE

Living on one's means that is!

MARTINE

Who's taken the very bed from under me.

SGANARELLE

You'll get up all the sooner!

MARTINE

Who hasn't left a single thing in the whole place!

SGANARELLE

All the easier to move house.

MARTINE

And does nothing but gamble and drink from morning to night.

SGANARELLE

That's to keep up my spirits.

MARTINE

I have our little children on my hands.

SGANARELLE

Put them on the floor.

MARTINE

They are crying for bread all the time.

SGANARELLE

Give'em a whipping. When I've had my fill I'll have everyone in the house be content.

MARTINE

And do you intend, you sot, that things shall continue to go on like this?

SGANARELLE

Now wife, take it easy, do.

MARTINE

Am I to go on putting up with your insolence and debauchery forever?

SGANARELLE

Don't let us get annoyed, my dear.

MARTINE

Do you think I don't know how to bring you to some sense of your duty?

SGANARELLE

What you do know, my dear, is that I'm not very long suffering and that I have a pretty strong arm.

MARTINE

I don't care what you do.

SGANARELLE

My dear little wifie, you are itching for trouble as usual.

MARTINE

I'll show you that I'm not afraid of you.

SGANARELLE

My dear better half, you really are asking for it.

MARTINE

Do you think I care for your threats?

SGANARELLE

My dear...

MARTINE

Wretch! Villain! Twister! Scoundrel! Gallows bird! Beggarly, scoundrelly, rascally thief . . .

SGANARELLE *[picking up a cudgel and beating her]*

Ah! So you will have it.

MARTINE

Ow! Ow! Ow!

SGANARELLE

That's the right way to quieten you!
(Enter MR ROBERT)

MR ROBERT

Hallo! Hallo! Hallo! Come, come! What's all this about? Disgraceful behaviour! Confound you, you scoundrel. Fancy beating your wife like that!

MARTINE *[facing MR ROBERT arms akimbo, gives a slap]*

Suppose I want him to beat me!

MR ROBERT

Ah! Then I heartily agree.

MARTINE

What are you butting in for?

MR ROBERT

It was wrong of me...

MARTINE

Is it any business of yours?

MR ROBERT

You are right.

MARTINE

Just fancy! The impertinence! Wanting to stop husbands beating their wives!

MR ROBERT

I apologize.

MARTINE

What have you to do with it?

MR ROBERT

Nothing.

MARTINE

What right have you to poke your nose in?

MR ROBERT

None at all.

MARTINE

Mind your own business then.

MR ROBERT

I won't say another word.

MARTINE

What if I like being beaten?

MR ROBERT

All right.

MARTINE

It doesn't hurt you.

MR ROBERT

That's true.

MARTINE

You are a fool to come meddling with what has nothing to do with you.
(She gives him another slap.)

(Mr Robert now goes towards SGANARELLE who addresses him similarly, forces him to retreat, beats him with his cudgel, and puts him to flight.)

MR ROBERT

I beg your pardon friend, most sincerely. Carry on, beat her and thrash her to your heart's content. I'll give you a hand if you like.

SGANARELLE

No I don't want to.

MR ROBERT

Ah! That's different then.

SGANARELLE

I'll beat her or not as I choose.

MR ROBERT

Very good.

SGANARELLE

She's my wife, not yours

MR ROBERT

Undoubtedly.

SGANARELLE

I don't take orders from you

MR ROBERT

Of course not.

SGANARELLE

I don't want your help either

MR ROBERT

Well, that suits me.

SGANARELLE

You are an idiot to interfere in other people's business.

(He beats MR ROBERT and chases him out. He turns to his wife and takes her hand.)

SGANARELLE

Suppose we make peace now. Your hand on it.

MARTINE

Oh yes! After you've beaten me like that!

SGANARELLE

That was nothing. Your hand.

MARTINE

I won't.

SGANARELLE

Eh!

MARTINE
No.

SGANARELLE
My dear little wife.

MARTINE
Not a bit of it.

SGANARELLE
Come on now.

MARTINE
No, I won't.

SGANARELLE
Come, come, come, come!

MARTINE
No! I'm annoyed and I mean it!

SGANARELLE
Bah! It was nothing! Come along!

MARTINE
Let me be.

SGANARELLE
Shake hands, I tell you.

MARTINE
You've treated me too badly.

SGANARELLE
All right then I'll say that I'm sorry. Shake hands on it!

MARTINE
I forgive you.
(Sganarelle drops the cudgel, gives Martine a slurpy kiss and exits grinning. Martine speaks to the audience.)

MARTINE
But I'll make him pay for it yet.
(She picks up the cudgel and exits as the Chorus enter.)

ALL
Fast forward!
>> Is it all made up? Kissed and forgotten?
>> Of course not!

ALL
Revenge!
>> The wife goes on to get her revenge with one of the funniest plots in French comedy.

>> She makes Sganarelle agree to pretend being a doctor, even if he has to be beaten into the act!

>> Here's how it goes.

>> In the nearby town lives a man, Geronte, who is determined to have his daughter marry a certain gentleman.

>> A wealthy gentleman.

>> Lucinde is the daughter. She has a young man of her own choice in mind.

>> And a mind of her own. She must find a way to put off meeting the man her father has chosen.

ALL

Ta-da! A typical Moliere plot is hatched.

>> Lucinde feigns an illness.

>> A special, rare illness. She loses her speech and appears in a daze.

>> The local physician has no clue what the illness is, or what to do about it.

>> Geronte sends his servants on a scouting mission to the countryside.

>> To find a doctor who can cure his daughter.

ALL

They arrive at Martine's backyard.

>> Does she know any good doctor?

>> One who can cure the beautiful young Lucinde of her strange malady.

ALL

Ta-da!

>> Of course she knows one – the best doctor ever.

>> Aah, but there is a catch.

>> He will not admit he is a doctor. He will need...Persuasion.

>> A sound thrashing!

>> The genius doctor in him comes out only with a sound thrashing!

(We see Sganarelle backing off, crying out load, as two men thrash him with the cudgel. The group moves from one side of the stage to the other.)

SGANARELLE

Stop! Oh, stop! All right! Yes, I was a physician once. No! Please. I am a physician still. Yes, I will come with you. Yes, I will examine the young lass. Stop now, please! All right, take me to her!

The Chorus completes the introduction.

>> He is marched off to the town.

>> Directly to the home of Geronte.

ALL

The physician in spite of himself!

EXCERPT: The Physician in Spite of Himself Scene VI (Abridged).

Lucinde is wheeled in on a bench turned into bed.

SGANARELLE

Is this the patient?

GÉRONTE

Yes she's my only daughter; and I would be very upset if she were to die.

SGANARELLE

She must not do anything of the kind. She must not die without the doctor's order.

GÉRONTE

Chairs, please!

SGANARELLE *[Seated between Géronte and Lucinde]*

This is not a bad looking patient, and I think a healthy man would be pleased to have her.

(Lucinde giggles.)

GÉRONTE

You have made her laugh, sir.

SGANARELLE

Excellent. When a doctor makes the patient laugh, it s a very good sign *(To Lucinde)*

Come now, what is the matter? What ails you? What is it you feel?

(Lucinde replies by motions, by putting her hand to her mouth, her head, and under her chin.)

LUCINDE

Ha, hi, ho, ha!

SGANARELLE

What? What are you saying?

LUCINDE *[Continues the same motions]*

Ha, hi, ho, ha, ha, hi, ho!

SGANARELLE

What?

LUCINDE

Ha, hi, ho!

SGANARELLE *[Imitating her]*

Ha, hi, ho, ha, ha! I don't understand you. What the devil is that language?

GÉRONTE

Sir, that's her disease. She has become dumb, and up to now, no one has been able to discover the cause; and this mishap has forced us to postpone her marriage.

SGANARELLE

Why?

GÉRONTE
The man she is supposed to marry wants to wait for her recovery.

SGANARELLE
And who is this fool who doesn't want his wife to be dumb? Would to Heaven mine had that complaint! I'd take great care not to have her cured.

GÉRONTE
In a word, Sir, we beseech you to use all your skill to cure her of this affliction.

SGANARELLE
Don't worry. But tell me, does this pain oppress her much?

GÉRONTE
Yes, Sir.

SGANARELLE
Good. Does she suffer acute pains?

GÉRONTE
Very acute.

SGANARELLE
That's excellent. Does she go to...you know where?

GÉRONTE
Er...yes.

SGANARELLE
Profusely?

GÉRONTE
Sir...I don't understand these things.

SGANARELLE
Is the substance healthy looking? What colour?

GÉRONTE
I am not versed in those things.

SGANARELLE *[Turning to the patient]*
Give me your hand. [To Géronte] This pulse tells me that your daughter is...dumb.

GÉRONTE
Yes, Sir, that is her illness; you've found it out at once.

SGANARELLE
Of course!
We great doctors, we discover things immediately. An ignoramus would have been puzzled, and would have said: it's this, it's that; but I hit the nail on the head from the very first, and I tell you that your daughter is dumb.

GÉRONTE
Yes; but I'd like you to tell me what causes this.

SGANARELLE

Nothing is easier; it is due to the fact that she has lost her speech.

GÉRONTE

All right! But, please, what is the reason for her having lost her speech?

SGANARELLE

Our best authorities will tell you that it is because there is an impediment to the movement of her tongue.

GÉRONTE

But, once more, your opinion on this impediment to the movement of her tongue.

SGANARELLE

Aristotle on this subject says...many wonderful things.

GÉRONTE

I dare say.

SGANARELLE

Ah! He was a great man!

GÉRONTE

No doubt.

SGANARELLE

Yes, a very great man.

(Holding out his arm, and putting a finger of the other hand in the bend). A man who was greater than I by this much. But to come back to our argument: I believe that this impediment to the movement of her tongue is caused by certain humours, which among us learned men, we call peccant humours; peccant that is to say...peccant humours; inasmuch as the vapours formed by the exhalations of the influences which rise up in the area of diseases, coming...so to say...Do you understand Latin?

GÉRONTE

No, I don't.

SGANARELLE *(Suddenly rising)*

You don't understand Latin?

GÉRONTE

No.

SGANARELLE *(Assuming various comic attitudes)*

Cabricias arci thuram, catalamus, singulariter, nominativo, hac musa, the muse, bonus, bona, bonum. Deus sanctus, estne oratio latinas? Etiam, Yes. Quare? Why.

Quia substantivo et adjectivum, concordat in generi, numerum, et casus.

GÉRONTE

Ah! Why didn't I complete my schooling?

SGANARELLE

And so, these vapours which I speak of, passing from the left side, where the liver is, to the right side, where the heart is, it so happens that the lungs, which in Latin we call armyan, having communication with the brain, which in Greek is termed nasmus, by means of the vena cava, which in Hebrew we call cubile, meet in their course the said vapours, which fill the ventricles of the shoulder blades; and because the said vapours...try to understand this argument, please...and because these said vapours are somewhat malignant...listen carefully to this, I beg you.

GÉRONTE

Yes, yes.

SGANARELLE

Are somewhat malignant...pay attention, if you please.

GÉRONTE

I do.

SGANARELLE

Because of the acridity of the humours engendered in the concavity of the diaphragm, it happens that these vapours. Ossabandus, nequeis, nequer, potarinum, quipsa milus. That is the reason why your daughter is dumb.

GÉRONTE

Your reasoning is most eloquent, of course. There is but one thing that surprised me: that's the position of the liver and the heart. It seems to me that you place them differently from where they are; that the heart is on the left side, and the liver on the right.

SGANARELLE

Yes; it was so formerly; but we have changed all that, and we now practise medicine in an entirely different way.

GÉRONTE

I didn't know that, and I apologize for my ignorance.

SGANARELLE

There is no harm done; and you don't have to be as clever as we are.

GÉRONTE

Of course. But what do you think, sir, ought to be done for this complaint?

SGANARELLE

What do I think ought to be done?

GÉRONTE

Yes.

SGANARELLE

My advice is to keep her in bed, and to make her take as a remedy plenty of bread soaked in wine.

GÉRONTE
Why so, sir?

SGANARELLE
Because there is in bread and wine mixed together a power which makes people speak. Don't you see that they give nothing else to parrots, and that, by eating it, they learn to speak?

GÉRONTE
That is true. Oh! The great man! Quick, plenty of bread and wine.
The actors exit quickly, wheeling out Lucinde.
The Chorus enters and introduces the next scene: The School for Wives.

....

Third narration

CHORUS
We meet Moliere's young wife, Armande, in many of his plays.
   >> She was present in the characters he created in the plays of that time.
   >> For instance, Moliere's frustration in coping with the quicksilver ways of Armande finds a solution in an invention.
   >> It is a special school for grooming a young wife for, well, a not so young gentleman.
Arnolphe and Chrysalde take their places.

CHORUS
The school for wives!
>> Arnolphe, a middle aged rogue, believes that the surest safeguard of a wife's honour is...ignorance.
   >> He reveals his intentions to his friend, Chrysalde.
   >> He has a plan for the young Agnes who he intends to marry.
The Chorus exits. Scene 2 is played out: The School for Wives.

SCENE 3

EXCERPTS from The School for Wives
Arnolphe shares his plan with Chrysalde.

ARNOLPHE
A man's not simple to take a simple wife.
Your wife, no doubt, is a wise, virtuous woman,
But brightness, as a rule, is a bad omen,
And I know men who've undergone much pain
Because they married girls with too much brain.
I want no intellectual, if you please,
Who'll talk of nothing but her Tuesday teas,

Who'll frame lush sentiments in prose and verse
And fill the house with wits, and fops, and worse,
While I, as her dull husband, stand about
Like a poor saint whose candles have gone out.

CHRYSALDE
Stupidity's your cup of tea, I gather.

ARNOLPHE
I'd choose a plain, stupid woman rather
Than a great beauty who was over-wise.

CHRYSALDE
But wit and beauty –

ARNOLPHE
Virtue is what I prize.

CHRYSALDE
So be it.

ARNOLPHE
Each man has his own design
For wedded bliss, and I shall follow mine.
I'm rich, and so can take a wife who'll be
Dependent, in the least respect, on me.
A sweet, submissive girl who cannot claim
To have brought me riches or an ancient name.
The gentle, meek expression which she wore
Endeared Agnes to me when she was four;
In a small convent, far from the haunts of man,
The girl was reared according to my plan:
I told the nuns what means must be employed
To keep her growing mind a perfect void,
And, God be praised, they had entire success.
As a grown girl, her simple-mindedness
Is such that I thank Heaven for granting me
A bride who suits my wishes to a T.
Farewell for now.
(He exits)

CHRYSALDE
The man's quite mad. A lunatic, in fact.
The Chorus brings in Agnes with an embroidery basket, seats her and exits.

CHRYSALDE *(Continuing as Narrator)*
Agnes is the girl Arnolphe has chosen to marry. Aah, but while Arnolphe
is away she has been spotted by a young man, Horace, who is the son of

an old friend of Arnolphe, and a newcomer to this town. Horace meets Agnes. Boy meets girl.

(Arnolphe enters and speaks as the second Narrator.)

ARNOLPHE *(as Narrator)*

Arnolphe gets to know. He proceeds to confront the young fiancée, Agnes, and to let her know what lies in store for her. He looks for a way to open the subject...

EXCERPT: Act II, Scene 5.

ARNOLPHE

The weather's mild.

AGNES

Oh, yes.

ARNOLPHE

Most pleasant.

AGNES

Indeed!

ARNOLPHE

What news, my child?

AGNES

The kitten died.

ARNOLPHE

Too bad, but what of that?
All men are mortal, my dear, and so's a cat.
While I was gone, no doubt it rained and poured?

AGNES

No.

ARNOLPHE

You were bored, perhaps?

AGNES

I'm never bored.

ARNOLPHE

During my ten days absence, what did you do?

AGNES

Six nightshirts, I believe; six nightcaps, too.

ARNOLPHE *(after a pause)*

My dear Agnes, this world's a curious thing.
What wicked talk one hears, what gossiping!
While I was gone, or so the neighbours claim,
There was a certain strange young man who came
To call upon you here, and was received.

But such a slander's not to be believed,
And I would wager that their so-called news –

AGNES

Heavens! Don't wager; you'd be sure to lose.

ARNOLPHE

What! Is it true, then, that a man –

AGNES

Oh, yes.
In fact, he all but lived at this address.

ARNOLPHE *(Aside)*

That frank reply would seem to demonstrate
That she's still free of guile, at any rate.
(Aloud) But I gave orders, Agnes, as I recall,
That you were to see no one, no one at all.

AGNES

I disobeyed you, but when I tell you why,
You'll say that you'd have done the same as I.

ARNOLPHE

Perhaps; well, tell me how this thing occurred.

AGNES

It's the most amazing story you ever heard.
I was sewing out on the balcony, in the breeze,
When I noticed someone strolling under the trees.
It was a fine young man, who caught my eye
And made a deep bow as he went by.
I, not to be convicted of a lack
Of manners, very quickly nodded back.
At once, the young man bowed to me again.
I bowed to him a second time, and then
It wasn't very long until he made
A third deep bow, which I of course repaid.
Indeed, had night not fallen, I declare
I think that I might still be sitting there,
And bowing back each time he bowed to me,
For fear he'd think me less polite than he.

ARNOLPHE *(Aside)*

The big question remains: Did he? Did she? Did they?
EXCERPT: Act II, Scene 5 continued.
Arnolphe and Agnes again. (The "ribbon scene")

ARNOLPHE

And when you were alone, what did he do?

AGNES

He swore he loved me with a matchless passion,
And said to me, in the most charming fashion,
Things which I found incomparably sweet,
And never tire of hearing him repeat,
So much do they delight my ear, and start
I know not what commotion in my heart.

ARNOLPHE *(Aside)*

O strange interrogation, where each reply
Makes the interrogator wish to die!
(To Agnes) Besides these compliments, these sweet addresses,
Were there not also kisses and caresses?

AGNES

Oh yes! He took my hands, and kissed and kissed
Them both, as if he never would desist.

ARNOLPHE

And did he not take...something else as well?
(He notes that she is taken aback) Agh!

AGNES

Well, he -

ARNOLPHE

Yes?

AGNES

Took-

ARNOLPHE

What?

AGNES

I dare not tell.
I fear that you'll be furious with me.

ARNOLPHE

No.

AGNES

Yes.

ARNOLPHE

No, no.

AGNES

Then promise not to be.

ARNOLPHE

I promise.

AGNES
He took my - oh, you'll have a fit.

ARNOLPHE
No.

AGNES
Yes.

ARNOLPHE
No, no. The devil! Out with it!
What did he take from you?

AGNES
He took...He took the pretty ribbon that you gave me.
Indeed, he begged so that I couldn't resist.

ARNOLPHE *(Taking a deep breath)*
Forget the ribbon. Tell me: once he'd kissed
Your hands, what else did he do, as you recall?

AGNES
Does one do other things?

ARNOLPHE
No, not at all;
But didn't he ask some further medicine
For the sad state of health that he was in?

AGNES
Why, no. But had he asked, you may be sure
I'd have done anything to speed his cure.

ARNOLPHE *(Aside)*
I've got off cheap this once, thanks be to God;
If I slip again, let all men call me a clod.
(To Agnes) Agnes, my dear, your innocence is vast;
I shan't reproach you; what is past is past.
But all that trifler wants to do – don't doubt it –
Is to deceive you, and then boast about it.

AGNES
Oh, no. He's often assured me otherwise.

ARNOLPHE
Ah, you don't know how that sort cheats and lies.
But do grasp this: To kiss your hands and fill you with 'commotion'
Is a great sin, for which your soul could die.

AGNES
A sin, you say! But please, Sir, tell me why.

ARNOLPHE

Why? Because, as all authority states,
It's just such deeds that Heaven abominates.

AGNES

Abominates! But why should Heaven feel so?
It's all so charming and so sweet, you know!
I never knew about this sort of thing
Till now, or guess what raptures it could bring.

ARNOLPHE

Yes, all these promises of love undying,
These sighs, these kisses, are most gratifying,
But they must be enjoyed in the proper way;
One must be married first, that is to say.

AGNES

And once you're married, there's no evil in it?

ARNOLPHE

That's right.

AGNES

Oh, let me marry, then, this minute!

ARNOLPHE

If that's what you desire, I feel the same;
It was to plan your marriage that I came.

AGNES

What! Truly?

ARNOLPHE

Yes.

AGNES

How happy I shall be!

ARNOLPHE

Yes, wedded life will please you, I foresee.

AGNES

You really intend that we two –

ARNOLPHE

Yes, I do.

AGNES

Oh, how I'll kiss you if that dream comes true!

ARNOLPHE

And I'll return your kisses, every one.

AGNES

I'm never sure when people are making fun.

Are you quite serious?

ARNOLPHE
Yes, I'm serious. Quite.

AGNES
We're to be married?

ARNOLPHE
Yes.

AGNES
But when?

ARNOLPHE
Tonight.

AGNES *(Laughing)*
Tonight?

ARNOLPHE
Tonight. It seems you're moved to laughter.

AGNES
Yes.

ARNOLPHE
Well, to see you happy is what I'm after.

AGNES
Oh, Sir, I owe you more than I can express!
With him, my life will be pure happiness!

ARNOLPHE
With whom?

AGNES
With...him.

ARNOLPHE
With him! Well, think again.

AGNES *(As Narrator)*
In the next visit Agnes is told firmly where she stands. And what is expected of a perfect wife.
EXCERPT: Act III, Scene 2 (The Maxims of Marriage)
Arnolphe has a small book in his hands

ARNOLPHE
Agnes, stop stitching and hear what I have to say.
Lift up your head a bit, and turn this way.
(Putting his finger to his forehead)
Look at me here while I talk to you, right there,
And listen to my every word with care.
My dear, I'm going to wed you, and you should bless

Your vast good fortune and your happiness.
Reflect upon your formal low estate,
And judge, then, if my goodness is not great
In raising you, a humble peasant lass,
To be a matron of the middle class,
To share the bed and the connubial bliss
Of one who's shunned the married state till this,
Withholding from a charming score or two
The honour which he now bestows on you.
Be ever mindful, Agnes, that you would be,
Without this union, a nonentity;
I have, in my pocket, a book of no small fame
From which you'll learn the office of a wife.
'Twas written by some man of pious life.
Study his teaching faithfully, and heed it.
Here, take the book; let's hear how well you read it.

AGNES *(Reading)*
The Maxims of Marriage
or
The Duties of a Married Woman
Together with Her Daily Exercises.
First Maxim:
A woman who in church has said
She'll love and honour and obey
Should get it firmly in her head,
Despite the fashions of the day,
That he who took her for his own
Has taken her for his bed alone.
(She looks up perplexed)

ARNOLPHE
I shall explain that; doubtless you're perplexed.
But, for the present, let us hear what's next.

AGNES *(Continuing)*
Second maxim:
Let her not daub her face
With paint and patch and powder-base
And creams which promise beauty on the label.
It is not for their husbands' sake
But vanity's, that women undertake
The labours of the dressing table.
Third Maxim:
Let her be veiled whenever she leaves the house,
So that her features are obscure and dim.

If she desires to please her spouse,
She must please no one else but him.
Fourth Maxim:
Except for friends who call
To see her husband, let her not admit
Anyone at all.
A visitor whose end
Is to amuse the wife with gallant wit
Is not the husband's friend.
The Chorus enters and takes over as Agnes and Arnolphe watch

ALL

The maxims of marriage!
>> Composed by men
>> To be practiced by women.

ALL

To continue with the maxims...
>> She must keep his rooms tidy, bring him three meals a day (to be eaten in his room),
>> keep his clothes and laundry in good order, and keep his bedroom and study neat.
>> She must not use his desk, of course.
>> She must not expect her husband to either sit with her, or accompany her outside of the house - and she must stop talking when he requests.
(Agnes looks into her book. She and Arnolphe stare at each other.)

ALL

Maxims!
>> That was not the old gentleman from Moliere's play. That was...
>> Somebody we all know from our times. Can you guess?
(They engage the audience)
>> It was Albert Einstein!
>> Nothing has changed, has it?

....

Fourth song and narration.
The Chorus sings. (Song to be developed.) When the song ends they stand still, heads bowed. Finally, one in the Chorus speaks.
>> Tartuffe!

ALL

Tartuffe!
>> Tartuffe. 1664.
>> The play was meant to be a short comedy, but it turned out into one long length of persecution for the group.

>> Even Moliere's friend, the king, could not protect him in the hounding that followed Tartuffe.

>> The play came under immense pressure from the aristocracy.

ALL

The court had to ban the play.

>> What was it about Tartuffe that attracted so much resentment?

>> It was the dig at unscruplous godmen. Tartuffe was one.

>> Swamijis of that time.

(Orgon and Dorine enter to take their places.)

DORINE

A play cannot be about the godman only. Godmen thrive after all on the gullibility of ordinary men.

ORGON

And women.

DORINE

Aah, women and swamijis, swamijis and women...

ORGON

Again... Things haven't changed in 350 years

DORINE

In this play the victim is a man. But not without a woman involved!

ORGON

His name is Orgon. A rich man, a weak and foolish head of a rich household, who falls prey to the wily charm of the imposter Tartuffe.

DORINE

Orgon appears possessed.

(By now Orgon and Dorine are in position for the scene.)

CHORUS

Orgon returns from an out of town trip

>> Dorine, the maid, worries about her mistress' health

>> Orgon talks only about Tartuffe

(The Chorus exits.

Five excerpts from Tartuffe follow.

Orgon, returning from a trip, asks about Tartuffe, the house guest, while Dorine worries about her Mistress' health.)

ORGON

Has all been well, these two days I've been gone?
What's been going on?

DORINE

Your wife, two days ago, had a bad fever,
And a fierce headache which refused to leave her.

ORGON
Ah. And Tartuffe?

DORINE
Tartuffe? Why, he's round and red,
Bursting with health, and excellently fed.

ORGON
Poor fellow!

DORINE
That night, the mistress was unable
To take a single bite at the dinner-table.
Her headache-pains, she said, were simply hellish.

ORGON
Ah. And Tartuffe?

DORINE
He ate his meal with relish,
And zealously devoured in her presence
A leg of mutton and a brace of pheasants.

ORGON
Poor fellow!

DORINE
After much ado, we talked her
Into dispatching someone for the doctor.
He bled her, and the fever quickly fell.

ORGON
Ah. And Tartuffe?

DORINE
He bore it very well.
To keep his cheerfulness at any cost,
And make up for the blood Madame had lost,
He drank, at lunch, four beakers full of port.

ORGON
Poor fellow!

DORINE
Both are doing well in short.
I'll go and tell Madame that you've expressed
Keen sympathy and anxious interest.
(The actors freeze briefly, then continue with the next link.)

DORINE

Very interestingly, Tartuffe appears on stage for the first time only in the third act of the play. We discover that Orgon has decided to give away his daughter Mariane in marriage...to Tartuffe.

ORGON

Mariane, of course, has a lover, Valere, who had earlier been approved by her parents.

Mariane enters and takes her place.
EXCERPT: Act II, Scenes 1 and 2.
Orgon proposes marriage with Tartuffe to Mariane. Dorine watches from behind.

ORGON

Mariane.

MARIANE

Yes, Father?

ORGON

A word with you; come here.

MARIANE

What are you looking for?

ORGON *(peering into a small closet)*

Eavesdroppers, dear.
The Maid, Dorine, enters, duster in hand and eavesdrops.
I'm making sure we shan't be overheard.
Someone in there could catch our every word.
Ah, good, we're safe. Now Mariane, my child,
You're a sweet girl who's tractable and mild,
Whom I hold dear, and think most highly of...
Now what d'you think of Tartuffe, our guest?

MARIANE

I, Sir?

ORGON

Yes. Weigh your answer; think it through.

MARIANE

Oh dear, I'll say whatever you wish me to.

ORGON

That's wisely said, my Daughter. Say of him, then,
That he's the worthiest of men,
And that you're fond of him, and would rejoice
In being his wife, if that should be my choice.
Well?... Well?

MARIANE

Forgive me, pray. Of whom, Sir, must I say
That I am fond of him, and would rejoice
In being his wife, if that should be your choice?

ORGON

Why, of Tartuffe.

MARIANE

But Father, that's false, you know.
Why would you have me say what isn't so?

ORGON

Because I am resolved it shall be true.
That it's my wish should be enough for you.

MARIANE

You can't mean Father...

ORGON

Yes, Tartuffe shall be
Allied by marriage to this family,
And he's to be your husband, is that clear? It's a father's privilege

EXCERPT: Dorine enters with MARIANE

ORGON *(to Dorine)*

What are you doing in here?
Is curiosity so fierce a passion
With you, that you must eavesdrop in this fashion?

DORINE

There's lately been a rumour going about –
Based on some hunch or chance remark, no doubt –
That you mean Mariane to wed Tartuffe.
I've laughed it off, of course, as just a spoof.

ORGON

You find it so incredible?

DORINE

All right, then: we believe you, sad to say.
But how a man like you, who looks so wise.
And wears a moustache of such splendid size,
Can be so foolish as to...

ORGON *(Pushing Dorine off to the corner)*

Silence, please!
My girl, you take too many liberties.
I'm master here, as you must not forget.

DORINE

Do let's discuss this calmly, don't be upset.
You can't be serious, Sir, about this plan.
What should that bigot want with Mariane?
Praying and fasting ought to keep him busy.
And then, in terms of wealth and rank, what is he?
Why should a man of property like you
Pick out a beggar son-in-law?

ORGON

That will do.
(He exits.
Valere enters and joins Dorine and Mariane. They provide the next link.)

MARIANE

Oh, there's plenty of comedy in the play.

DORINE

Remember, the play was written as a comedy.

VALERE

For instance, when Valere confronts Mariane on hearing about her proposed marriage to Tartuffe, there is a lovers quarrel that is soon going into a tailspin.

EXCERPT: Act II, Scene 4.
Valere, Mariane and Dorine.

MARIANE

Go then: console yourself; don't hesitate.
I wish you to; indeed, I cannot wait.

VALERE

You wish me to?

MARIANE

Yes.

VALERE

That's the final straw.
Madam, farewell. Your wish shall be my law.
(He starts to leave, and then returns. This happens repeatedly)

MARIANE

Splendid.

VALERE

(Coming back again)
This breach, remember, if of your making;
It's you who've driven me to the step I'm taking.

MARIANE
Of course.

VALERE *(Coming back again)*
Remember, too, that I am merely
Following your example.

MARIANE
I see that clearly.

VALERE
Enough. I'll go and do your bidding, then.

MARIANE
Good.

VALERE *(Coming back again)*
You shall never see my face again.

MARIANE
Excellent.

VALERE *(Walking to the door, then turning about:)*
Yes?

MARIANE
What?

VALERE
What's that? What did you say?

MARIANE
Nothing. You're dreaming.

VALERE
Ah. Well, I'm on my way.
Farewell, Madame.
He moves away...slowly.

MARIANE
Farewell.

DORINE *(to Marianne)*
If you ask me,
Both of you are mad as mad can be.
Do stop this nonsense, now. I've only let you
Squabble so long to see where it would get you.
Whoa there, Monsieur Valere!
(She goes and seizes Valere by the arm; he makes a great show of resistance.)

VALERE
What's this, Dorine?

DORINE
Come here.

VALERE
No, no, my heart's too full of spleen.
Don't hold me back; her wish must be obeyed.

DORINE
Oh, pooh!

MARIANE
He hates the sight of me, that's plain.
I'll go, and so deliver him from pain.

DORINE
And now you run away! Get back.

MARIANE
No, no.
Nothing you say will keep me here. Let go!

VALERE
She cannot bear my presence, I perceive.
To spare her further torment, I shall leave.

DORINE
Again! You'll not escape, Sir; don't you try it.
Come here, you two. Stop fussing, and be quiet.

VALERE *(to Dorine)*
What do you want of me?

MARIANE *(to Dorine)*
What is the point of this?

DORINE
We're going to have a little armistice.
(to Valere) Now weren't you silly to get so overheated?

VALERE
Didn't you see how badly I was treated?

DORINE *(to Mariane)*
Aren't you a simpleton, to have lost your head?

MARIANE
Didn't you hear the hateful things he said?

MARIANE *(to Valere)*
You're both great fools.
Her sole desire, Valere,
Is to be yours in marriage. To that I'll swear.
(To Mariane) He loves you only, and he wants no wife
But you, Mariane. On that I'll stake my life.

MARIANE *(to Valere)*
Then why you advised me so, I cannot see.

VALERE *(to Mariane)*
On such a question, why ask advice of me?

DORINE
Oh, you're impossible. Give me your hands, you two.
(To Valere) Yours first.

VALERE *(giving Dorine his hand)*
But why?

DORINE *(To Mariane)*
And now a hand from you.

MARIANE *(Also giving Dorine her hand)*
What are you doing?

DORINE
There: a perfect fit.
You suit each other better than you'll admit.
(Valere and Mariane hold hands for some time without looking at each other.)

VALERE *(turning towards Mariane)*
Ah, come, don't be so haughty. Give a man
A look of kindness, won't you, Mariane?
(Mariane turns towards Valere and smiles.
The actors freeze briefly. Mariane and Valere set the next scene and then exit, arm in arm.
Dorine continues with the link.)

DORINE
I tell you, lovers are completely mad!
(Tartuffe appears late in the play. Almost immediately on his appearance we have a scene between him and Elmire, Orgon's wife.)

EXCERPT: Act III, Scene 3.
Elmire and Tartuffe – the first seduction.

TARTUFFE
May Heaven, whose infinite goodness we adore,
Preserve your body and soul forevermore,
And bless your days, and answer thus the plea
Of one who is its humblest votary.

ELMIRE
I thank you for that pious wish. But please,
Do take a chair and let's be more at ease.
(They sit down.)

TARTUFFE
I trust you are once more well and strong?

ELMIRE

There's a private matter I'm anxious to discuss.
I'm glad there's no one here to hinder us.

TARTUFFE

I too am glad; it floods my heart with bliss
To find myself along with you like this.
For just this chance I've prayed with all my power –
But prayed in vain, until this happy hour.

ELMIRE

This won't take long, Sir, and I hope you'll be
Entirely frank and unconstrained with me.

TARTUFFE *(Taking Elmire's hand and pressing her fingertips)*

Quite so; and such great fervour do I feel.

ELMIRE

Ooh! Please! You're pinching.

TARTUFFE

'Twas from excess of zeal.
I never meant to cause you pain, I swear.
I'd rather...
(He places his hand on Elmire's knee)

ELMIRE

What can your hand be doing there?

TARTUFFE

Feeling your gown; what soft, fine-woven stuff!

ELMIRE

Please, I'm extremely ticklish. That's enough.
She draws her chair away; Tartuffe pulls his after her.

TARTUFFE *(Fondling the lace collar of her gown)*

My, my, what lovely lacework on your dress!
The workmanship's miraculous, no less.
I've not see anything to equal it.

ELMIRE

Yes, quite. But let's talk business for a bit.
They say my husband means to break his word.
And give his daughter to you, Sir. Had you heard?

TARTUFFE

He did once mention it. But I confess
I dream of quite a different happiness
It's elsewhere, Madam, that my eyes discern
The promise of that bliss for which I yearn.

ELMIRE
I see: you care for nothing here below.

TARTUFFE
Ah well – my heart's not made of stone, you know.

ELMIRE
All your desires mount heavenward, I'm sure,
In scorn of all that's earthly and impure.

TARTUFFE
A love of heavenly beauty does not preclude
A proper love for earthly pulchritude;
I vowed to flee the sight of you, eschewing
A rapture that might prove my soul's undoing;
But soon, fair being, I became aware
That my deep passion could be made to square
With rectitude, and with my bounden duty.
I thereupon surrendered to your beauty.

ELMIRE
Your declaration is most gallant, Sir,
But don't you think it's out of character?
It ill becomes a pious man like you...

TARTUFFE
I may be pious, but I'm human too:
With your celestial charms before his eyes
A man has not the power to be wise.
(Elmire and Tartuffe freeze briefly. Tartuffe repositions himself for the next excerpt.
Elmire provides a short link.)

ELMIRE
Elmire, of course, is not surprised at all with Tartuffe's behaviour.
She just about manages to convince Orgon to hide and watch what happens when she meets Tartuffe again. There is another scene with Elmire and Tartuffe where she suggests that it would be in order for Tartuffe to continue from where he left things earlier.
(Orgon enters on tip-toe with a lampshade on his head and positions himself. Tartuffe enters.)

EXCERPT: Act IV, Scene 5.
Elmire and Tartuffe – the second seduction. Orgon watches from behind.

TARTUFFE
Madam, no happiness is so complete
As when, from lips we love, come words so sweet;
And yet I must beg leave, now, to confess

Some lingering doubts as to my happiness.
Might this not be a trick? Might not the catch
Be that you wish me to break off the match
With Mariane, and so have feigned to love me?
I shan't quite trust your fond opinion of me
Until the feelings you've expressed so sweetly
Are demonstrated somewhat more concretely.

ELMIRE

(She coughs, to warn her husband)
Why be in such a hurry? Must my heart
Exhaust its bounty at the very start?

TARTUFFE

Well, if you look with favour upon my love,
Why, then, begrudge me some clear proof thereof?

ELMIRE

Must not one be afraid of Heaven's wrath?

TARTUFFE

Madam, forget such fears, and be my pupil,
And I shall teach you how to conquer scruple.
Some joys, it's true, are wrong in Heaven's eyes;
Yet Heaven is not averse to compromise;
There is a science, lately formulated,
Whereby one's conscience may be liberated,
And any wrongful act you care to mention
May be redeemed by purity of intention.
I'll teach you, Madam, the secrets of that science;
Meanwhile, just place on me your full reliance.
Assuage my keen desires, and feel no dread:
The sin, if any, shall be on my head.
(Elmire coughs again, this time more loudly)
If you're still troubled, think of things this way:
No one shall know our joys, save us alone,
And there's no evil till the act is known;
It's scandal, Madam, which makes it an offence,
And it's no sin to sin in confidence.

ELMIRE

(Having coughed once more):
Well, clearly I must do as you require,
And yield to your importunate desire.
It is apparent, now, that nothing else
Will satisfy you, and so I acquiesce

TARTUFFE
Madam, the fault is mine, if fault there be,
And...

ELMIRE
Open the door a little, and peek out;
I wouldn't want my husband poking about.

TARTUFFE
Why worry about that man? Each day he grows
More gullible; one can lead him by the nose.
To find us here would fill him with delight,
And if he saw the worst, he'd doubt his sight.

ELMIRE
Nevertheless, do step out for a minute
Into the hall, and see that no one's in it.

ORGON
(Coming out from hiding)
That man's a perfect monster, I must admit!
I'm simply stunned. I can't get over it.

ELMIRE
What, coming out so soon? How premature!
Get back into hiding, and wait until you're sure.

ORGON
Hell never harboured anything so vicious!

ELMIRE
Tut, don't be hasty. Try to be judicious.

TARTUFFE *(Not seeing Orgon)*
Madam, all things have worked out to perfection;
I've given the neighbouring rooms a full inspection;
No one's about; and now that I may at last...

ORGON *(Intercepting him)*
Hold on, my passionate fellow, not so fast!
I should advise a little more restraint.
Well, so you thought, you'd fool me, my dear saint!
How soon you wearied of the saintly life –
Wedding my daughter, and coveting my wife!

TARTUFFE
Brother...

ORGON
Spare me your falsehoods and get out of here.

TARTUFFE
No, I'm the master, and you're the one to go!

This house belongs to me, I'll have you know,
And I shall show you that you can't hurt me
By this contemptible conspiracy,
That those who cross me know not what they do,
And that I've means to expose and punish you,
Avenge offended Heaven, and make you grieve
That ever you dared order me to leave.
(Tartuffe exits.)

ELMIRE
What was the point of all that angry chatter?

ORGON
Dear God, I'm worried. This is no laughing matter.

ELMIRE
How so?

ORGON
I fear I understood his drift.
I'm much disturbed about that deed of gift.

ELMIRE
You gave him...?

ORGON
Yes, it's all been drawn and signed.
(The actors freeze briefly and exit.
The chorus enters and provides the next link.)

Fifth narration
The Chorus enters – without a song this time.

CHORUS *(Together)*
No, it is not tragedy.
>> It is still comedy.
>> Yes, the play does have comic scenes.
>> And a happy ending. A typical Moliere clever ending.
>> But for the group, and Moliere in particular, Tartuffe turned out to be an extended ordeal.
>> That did nothing to quell Moliere's knack for controversy.
>> He went straight ahead and wrote Don Juan in retaliation.
>> It was performed in 1665.
>> As if Tartuffe was not enough...
>> That play too was forced to be withdrawn by the religious authorities after fifteen performances, and never performed again.
(The chorus chants a brief lament. (To be devised by the performing group)
Two members of the chorus escort the actor playing Don Juan, who enters hesitantly.)

DON JUAN

What makes you think somebody in the audience here will not get worked up? Write a letter to the Censor Board tomorrow, or worse, to you-know-who, asking for a ban on this show?

>> We'll cross that bridge when we get there. Get on with it.

DON JUAN

Well...Alright...

ALL

Get on with it.

(Don Juan turns his back to the audience, transforms into Don Juan, turns back, and does an excerpt from Don Juan: the monologue in Act I.)

SCENE 5

EXCERPT from Don Juan: the monologue.
The actor uses the stage space imaginatively.

DON JUAN

What! Would you have a man tie himself up to the first woman that captured his fancy, renounce the world for her, and never again look at anyone else? That is a fine idea, I must say, to make virtue of faithfulness, to bury oneself for good and all in one single passion and remain blind ever after to all the other beauties that might catch one's eye! No! Let fools make a virtue of constancy! All beautiful women have a right to our love, and the accident of being the first comer shouldn't rob others of a fair share in our hearts. As for me, beauty delights me wherever I find it and I freely surrender myself to its charms. No matter how far I'm committed, the fact that I am in love with one person shall never make me unjust to the others. I keep an eye for the merits of all of them and render each one the homage, pay each one the tribute that nature enjoins. Come what may, I cannot refuse love to what I find lovable, and so, when a beautiful face is asking for love, if I had ten thousand hearts I would freely bestow every one of them. After all, there is something inexpressibly charming in falling in love and, surely, the whole pleasure lies in the fact that love isn't lasting. How delightful, how entrancing it is to lay siege with a hundred attentions to a young woman's heart; to see, day by day, how one makes slight advances; to pit one's exaltation, one's sighs and one's tears, against the modest reluctance of a heart unwilling to yield; to surmount, step by step, all the little barriers by which she resists; to overcome her proud scruples and bring her at last to consent. But once one succeeds, what else remains? What more can one wish for? All that delights one in passion is over and one can only sink into a tame and slumberous affection...until a new love comes along to awaken desire and offer the charm of new conquests. There is no pleasure to compare with the conquest of beauty, and my ambition is that of all the great conquerors who could never find it in them to set bounds to their ambitions, but must go on forever from conquest to conquest. Nothing can restrain my impetuous desires. I feel it is in me to love the whole world and like Alexander still wish for new worlds to conquer.

(At the end of the monologue Don Juan freezes briefly and then retransforms himself into the reticent actor.

The chorus enters and applauds him.!)

DON JUAN *(To audience)*

It's a part every actor wants to sink his teeth into. I don't know...Maybe I will get it right one of these days. Playing Don Juan is like playing Moliere himself. Frightening!

The actor exits

Sixth song, Sixth narration.

On stage already, the Chorus sings. (Song to be developed.)

CHORUS

The mocking continued!

\>> If it wasn't doctors and lawyers, it was the page 3 people of his times!

\>> Le Bourgeois Gentilhomme...

\>> A hugely successful comedy.

ALL

The Would-be Gentleman!

\>> M. Jourdain!...has come into great wealth.

\>> What he wants now is culture. More correctly, what he wants to do now is to buy culture.

\>> More more correctly, that means finding his way into the elite circle of "quality people". He has big plans.

\>> Including a suitable husband for his daughter Lucille.

\>> Who, of course, is in love already with another young man, a handsome young man called Cleonte!

\>> Mme. Jourdain has her own ideas about marriage for her daughter.

M Jourdain and the music, fencing and dancing masters enter. There is also a philosophy master. (Called Music, Fencing, Dance and Philosophy below.) They are helping him put on his make shift costume.

\>> For a start, M. Jourdain decides to hire an expensive tailor for a completely up to date wardrobe.

JOURDAIN

Of course he is taken for a ride, and ends up looking quite ridiculous in his new clothes.

MUSIC
And then he hires *(himself)* a Music Master –
(He adds on costume/props items)

DANCE *(Himself)*
A Dance Master –
(He adds on costume/props items)

FENCING *(Himself)*
A Fencing Master, all of them to teach him the gentlemanly arts.
(He adds on costume/props items)

JOURDAIN
Essential qualifications for entry into the court circle.
>> And a philosophy Master to teach him, well, to read and write.
>> One day, the teachers arrive one after the other at M. Jourdain's home.

ALL
They all set to work on him...having fun at his expense.
The Chorus exits.
The excerpts from The Would-be Gentleman follow.

SCENE 6

The Would-be Gentleman
EXCERPT: Act II. The quarrel among the music, dance and fencing masters, with the philosophy master joining in.
M. Jourdain is attempting to pirouette. He is clumsy.

MR JOURDAIN
Phew! Learning dance is not easy!

DANCE
You do splendidly.
(It is the Fencing Master's turn. He steps forward.)

FENCING
I have told you before that the whole art of sword-play lies in two things only – in giving and not receiving. And, as I showed you the other day by logical demonstration, it is impossible for you to receive a hit if you know how to turn your opponent's sword from the line of your body, for which all that is needed is the slightest turn of the wrist – inward or outward.

MR JOURDAIN
At that rate, then, a fellow can be sure of killing his man and not being killed himself...without need of courage.

FENCING
Exactly! Didn't you follow my demonstration?

MR JOURDAIN

Oh yes.

FENCING

Well then, you see what respect should be paid to men of my profession and how much more important is skill in arms than such futile pursuits as dancing and music.

DANCE

Go easy, Mr Scabbard Scraper. Mind what you say about dancing.

MUSIC

And try to treat music with a little more respect if you please.

FENCING

A fine lot of jokers you are, to think of comparing your professions with mine.

MUSIC

Just listen who's talking.

DANCE

The ridiculous creature, with his leather upholstered belly!

FENCING

My little dancing master, I could make you skip if I had a mind to, and as for you, sing to my tune!

DANCING MASTER

Mr sabre-rattler, I shall have to teach you your trade.

MR JOURDAIN *(to dancing master)*

You must be mad to quarrel with a man who knows all about tierce quart and can kill a man by logical demonstration.

DANCE

I don't give a rap for his logical demonstration, his tierce, or his quart.

MR JOURDAIN *(to dancing master)*

Do be careful, I tell you.

FENCING *(to dancing master)*

You impertinent jackanapes!

MR JOURDAIN

Oh, Mr Fencing Master!

DANCE

You great cart horse!

MR JOURDAIN

Oh, Mr. Dancing Master!

FENCING

If I once set about you –

MR JOURDAIN (*to dancing master*)
Gently there – gently!

DANCE
If I once get my hands on you –

MR JOURDAIN
Easy now! Easy!

FENCING
I'll let a little daylight into you.

MR JOURDAIN (*to fencing master*)
Please – please – if you please.

DANCE
I'll give you such a drubbing.

MR JOURDAIN (*to dancing master*)
I ask you – I – I –

MUSIC
Just give us a chance and we will teach him how to talk to –

MR JOURDAIN (*to music master*)
Do for goodness sake stop!
(*The Philosophy Master enters*)

MR JOURDAIN
Ah, M'sieur Philosopher. You have arrived in the nick of time with your philosophy. Come and make peace between these fellows.

PHILOSOPHER
What is it? What is it all about, gentlemen?

MR JOURDAIN
They have got so worked up about which of their professions is the most important that they have started slanging each other and very nearly come to blows.

PHILOSOPHER
Come, come, gentlemen ! Why let yourselves be carried away like this? Have you not read Seneca on passion which reduces men to the level of animals ! Surely, surely, reason should control all our actions!

DANCE
But my good Sir, he has just been black-guarding the pair of us and disparaging music, which is this gentleman`s profession, and dancing which is mine.

PHILOSOPHER
A wise man is superior to any insults which can be put upon him, and the best reply to unseemly behaviour is patience and moderation.

FENCING

They had impudence to compare their professions with mine.

PHILOSOPHER

Well friend, why should that move you? We should never compete in vainglory or precedence. What really distinguishes man one from another is wisdom and virtue.

DANCE

I maintain that dancing is a form of skill, a science, to which sufficient honour can never be paid.

MUSIC

And I that music has been held in foremost esteem all down the ages.

FENCING

And I still stick to my points against the pair of them that skill in arms is finest and most necessary of all the sciences.

PHILOSOPHER

In that case where does philosophy come in? I consider you are all three presumptuous to speak with such assurance before me and impudently give the title of science to a set of mere street accomplishments which does not even deserve the name of arts and can only be adequately described under their wretched trades of gladiator, ballad singer, and mountebank!

FENCING

What?! Oh get out! You dog of a philosopher!

MUSIC

Get out ! You miserable pedant!

DANCING

Get out ! You beggarly usher!

PHILOSOPHER

What! Rascals like you dare to –
(He burls himself upon them and all three set about him.)

MR JOURDAIN

Mr. Philosopher!

PHILOSOPHER

Scoundrels, rogues, insolent –

MR JOURDAIN

Mr. Philosopher!

FENCING MASTER

Confound the brute!

MR JOURDAIN

Gentlemen!

PHILOSOPHER
Insolent scoundrels!

MR JOURDAIN
Oh, Mr. Philosopher!

DANCING
The devil take the ignorant blockhead!

MR JOURDAIN
Gentlemen!

PHILOSOPHER
Villains!

MR JOURDAIN
Mr. Philosopher!

MUSIC
Down with him *(her)*!

MR JOURDAIN
Gentlemen!

PHILOSOPHER
Rogues! Traitors! Impostors! Mountebanks!

MR JOURDAIN
Mr. Philosopher, Gentlemen, Mr. Philosopher, Gentlemen, Mr. Philosopher, Gentlemen...
(They rush out still fighting. M. Jourdain sinks into a seat wiping his brow. A great big crash is heard offstage. Jourdain is alarmed. Another crash. The Philosophy Master enters.)

PHILOSOPHER *(as Narrator)*
When things cool down, the philosophy lesson begins. Would M. Jourdain like to begin with Latin?

JOURDAIN *(as Narrator)*
Well... not easy on the tongue.

PHILOSOPHER
Some moral philosophy, then?

JOURDAIN
Moral? Oh dear...

PHILOSOPHER
Logic? Natural sciences?

JOURDAIN
Too much of a rigmarole.

EXCERPT: Act II. The philosophy master instructs Jourdain on vowels.

PHILOSOPHER

Then what am I to teach you?

JOURDAIN

Teach me to spell.

PHILOSOPHER

Willingly.

JOURDAIN

And then you can teach me the almanac so that I shall know if there will be a moon or not.

PHILOSOPHER

Very well. Now, to meet your wishes and at the same time treat the matter philosophically, one must begin, according to the proper order of these things, with the precise recognition of the nature of the letters of the alphabet and the different ways of pronouncing them, and, in this connexion, I must explain that the letters are divided into two varieties: vowels and consonants, so named because they express the various sounds pronounced `con`, or with, the vowels and serve only to differentiate the various articulations of the voice. There are five vowels, A,E,I,O,U.

Note: The vowels A/E/I/O/U are to be pronounced the French way:

A: AAH

E: EH / EY

I: EE

O: OH

U: OO

(The formation of the mouth/jaw that the Philosopher teaches conform to that.)

MR JOURDAIN

Ah, I understand all that.

PHILOSOPHER

The vowel A is pronounced with the mouth open wide. So – A , Aah, Aah.

MR JOURDAIN

Ah, Ah. Yes.

PHILOSOPHER

The vowel E is pronounced by bringing the jaws near together. So, A, E...Aah, Eh.

MR JOURDAIN

A, E. Ah, Eh. Now that is fine.

PHILOSOPHER

For the vowel I, bring the jaws still nearer together and stretch the mouth corners towards the ears, so –A, E, I...Aah, Eh, Eee.

MR JOURDAIN

A, E, I, Ah, Eh, Eee. It is quite right, Oh ! what a wonderful thing is knowledge!

PHILOSOPHER

To pronounce the vowel O you must open the mouth again and round the lips so...Oh.

MR JOURDAIN

Oh, you're right again! Ah, Eh, Ee, Oh. Splendid. Ee – Oh – Ee – Oh – Ee – Oh – Ee – Oh.

PHILOSOPHER

The opening of the mouth is exactly the shape of the letter O.

MR JOURDAIN

Oh, O. You are right. Oh. How wonderful to know such things!

PHILOSOPHER

The vowel U is pronounced by bringing the teeth close together, but without quite meeting and pushing your lips forward ever so lightly, you happen to show that you only need say You!

MR JOURDAIN

U, you. It's perfectly true. Oh why didn`t I learn all this earlier?

PHILOSOPHER

Tomorrow we will take the other letters, the consonants.
(The Philosopher exits.
Mrs. Jourdain and Cleonte enter and provide a brief link.)

MRS. JOURDAIN

Meanwhile, Cleonte and Lucille have been seeing each other, and the time has come, they think, for Cleonte to talk to M. Jourdain.

CLEONTE

Jourdain refuses to budge when approached by Mrs. Jourdain on behalf of the young couple.

MRS. JOURDAIN

Cleonte. decides to meet M. Jourdain himself and ask for the hand of Lucille

CLEONTE

Mrs. Jourdain stays and watch from behind.
(Mrs. Jourdain steps behind.)

EXCERPT: Act III. Cleonte and Jourdain,

CLEONTE

Sir, I wanted to put to you myself, rather than through a third person, a request I have long been considering, so, without further preliminaries, may I ask you to accord me the honour and the privilege of becoming your son-in-law?

JOURDAIN

Before giving you a reply, sir, I must ask you to answer one question. Are you a gentleman?

CLEONTE

Most men would have little hesitation, sir, in answering that question in the affirmative. Such a matter is quickly decided. The title is easy enough to assume, and custom today appears to sanction the appropriation. I myself am a little more scrupulous. I believe that any form of deception is unworthy of an honourable man and that it is wrong to disguise the estate to which it has pleased Heaven to call one, to appear in the eyes of the world under an assumed title, to pretend to be what one is not. I was born, sir, of honourable parentage. I have served for six years in the army and with some credit, and have, I believe, means sufficient to maintain a pretty fair position in the world we are born in.

Nevertheless, I make no pretence to a title which others in my place might very well consider themselves entitled to assume. I, therefore, tell you frankly that I am not, as you put it, a gentleman.

JOURDAIN

That settles it, then. My daughter is not for you.

CLEONTE

What!

JOURDAIN

If you aren't a gentleman, you can't have my daughter.

MRS JOURDAIN *(Stepping forward)*

What are you talking about? You and your gentleman! Do you reckon we are of the blood of St Louis?

JOURDAIN

Be quiet! I know what you are getting at.

MRS JOURDAIN

What are we, either of us, but plain, decent folk?

JOURDAIN

What a way to be talking!

MRS JOURDAIN

Wasn't your father a tradesman, the same as mine?

JOURDAIN *(Aside)*

Aagh! Confound the woman! She never fails to bring that up! *(To her)*

If your father was a tradesman, so much the worse for him. But as for mine, people who make such a statement don't know what they are talking about. And what I do say is that I insist on having a gentleman for my son-in-law.

MRS JOURDAIN

And I say that our daughter should marry someone of her own sort. Far better a decent man, good looking and comfortably off, than a beggarly gentleman who is neither use nor ornament.

JOURDAIN

I can afford to see that my daughter goes up in the world. And I mean to make her a marchioness.

MRS JOURDAIN

A marchioness!

JOURDAIN

Yes! A marchioness!

MRS JOURDAIN

Heaven forbid!

JOURDAIN

I have made up my mind on it.

MRS JOURDAIN

Yes, and I have made up mine too, and I will never consent. Marrying above one's station always brings trouble. I don't want a son-in-law who'll look down on my daughter because of her parentage. And I don't want her children to be ashamed to call me their grandmother neither, nor to have her coming to see me in style and perhaps forgetting to say 'How d'ye do' to one of the neighbours. Folk wouldn't fail to say all sorts of ill-natured things. 'See the grand lady with her high and mighty airs,' they would say, 'it's old Jourdain's daughter. She's gone up in the world now, but both her grandparents sold cloth in the market by the church. You don't get as rich as that by remaining honest.' No, I don't want that sort of gossip. I want a man who will be grateful to me for my daughter so that I shall be able to say to him, 'Sit down and have dinner with us, lad.'

JOURDIAN

That all shows what a little mind you have – not to want to rise in the world. It's no use arguing, I shall make my daughter a marchioness if all the world is against me, and if you provoke me any further I will make her a duchess!

(He goes out.
Mrs. Jourdain provides a brief link.)

MRS. JOURDAIN

But boy-meets-girl-boy-marries-girl simply must go through. This calls for a proper Moliere plot.

(Enter Covielle with Head dress)

COVIELLE

Cleonte's clever valet, Covielle! He takes the help of a drama company, Bendakallais Little Theatre, borrowing their costumes and props, and stages an elaborate prank on the unsuspecting Jourdain.

MRS JOURDAIN

Covielle, disguised in so-called Turkish attire, approaches Jourdain. *(She exits, leaving Covielle and M. Jourdain on stage.)*

EXCERPT: Act IV. Covielle in disguise convinces Jourdain to give Lucille in marriage to the Grand Turk's son and be initiated as a Paladina.

COVIELLE

Sir! I don't think I have the honour of being known to you.

JOURDAIN

No, sir.

COVIELLE

But I knew you when you were only so high (indicating with his hand).

JOURDAIN

Me?

COVIELLE

Yes. You were the prettiest child I ever saw. All the ladies were forever picking you up and cuddling you.

JOURDAI

Cuddling me!

COVIELLE

Yes. You see I was a great friend of the late gentleman, your father.

JOURDAIN

The late...my father...gentleman?

COVIELLE

Yes, a very worthy gentleman he was too.

JOURDAIN

What's that you say?

COVIELLE

I said a very worthy gentleman he was too.

JOURDAIN

My father?

COVIELLE

Of course.

JOURDAIN

Did you know him well?

COVIELLE
Certainly.

JOURDAIN
And you knew him to be a gentleman?

COVIELLE
Undoubtedly.

JOURDAIN
I don't understand what people mean, then.

COVIELLE
What is the trouble, sir?

JOURDAIN
There are foolish people about who will have it that my father was a shopkeeper.

COVIELLE
In trade! Sheer slander! Never in his life! It was just that he was obliging, anxious to be helpful, and as he knew all about cloth he would go round and select samples, have them brought to his house and give them to his friends –for a consideration.

JOURDAIN
I'm delighted to know you. You will be able to testify that my father was a gentleman.

COVIELLE
I'll maintain it before everybody.

JOURDAIN
Ohh!

COVIELLE
Have you heard that the Grand Turk's son is here?

JOURDAIN
No, I didn't know.

COVIELLE
Why! He has a splendid retinue of attendants, and everybody is running around to get a look at him. He is being received here as a personage of the greatest distinction.

JOURDAIN
Upon my word! I didn't know that.

COVIELLE
What is so fortunate for you is that he has fallen in love with your daughter.

JOURDAIN
The son of the Grand Turk?

COVIELLE

Yes, and he won't be happy until he's your son-in-law.

JOURDAIN

My son-in-law! The Grand Turk's son?

COVIELLE

That's it. The son of the Grand Turk, your son-in-law. I have been to see him and, knowing the language, of course, had quite a chat.

JOURDAIN

You – know – the Grand Turk's – son?

COVIELLE

Of course! In the course of the conversation he said, 'Acciam croc soler onch alla moustaph gidelum amanahem varahini oussere carbulath', meaning 'Have you ever come across a very beautiful young lady, the daughter of M. Jourdain, a gentleman of Paris?'

JOURDAIN

The Grand Turk's son said that about me?

COVIELLE

He did. And when I told him that I knew you personally and had met your daughter, he said, 'Marababa sahem'', which means 'Ah, how I love her!'

JOURDAIN

'Marababa Sahem' means 'Ah, how I love her!'

COVIELLE

That's it.

JOURDAIN

My goodness, I am glad you told me. I should never have thought that 'Marababa Sahem' meant 'Ah, how I love her!' What a wonderful language Turkish is!

COVIELLE

You'd be surprised. Do you know what 'cacaaracamouchen' means?

JOURDAIN

'Cacaracamouchen'? No.

COVIELLE

It means 'Dear Heart!'

JOURDAIN

'Cacaracamouchen' means 'Dear Heart'?

COVIELLE

Yes.

JOURDAIN
Well, isn't that wonderful! 'Cacaracamouchen'…'Dear Heart'. Who would ever have thought it!
It's amazing.

COVIELLE
But to conclude my mission, he is on his way here to ask to marry your daughter and in order that his father-in-law may be worthy of him he wants to make you a Mamamouchi, a title of great rank in his country.

JOURDAIN
Mamamouchi?

COVIELLE
Mamamouchi, or as we should say, a Paladin. Paladins are the former… paladins. There's no higher rank anywhere in the world. You'll be on an equal parity with the greatest of noblemen.

JOURDAIN
Well, I'm very much obliged to the son of the Grand Turk. Please take me to him so that I can thank him.

COVIELLE
But I told you, he is coming here.

JOURDAIN
Coming here!

COVIELLE
Yes, and he's bringing everything needed for the ceremony.

JOURDAIN
It's all very sudden.

COVIELLE
His love brooks no delay.

JOURDAIN
The only thing that worries me is that my daughter is a most obstinate girl, and she's taken a fancy to an ordinary fellow called Cleonte, and swears that she'll marry nobody else.

COVIELLE
You'll see she'll change her mind when she sees the Grand Turk's son. By a most remarkable coincidence he is very like Cleonte, whom I've had pointed out to me, and her love for the one can easily be transferred to the other. Ah, but I hear him coming. Here he is.
(Cleonte enter. He is dressed in a cape and other paraphernalia, accompanied by a retinue. Covielle nudges Jourdain and makes him bow to Cleonte.)

CLEONTE
Amboushahim oquiboraf, Jordina! Salaamalequi!

COVIELLE *(to MR JOURDAIN)*

Which is, being interpreted, Mr Jourdain, may your heart be all the year like a rose tree in flower.

These are the usual forms of polite greeting in his country.

JOURDAIN

I am his Turkish Highness's most humble servant.

COVIELLE

Carigar camboto oustin moraf.

CLEONTE

Oustin yoc catamalequi basum base alla moran.

COVIELLE

He prays that Heaven may endow you with the strength of lions and the wisdom of serpents.

JOURDAIN

His Turkish Highness is too kind. Say I wish him every prosperity.

COVIELLE

Ossa binamin sadoc babally oracaf ouram.

CLEONTE

Bel men.

COVIELLE

He requests that you go with him at once to prepare for the ceremony, so that he may then meet your daughter and conclude the marriage.

JOURDAIN

All that in two words?

COVIELLE

Yes. That's what the Turkish language is like. You can say a great deal in few words.

Follow where he wants you to go.

(MR JOURDAIN follows CLEONTE and his pages.)

COVIELLE *(alone).*

Oh, ho ho! My goodness! What a lark! And what a fool! If he had learned his part by rote he couldn't play it better. Oh, I'm off! Or I'll be late for the ceremony.

(He exits.)

The scene changes dramatically for the ceremony to follow.

EXCERPT: Act IV. The initiation ceremony by a Mufti. All else in the cast chip in as dancers and Turks.

The ceremony is a colourful and wild fantasy, a stereotype of all things "Arabian". It builds up the atmosphere for the finale. For instance:

• *Enter Jourdain from L under a canopy carried by two dancers. He is looking around nervously.*

• *We hear the strains of supposedly Turkish folk music. Enter dancers from two directions.*

• *Dancers then move to four sides of Jourdain and dance around him. They move him, spin him around, etc.*

• *Attendants enter with a robe and other props for the ceremony.*

• *More "Turk" attendants enter heralding the Grand Mufti. They chant and enter as the dancers move into a line to strains of Turkish folk music.*

• *Turks stop UL. They create an aisle for the Mufti to enter and chant 'Awooaah'.*

• *Mufti strides in. Turks chant the second Awooaahh... then BurrBurr!*

• *Mufti walks up to Jourdain, looks him up and down and takes his place for the ceremony – a raised box.*

• *More chants of Aawooaah... BurrBurr!*

• *Mufti signals to attendants to turn MJ around.*

• *Mufti claps and all freeze in silence.*

• *Mufti begins a chant to a rap beat.*

In the first Bangalore production a woman played the Mufti – as a Muftina!

THE MUFTI *(in a rap beat)*

If him com-pree him say yum yum!

If no com-pree him-a keepee mum. Me am Mufti and what am-a he? Him no compree?

ALL

No compree! No-No compree! No-no compree !

MUFTI

Speakee a-quickly, what am he?

ONE

Him-a no heathen? Him-a no Jew?

ANOTHER

Him no Buddhist? No Hindu

ALL

No, no, no-no! No, no, no-no!

ONE

Him no coffir? No puritan?

ANOTHER

Him no Hussite? Lutheran?

ALL

No, no, no-no! No, no, no-no!

MUFTI

What am he? Morang-utan?

ALL
Hanh-Hanh-Hanh, to be to be!
Hanh-Hanh-Hanh, to be to be!

MUFTI
Him called how? How him called?

ONE
Him called Jourdaan

ANOTHER
Jourdain.

ANOTHER
Jourdinaaaaa
(Mufti signals for Jourdain to be dropped to his knees. Mufti then claps his hands together to begin chanting prayer. All follow.)

MUFTI
We pray for Mr Jourdain...
To Morang-utan night and mornain',
Going to make a Paladina.
Of Jourdina, of Jourdina.
Give him sabre, give him turban.

ALL
Give him sabre! Give him turban!
(Two attendants ceremoniously bring in sabre and turban to put on to MJ)

MUFTI
Give him galley, brigantina
Him go fight for Palestina
Good Morang-utan! Jourdina!
Him be good Turk Jourdina?

ALL
Hey Valla! Hey Valla!
MUFTI *(singing)*
Ha la ba, ba la da!
Ha la ba, ba la da!

ALL
Ha la ba, ba la da!
Ha la ba, ba la da!
Ha la ba, ba la ba, ba la da, ba la CHOO !
• *While the Jourdain theme is being chanted an attendant ceremoniously brings in the Holy Book.*
   • *Attendants make Jourdain go on an all fours.*
   • *One sets the Holy Book on Jourdain's back.*

• At the end of the Jourdain theme Mufti steps down, reads from the book, makes a second invocation, ending with a loud HOO!
• Another then takes the Holy Book off Jourdain's back.

MUFTI *(rapping)*
Him no scoundrel, him no knave?

ALL
No, no, no-no! No, no, no-no!

MUFTI *(as before)*
Him no coward, him be brave?

ALL
Him be brave! Him be brave!

MUFTI
Take then, take the scimitar.
Mufti takes scimitar out of his waist band

THE MUFTI *(singing, getting off his seat and whacking Jourdain on the backside)*
Give him, give him Bastonnade!
Give him, give him Bastonnade!

ALL
Thus Jourdain Morang-utan made.

MUFTI
Ha la ba, ba la da!

ALL
Ha la ba, ba la da Ha la ba, ba la da! Ha la ba, ba la da!

MUFTI *(interrupting and whacking Jourdain one last time)*
Be not offended! All is ended.

ALL
Be not offended! All is ended!
Music begins and all begin to dance around Jourdain and Mufti. All exit in a file UL.
Mufti walks up to Jourdain ceremoniously gives him a loud slurpy kiss on both cheeks and strides out.
The action flows into the next EXCERPT:

Act V. Mrs. Jourdain sees Jourdain as the converted Paladina.
JOURDAIN is making obeisance and singing Turkish phrases as she enters.

MRS JOURDAIN
Oh Lord have mercy on us! Whatever is he up to now? What a sight! Are you going mumming? Is this a time to be in fancy dress? What's it all about? Who on earth has you togged up like this?

JOURDAIN
The impertinence of the woman! How dare you talk like that to a Mamamouchi?

MRS JOURDAIN
A what?

JOURDAIN
You'll have to be more respectful now that I've been made a Mamamouchi.

MRS JOURDAIN
What on earth is the man talking about, with his Mamamouchi?

JOURDAIN
I tell you I am a Mamamouchi.

MRS JOURDAIN
And whatever sort of creature is that?

JOURDAIN
A Mamamouchi is what we should call a Paladin.

MRS JOURDAIN
You ought to know better than go a-balladin' at your age.

JOURDAIN
The ignorance! The title of Paladin is a dignity that has just been conferred upon me.
I come straight from the ceremony.

MRS JOURDAIN
What sort of ceremony?

JOURDAIN *(singing and dancing)*
Good Morang-utan Jourdina!

MRS JOURDAIN
And what does that mean?

JOURDAIN
Jourdina means Jourdain.

MRS JOURDAIN
And what about old Jourdain?

JOURDAIN *(sings)*
Going to make a Paladina – of Jourdina, of Jourdina!

MRS JOURDAIN
Eh?

JOURDAIN *(sings)*
Give him galley, brigantina!

MRS JOURDAIN
I don't understand a word of it!

JOURDAIN *(sings)*
Him go fight for Palestina.

MRS JOURDAIN
What on earth...

JOURDAIN *(as before)*
Give him, give him Bastonnade!

MRS JOURDAIN
Whatever is this nonsense?

JOURDAIN *(as before)*
Be not offended! All is ended!

MRS JOURDAIN
What on earth!

JOURDAIN *(dancing and clapping his hands)*
Ba la ba, ba la CHOO! *(He tumbles over)*

MRS JOURDAIN
Oh my goodness! He is off his head.

JOURDAIN *(as he picks himself up and goes off)*
Silence! Show more respect to a Mamamouchi!
He drops to his knees with a loud Ba la ba, ba la HOO!
Mrs. Jourdain rushes out shrieking.
Black out.
The lights return on an empty stage. The Chorus enters in a procession.
They sing. Song to be developed (Optional).
The procession turns into the curtain call, with the whole cast.

MUFTI
Ha la ba Ba la da
Ha la ba Ba la da

ALL
Ha la ba Ba la da
Ha la ba Ba la da
Ha la ba Ba la da Ba la ba Ba la chou!
Cast takes three bows
MUFTI: Be not offended! All has ended!

....

*(In one of the Bangalore productions the entire cast appeared on the stage at
the end of this excerpt for a sign-off. Shown below.)*
The chorus enters in a procession.
They sing. Song to be developed (Optional).
The whole cast appears on stage.

MUFTI

Ha la ba Ba la da
Ha la ba Ba la da

ALL

Ha la ba Ba la da
Ha la ba Ba la da
Ha la ba Ba la da Ba la ba Ba la chou!

MUFTI

Be not offended! All has ended!
They exit, leaving the Chorus on stage.

SCENE 7

Reprise: The Imaginary Invalid
The Chorus sets up the stage for the scene for the Imaginary Invalid as at the start. The actors playing Beralde and Argan take their places.

ALL

1666.

>> When the play Le Misanthrope was performed, Moliere was showing the first signs of a serious illness of the lungs.

>> By then he had written over thirty plays. Comedy had come to rival tragedy in French theatre.

>> The deteriorating health provided the setting, it seems, for The Imaginary Invalid.

ALL

Moliere said this of himself...

>> Sometimes I wondered if I had turned my slapstick on myself in this one.

>> Was I really ill and dying, or was I being a hypochondriac, deluding myself about it?

>> Had imagination invaded reality, or was it the other way about? I wasn't really sure.

ALL

The play opened in 1673.

>> Argan is the hypochondriac.

>> His brother, Beralde, tries to counsel him about good health, medicines and doctors.

(They return to the opening scene from The Imaginary Invalid.)

BERALDE

I'm not taking it upon myself to attack medical science, brother; not at all. Everybody can believe what he likes at his own risk and peril. All I'm

saying is just between ourselves and I only wish I could have taken you,
to one of Moliere's plays on this subject.

ARGAN

I have no patience with your Moliere and his plays. It's all very amusing
I must say to be holding up worthy people like doctors to ridicule.

BERALDE

It's not the doctors themselves he makes fun of but the absurdities of
medical science.

ARGAN

It's very becoming I must say for him to take it on himself to put medicine
in order. A fine sort of simpleton he must be, a good conceit he must
have of himself to mock at consultations and prescriptions, set himself up
against the whole faculty and put respectable people like doctors on stage.

BERALDE

What could he do better than put on the stage men of all professions?
Princes and kings are put on the stage everyday and they aren't of less
consequence than doctors.

ARGAN

The devil! If I were a doctor I'd have my own back on him for his
impertinence. If he were ill I wouldn't help him though he were at death's
door. He wouldn't get the slightest bleeding or the smallest injection
however much he begged and prayed for 'em. 'Die and be damned', I'd
say, 'and that'll teach you to make fun of doctors!'

BERALDE

You are down on him aren't you!

ARGAN

He is a very foolish fellow and if the physicians are wise they'll do what
I've told you.

BERALDE

He'll be wiser than the doctors not to ask them for help.

ARGAN

So much the worse for him if he has no medicines to help him.

BERALDE

He has his own reasons for not wanting to have anything to do with
them. He thinks only the strongest and the most vigorous of men can
stand up to malady and medicine at the same time and that, so far as he's
concerned, it's as much as he can do to bear his illness.

ARGAN

What ridiculous arguments! Come, brother, don't let us talk any more
about the fellow. It rouses my bile. You'll be making me ill.

(Beralde, disappointed, steps back...as the Chorus enters.)

SCENE 8: CLOSE

The Chorus returns, along with all the actors. They form a tight semi-circle at Centre above the actor playing Argan, seated.

>> During the fourth performance of the play, Moliere was overcome by convulsive coughing.

>> He died soon afterwards.

>> Madeline Bejart had died the year before.

>> A reconciliation with Armande had followed. Yet, it was to be a death in the pain of loneliness.

>> At first, permission for internment in any sacred ground was stoutly refused.

>> On the king's intervention, he was allowed a burial, but it was at night, without ceremony.

>> He never really thought much about his life as he lived it.

>> Who does? Looking back, he thought that the real injury he did to his audience was that he made them laugh a little louder than they could.

>> They envied him for that ever since he came to Paris.

ALL

He said to himself:

ARGAN

They loved to criticize my plays. All the better! Heaven forbid that these plays should ever please them. I'd be most unhappy about that!

Fade out
Close of play

BANGALORE LITTLE THEATRE

Six Decades of Wholesome Community Theatre

In 1960, a small group of committed persons in Bangalore sought a theatre experience that could be a genuine alternative to the order of the day that was called BBC Theatre – British Bedroom Comedy. The group included the talented couple, Scott and Margaret Tod, and at least four other expats, along with a handful of Bangaloreans. They had a vision of a Community Theatre best described by the slogan invented 25 years later: *Think Globally, Act Locally.* Bangalore Little Theatre came into existence with a play reading in the last week of September that year. The first production on boards in December 1960 was Moliere's *The Prodigious Snob*, more commonly known as *The Would-be Gentleman.*

In 1962, within a year of inception, BLT arrived at a character and identity for itself: to maintain pride in its strictly amateur status, but to conduct its affairs in a thoroughly professional manner. The group gave itself a constitution and, through that, a participatory style of functioning. The group was seen as belonging to a membership, and therefore to be managed transparently by an elected management committee. The founding members were the first to give way to younger members to take the group forward.

Way back in 1963, BLT produced its first Indian play in English, an original adaptation of *Mrichhakatika* (The Toy Cart of Clay) by a founder-member, Prof B Chandrasekhara. Since then, the group has maintained the conscious policy of producing Indian plays periodically – translations, adaptations, original scripts, by its own members and others. Not surprisingly, two of the six awards for contemporary playscripts instituted for the first time by *The Hindu* in 1993 landed in BLT. The first prize was for the play by Vijay Padaki, *Credit Titles,* a political satire on intellectual property rights for patenting life forms. A Special Prize was awarded to another member, Ambika (Poile) Sengupta.

Old-timers of BLT have often been asked the secret of the group's long life when, in contrast, we see hundreds of cases of groups starting with a bang and dropping by the wayside in a couple of years. The difference, it seems, is in the simple fact that BLT is a community-based organisation and, therefore, a membership-driven group. From this fact has followed a number of guiding principles that appear to have served BLT well over the years. For instance:

- The participatory and transparency principles in management (with all financial transactions completely open and made available to the entire membership)
- The highly open leadership structure around an elected Managing Committee (rather than being founder-centric or personality-driven)
- The constant development of new talent, including new directors (rather than being dependent on the same old hands or breeding star complexes)
- The pursuit of the higher purpose, the constitutionally-enshrined objective of promoting the theatre and related arts in Bangalore (rather than the attitude of 'let's do another play')

All of this actually makes it far more difficult to 'manage' the organisation. It is so much easier to let a charismatic leader take charge and 'run' the group as he (or she) wishes.

The significance of these principles is understood better when we see that a sizeable majority of the theatre talent in Bangalore, including the more recognised names, has been in BLT productions, workshops and training programmes earlier. They continue their affiliation with BLT even if they perform under other banners.

Related to this point is one other indisputably important feature of BLT. It is the only English-language theatre group in Bangalore (perhaps anywhere in India) with strong links to the local-regional theatre, building bridges across language divides. Many of the stalwarts on the Kannada stage and screen have been either life members of BLT or have been prominently involved in some capacity or the other. After all, among the founders were personalities like Prof. B Chandrasekhara, Nani, Shivaram, Seetharam, V Ramamurthy and S Ramaswamy. Then there were CR Simha, Vimala Rangachar, SG Ramachandra, KC Sekhar, Suresh Heblikar, Paddu, Shankar and Arundhati Nag, Ashok Rao.... And many many more – including some who went on to become Presidents of Karnataka Nataka Academy! Indeed, BLT has been a substantial support to Kannada theatre groups in their start-up stages.

BLT has invested heavily in training and outreach activity. In the late 1970s, BLT introduced for the first time in Bangalore a comprehensive introductory programme for newcomers to the theatre, based on the Stella Adler system. Since the mid '80, the group has made its Summer Project on Theatre (SPOT) a regular training event. It has come to be recognised as the most prestigious training event in the city, because of the quality of inputs provided. And it continues to be a part of BLT's social commitment. Other groups and productions snap up the talent from these training projects.

In 1993, the group initiated an annual Festival of Short Plays (SHORTS), aimed at promoting theatre activity among the college and youth population. With the audience response as enthusiastic as seen, the scale of the Festival may well be enhanced considerably in the coming years.

As a socially-responsible theatre society, BLT has readily taken on many a fundraising production for worthy causes. In 1970-71, BLT's production of the new play by Badal Sircar, *Evam Indrajit*, was the first fundraising event to contribute to the Prime Minister's Fund for the Bangladeshi (then East Bengal) refugee crisis. An original script, *Head Start*, by Vijay Padaki, was produced for CRY in January 1996. Since then BLT has made a constitutional commitment to dedicate one production for a charity every year. The group also provides various kinds of help to theatre projects in colleges, schools, clubs and other institutions.

With the high repute in training and outreach activity, it was only logical for BLT to set up an Academy of Theatre Arts in 2008. The stated mission of the Academy is to enrich the theatre institutional system through the thrust programme of *Theatre Education,* thus building the societal base for the true appreciation of the theatre and, indeed, all of the performing arts.

THE SERIES EDITOR

Vijay Padaki is a Theatre Educator based in Bangalore. He has worn two caps for most of his life with equal facility. He has been active in the theatre for sixty years. He has been a management professional for over forty-five years.

Vijay is a psychologist and behavioural scientist by training, and founder-director of The P&P Group, a management resource centre that has programmes of research, consulting and training in the areas of Organisation and Institutional Development. A good part of the work of The P&P Group is devoted to the effectiveness of large development programmes. Among his earlier assignments he headed the Human Resources Division of India's oldest cooperative R&D institution, Ahmedabad Textile Industry's Research Association (ATIRA), which also helped set up the first Indian Institute of Management in Ahmedabad. Later, he was a member of the founding faculty at Indian Institute of Management, Bangalore, the founder of a Centre for Management for the textile industry in Ahmedabad, and a Visiting Professor at Indian Institute of Science, Bangalore to initiate a programme in R&D Management. He was a Senior Associate at the National Institute of Advanced Studies in its early years.

Vijay joined Bangalore Little Theatre in 1960, the year of its inception, and later served the company in many capacities–as actor, director, trainer, writer, designer and administrator, including two stints each as Secretary and President. In 2008, the institutional set up was restructured. Bangalore Little Theatre Foundation was created as a Public Charitable Trust. It was done with the purpose of reinforcing the organisation's strengths in outreach activity, and thus rededicating the commitment to social development goals beyond performance. The Trust requested Vijay to provide the leadership to a newly-created Academy of Theatre Arts in its formative years. The Academy is developing a long term programme thrusts to strengthen the institution of theatre education and practice in India.

Vijay has been responsible for institutionalising several activities of BLT, such as the annual summer workshop for newcomers to the theatre

(SPOT), from which has emerged a large number of the theatre personalities in Bangalore, the History of Ideas programme of biographical plays, the Courtyard Theatre programme, and the Children's Theatre programme, which includes the annual flagship children's play as a partnership production to support a charity. Vijay conceived and initiated the highly successful Trainer-Training programme and the Directors Training programme in Bangalore.

He has forged several international partnerships with BLT over the years. The John F Kennedy Centre for Performing Arts in Washington invited him to serve as an advisor to the India Festival in 2011. The same year, he gave the Harold Clurman lecture at the Stella Adler Studio in New York. More recently, the Ministry of Culture invited Vijay to initiate a programme of Arts and Heritage Management in India.

Vijay has written over 50 original plays. He has also adapted or translated several play scripts. Seagull Books has published a volume of two Gujarati plays translated by him. In 1993, Vijay won the award for the best contemporary play script instituted by The Hindu for the play Credit Titles.

In May 2024 Vijay was honoured with the Lifetime Achievement Award by ASSITEJ International, a world-wide body of artists committed to Theatre for Children and Young Audiences.

PUBLICATIONS IN THE SERIES

Volume 1: FOUR CLASSICS
on the Indian Stage

Contains original English language adaptations of Indian classics. These include *The Toy Cart of Clay,* an adaptation of the Sanskrit Classic *Mrichhakatika* by Sudraka; *The Anklet,* an adaptation from Ilango Adigal's Tamil Classic *Silappadikaram; Kurukshetra Burning!* based on *Smashana Kurukshetra* in Kannada by Kuvempu; *The Echo,* an adaptation of *Chomana Dudi* in Kannada by Shivarama Karanth.

Volume 2: THE HISTORY OF IDEAS
Programme of new plays

From BLT's highly acclaimed History of Ideas programme, plays include *The Prophet and the Poet,* based on the Gandhi-Tagore exchanges; *Finding Ananda,* rediscovering the life and work of Swami Vivekananda, with the Bengal Renaissance as the backdrop; *Tiger! Tiger!* revealing the humanistic side of Tipu Sultan; *Monsters in the Dark,* an original adaptation of the Pulitzer award book *The Emperor of All Maladies* by Siddhartha Mukherjee, sub-titled A Biography of Cancer; *Einstein's Dreams,* an original dance theatre adaptation of the novel by the same title by Alan Lightman.

Volume 3: CHILDREN'S THEATRE
Programme of Annual Productions

Containing plays from BLT's hugely successful Children's Theatre programme, this volume includes *The Ungrateful Man,* a tale from the Panchatantra; *The Magic Drum,* a collection of stories from the book by the same title by Sudha Murty; *Ali Oh Baba,* a retelling of the tale from the 1001 Arabian Nights; and *The Court Jester,* the tales of Tenali Rama.

Volume 4:
FOOTPRINTS and other plays

These plays were written by *Vijay Padaki* in the period 1986 to 2002 and represent explorations in combining form with content. There is a humanistic undercurrent in the plays, an affirmation of the human spirit, the innate ability to question the given, so often remaining suppressed, and the ability to find alternatives. It is known that a lot of his writing has been influenced by field experiences in his professional engagements. The content of the play has often (not always) begun as a case study, intriguing in itself, but demanding an alternative perspective. The alternative perspectives have provided the raw material for the play scripts. The play scripts should explain themselves. Footprints is presented as 'fictional science', raising the serious question of the human species being Nature's mistake, the price to be paid by the rest of the earth.

Volume 5:
MANDAP and other plays

The plays included in this Volume represent two main periods of Vijay Padaki's writing. The first is when he was deeply involved in social-development programmes that had field projects in rural areas. They were all addressing the issues of human rights and social justice, although from different 'sectoral' perspectives. It was the absence of rights and justice that was coming in the way of development in real terms. Violence was not ruled out. *Mandap* is the play from that period. The dynamics of rights and justice are seen in the urban setting too. The next five plays in this volume represent a period of writing in which the writer was increasingly drawn to developmental issues in the urban setting. The plays form a set that came to be called *Tales From the City*. They are grouped in this Volume as two double-bills and one play by itself. Violence is the recognizable undercurrent in all these plays. *Second Shift Muster* is the oldest of the play scripts appearing in this volume. The one-act play is included in this volume for a variety of reasons. As with the other tales, this play explores a lesser known city-based occupation in changing times, with changing value systems.

Volume 6:
SALT LICKS and other plays

The plays in Volume 6 reflect on the continued Western orientation of Indian communities till today. As a character in *Salt Licks* says: 'Go West, young man, to rediscover the East. And don't be in a hurry to get back'. The first play in the publication series refers to a peculiarly Bangalore society of elders fixated in the Raj, calling themselves the Empire Loyalists. If it was 'Great Britain' at one time, it was the American Dream later. In the pre-liberalised economy, young people went to extremes to get admission in American colleges and universities. Any university, any course, any location, it was only important to get there first. And yet...there was something so human in their dreams. The collection in this Volume can be called *Vijay Padaki's early plays.* The stories are set in the period early 'seventies to early 'nineties. The ubiquitous 2-in-1 music system in the plays creates a special place for itself. Two plays in the set need further explanation. ***Gold and Silver*** was written at the time of an exchange project with the Royal National Theatre celebrating India's Golden Anniversary of Independence. ***Evening Shadows*** is an original English language adaptation of *Sandhya Chhaya* by the Marathi playwright Jaywant Dalvi. The loneliness of an elderly couple is compounded by the son not returning from America.

Volume 7:
Short Plays & Sketches

The principle of economy of force applies even at the stage of conceiving a play. Many good ideas can be put across on the stage in a short play or a one-act play. They need not be put on the rack and stretched to a full length script. (It is cruelty to the audience.) This is the reason so many full length plays in English in India are bright and attractive in the first half an hour and run out of steam after the intermission. Not surprisingly many movie scripts are the same.

We have avoided the label 'one-act plays', preferring to call this compilation short plays. One-act plays had a historical context in the West, and served that context well. The context is different today, especially in countries like India where the 'ecosystem' of theatre performances makes its own demands on the performers. The short play has a legitimate place here. A one-act play will qualify as a short play, but not all short plays are one-act plays. And then there are the sketches. How does one define a sketch? Theatre folks have not found a satisfactory definition yet! The last sketch in this Volume, ***Ringaling***, has no spoken word. It is done entirely with moves and sound effects – a wide variety of ring tones of mobile phones.

Volume 8:
More Children's Theatre

Beginning with a one-off production in 1966, *The Ungrateful Man*, there was a steady build-up of projects and activities in Bangalore Little Theatre to comprise a full-fledged programme thrust committed to schools and young audiences. The five plays in Volume 8 bring us to the year 2021 in the Children's Theatre programme. Volume 3 was the first compilation of Children's Theatre plays. The two Volumes include only the plays presented as performances in the programme series. They do not reveal a lot else done in parallel in reaching schools. There are also the plays developed specifically for the Theatre-in-Education programme. We will see some of that work in Volume 9.

The plays in this Volume, and ***A Bellyful of Paradise*** in particular, reiterate BLT's position that children are capable of far higher levels of comprehension than we care to recognize. (Indeed, they have often absorbed play scripts that went over the heads of adult audiences.) Children's Theatre is too often equated with fun and froth on stage, dumbing down the storyline, and actors talking down to the children. It need not be so. Going by the credo of Theatre for Young Audiences (TYA) it must not be so. The plays by BLT are designed to tour schools. They include schools in rural areas and schools reaching underprivileged communities. The response of the children to the plays is the greatest testimony to what we have set out to do in Children's Theatre.

Volume 9:
Plays in Education

What is Theatre-in-Education? The totality of the field of TIE is explained in the Preface to this Volume. Contrary to popular perception TIE is not limited to just "enactment" or performance of plays. It will be seen that performances are one part of the totality. TYA (performances *for* students) can be a part of TIE too, but as just one component. Theatre techniques have been applied over the years in many other spheres. One of the earliest areas of application has been education. Theatre-in-Education is the use of theatre/drama techniques to aid the learning process. Its function is primarily pedagogic. TIE is aligned to the philosophy of education that upholds *child-centered learning*. The emphasis on doing things first makes it heavily experiential in nature. TIE aims to incorporate theatre and drama activities in curriculum subjects that the students are examining in their classes.

The TIE programme in Bangalore Little Theatre has had a specialized interest in Environment-Sustainability Education. The plays included in Volume 9 reflect the emphasis. A special feature of the Volume is an entire collection of short plays based on Folk Tales gathered from all parts of India. The plays are meant for classroom use and to enhance curricular learning.